Progress Chart

This chart lists all the topics in the book. Once you have completed each page, stick a star in the correct box below.

Page	Topic	Star	Page	Topic	Star	Page	Topic	Star
2	Multiplying by 10, 100, and 1,000	★	13	Decimal addition	★	24	Perimeter of shapes	★
3	The simplest form of fractions	★	14	Decimal addition	★	25	Decimal place value	★
4	Changing improper fractions to mixed numbers	★	15	Decimal subtraction	★	26	Speed problems	★
5	Rounding decimals	★	16	Decimal subtraction	★	27	Conversion table	★
6	Adding with different numbers of digits	★	17	Multiplying larger numbers by ones	★	28	Interpreting circle graphs	★
7	Adding with different numbers of digits	★	18	Multiplying larger numbers by ones	★	29	Probability scale 0 to 1	★
8	Subtracting one number from another	★	19	Real-life multiplication problems	★	30	Likely outcomes	★
9	Subtracting one number from another	★	20	Comparing and ordering decimals	★	31	Naming quadrilaterals	★
10	Real-life problems	★	21	Converting units of measure	★	32	Speed trials	★
11	Everyday problems	★	22	Converting units of measure	★	33	All the 3s	★
12	Everyday problems	★	23	Areas of rectangles and squares	★	34	All the 3s again	★

Page	Topic	Star	Page	Topic	Star	Page	Topic	Star
35	All the 4s	☆	49	Speed trials	☆	63	Line of symmetry	☆
36	All the 4s again	☆	50	Some of the 9s	☆	64	Ordering large numbers	☆
37	Speed trials	☆	51	The rest of the 9s	☆	65	Rounding whole numbers	☆
38	Some of the 6s	☆	52	Practice the 9s	☆	66	Choosing units of measure	☆
39	The rest of the 6s	☆	53	Speed trials	☆	67	Comparing fractions	☆
40	Practice the 6s	☆	54	Times tables for division	☆	68	Converting fractions to decimals	☆
41	Speed trials	☆	55	Times tables for division	☆	69	Adding fractions	☆
42	Some of the 7s	☆	56	Times tables for division	☆	70	Subtracting fractions	☆
43	The rest of the 7s	☆	57	Times tables for division	☆	71	Adding fractions	☆
44	Practice the 7s	☆	58	Times tables for division	☆	72	Adding fractions	☆
45	Speed trials	☆	59	Times tables practice grids	☆	73	Subtracting fractions	☆
46	Some of the 8s	☆	60	Times tables practice grids	☆	74	Adding mixed numbers	☆
47	The rest of the 8s	☆	61	Times tables practice grids	☆	75	Subtracting mixed numbers	☆
48	Practice the 8s	☆	62	Speed trials	☆	76	Adding mixed numbers and fractions	☆

Page	Topic	Star	Page	Topic	Star	Page	Topic	Star
77	Simple use of parentheses	☆	91	Conversion tables	☆	105	Real-life problems	☆
78	Simple use of parentheses	☆	92	Reading bar graphs	☆	106	Multiplication by 2-digit numbers	☆
79	Simple use of parentheses	☆	93	Expanded form	☆	107	Division by ones	☆
80	Multiplying decimals	☆	94	Cubes of small numbers	☆	108	Dividing larger numbers	☆
81	Multiplying decimals	☆	95	Multiplying fractions	☆	109	Division of 3-digit decimal numbers	☆
82	Real-life problems	☆	96	More complex fraction problems	☆	110	Division of 3-digit decimal numbers	☆
83	Real-life problems	☆	97	Finding percentages	☆	111	Real-life problems	☆
84	Real-life problems	☆	98	Addition	☆	112	Rounding money	☆
85	Conversions: length	☆	99	More addition	☆	113	Estimating sums of money	☆
86	Conversions: capacity	☆	100	Dividing by ones	☆	114	Estimating differences of money	☆
87	Fraction of a number	☆	101	Dividing by tens	☆	115	Estimating sums and differences	☆
88	Showing decimals	☆	102	Dividing by larger numbers	☆	116	Estimating products	☆
89	Area of right-angled triangles	☆	103	Everyday problems	☆	117	Estimating quotients	☆
90	Speed problems	☆	104	Real-life problems	☆	118	Rounding mixed numbers	☆

Page	Topic	Star	Page	Topic	Star	Page	Topic	Star
119	Calculate the mean	☆	133	Problems involving time	☆	145	Fraction models	☆
120	Mean, median, and mode	☆	134	Elapsed time	☆	146	Multiplying by one-digit numbers	☆
121	Line graphs	☆	135	Recognizing multiples	☆	147	Multiplying by one-digit numbers	☆
122	Coordinates	☆	136	Bar graphs	☆	148	Real-life problems	☆
123	Drawing angles	☆	137	Triangles	☆	149	Real-life problems	☆
124	Reading and writing numbers	☆	138	Place value to 10,000,000	☆	150	Problems involving time	☆
125	Multiplying and dividing by 10	☆	139	Multiplying and dividing by 10	☆	151	Multiplying and dividing	☆
126	Identifying patterns	☆	140	Appropriate units of measure	☆	152	Identifying patterns	☆
127	Recognizing multiples of 6, 7, and 8	☆	141	Identifying patterns	☆	153	Products with odd and even numbers	☆
128	Factors of numbers from 1 to 30	☆	142	Factors of numbers from 31 to 65	☆	154	Factors of numbers from 66 to 100	☆
129	Recognizing equivalent fractions	☆	143	Greatest common factor	☆	155	Multiplying by two-digit numbers	☆
130	Rounding decimals	☆	144	Writing equivalent fractions	☆	156	Multiplying by two-digit numbers	☆
131	Real-life problems	☆						
132	Real-life problems	☆						

When you have completed the progress chart in this book, fill in the certificate at the back.

Math
made easy
Grade 5 - ages 10-11
Workbook

Author
John Kennedy

Consultant
Sean McArdle

DORLING KINDERSLEY

Published by the Penguin Group
Penguin Group (USA) Inc., 375 Hudson Street, New York, New York 10014, U.S.A.
Penguin Books Ltd, Registered Offices: 80 Strand, London WC2R 0RL, England

First published in the United States by DK Publishing, Inc. in 2003
Reprinted 2004

Printed and bound in China by L. Rex Printing

LONDON • NEW YORK • SYDNEY • MOSCOW • DELHI

Multiplying by 10, 100, and 1,000

Write the answers in the boxes.

472 x 10 = 4,720   324 x 100 = 32,400   57 x 1,000 = 57,000

Write the answers in the boxes.

426 x   10 =   319 x   10 =   584 x   10 =
740 x   10 =   985 x   10 =   612 x   10 =
102 x 100 =   725 x 100 =   383 x 100 =
909 x 100 =   651 x 100 =   737 x 100 =
4,000 x   10 =   5,649 x   10 =   8,714 x   10 =
6,302 x 100 =   9,711 x 100 =   4,826 x 100 =

Find the number that has been multiplied by 100.

            x 100 = 163,100   x 100 = 562,300
            x 100 = 841,300   x 100 = 864,700
            x 100 = 636,500   x 100 = 839,100
            x 100 = 521,000   x 100 = 537,000

Write the answers in the boxes.

4,732 x 1,000 =   9,105 x 1,000 =
6,211 x 1,000 =   4,711 x 1,000 =
11,264 x 1,000 =   84,322 x 1,000 =
47,544 x 1,000 =   75,543 x 1,000 =
59,223 x 1,000 =   84,326 x 1,000 =

Find the number that has been multiplied by 1,000.

            x 1,000 =   764,000   x 1,000 = 9,810,000
            x 1,000 = 5,372,000   x 1,000 = 6,141,000
            x 1,000 = 4,169,000   x 1,000 = 8,399,000

The simplest form of fractions

Make these fractions equivalent by putting a number in the box.
$$\frac{70}{100} = \frac{7}{10} \qquad \frac{4}{12} = \frac{1}{3}$$

Make these fractions equivalent by putting a number in each box.

$\dfrac{30}{100} = \dfrac{}{10}$ $\dfrac{8}{100} = \dfrac{}{25}$ $\dfrac{40}{100} = \dfrac{}{10}$ $\dfrac{15}{100} = \dfrac{}{20}$

$\dfrac{5}{20} = \dfrac{}{4}$ $\dfrac{25}{100} = \dfrac{}{4}$ $\dfrac{12}{60} = \dfrac{}{5}$ $\dfrac{8}{20} = \dfrac{}{5}$

$\dfrac{16}{40} = \dfrac{}{5}$ $\dfrac{2}{6} = \dfrac{}{3}$ $\dfrac{10}{60} = \dfrac{}{6}$ $\dfrac{2}{12} = \dfrac{}{6}$

$\dfrac{9}{18} = \dfrac{}{2}$ $\dfrac{10}{18} = \dfrac{}{9}$ $\dfrac{4}{24} = \dfrac{}{6}$ $\dfrac{7}{28} = \dfrac{}{4}$

$\dfrac{4}{6} = \dfrac{2}{}$ $\dfrac{6}{10} = \dfrac{3}{}$ $\dfrac{9}{15} = \dfrac{3}{}$ $\dfrac{8}{12} = \dfrac{2}{}$

$\dfrac{18}{20} = \dfrac{9}{}$ $\dfrac{21}{28} = \dfrac{3}{}$ $\dfrac{6}{8} = \dfrac{3}{}$ $\dfrac{5}{50} = \dfrac{1}{}$

$\dfrac{15}{25} = \dfrac{3}{}$ $\dfrac{4}{16} = \dfrac{1}{}$ $\dfrac{12}{20} = \dfrac{3}{}$ $\dfrac{12}{18} = \dfrac{2}{}$

$\dfrac{3}{15} = \dfrac{1}{}$ $\dfrac{9}{36} = \dfrac{1}{}$ $\dfrac{9}{27} = \dfrac{1}{}$ $\dfrac{30}{50} = \dfrac{3}{}$

Make these rows of fractions equivalent by putting a number in each box.

$\dfrac{1}{9} = \dfrac{}{18} = \dfrac{3}{} = \dfrac{}{36} = \dfrac{}{45} = \dfrac{6}{}$

$\dfrac{1}{10} = \dfrac{}{20} = \dfrac{3}{} = \dfrac{4}{} = \dfrac{}{50} = \dfrac{}{60}$

$\dfrac{3}{5} = \dfrac{12}{} = \dfrac{}{25} = \dfrac{18}{} = \dfrac{}{35} = \dfrac{24}{}$

$\dfrac{5}{6} = \dfrac{}{12} = \dfrac{15}{} = \dfrac{20}{} = \dfrac{25}{} = \dfrac{30}{}$

$\dfrac{1}{7} = \dfrac{}{14} = \dfrac{}{21} = \dfrac{}{28} = \dfrac{5}{} = \dfrac{}{42}$

$\dfrac{3}{11} = \dfrac{}{44} = \dfrac{}{77} = \dfrac{27}{} = \dfrac{}{110} = \dfrac{33}{}$

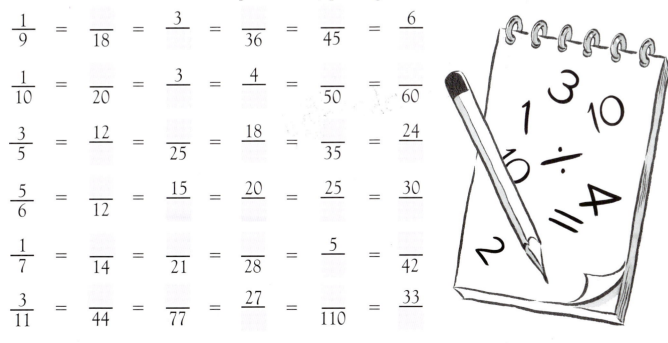

Changing improper fractions to mixed numbers

Change this improper fraction to a mixed number.
(Remember you may need to cancel.)

$$\frac{27}{12} = 2\frac{3^{1}}{12_{4}} = 2\frac{1}{4}$$

Change these mixed numbers to improper fractions.

$$2\frac{3}{4} = \frac{11}{4} \qquad 4\frac{1}{2} = \frac{9}{2}$$

Change these improper fractions to mixed numbers.

$$\frac{25}{3} = \qquad \frac{15}{12} = \qquad \frac{40}{7} =$$

$$\frac{17}{6} = \qquad \frac{11}{9} = \qquad \frac{12}{5} =$$

$$\frac{27}{5} = \qquad \frac{26}{3} = \qquad \frac{32}{5} =$$

$$\frac{9}{2} = \qquad \frac{19}{2} = \qquad \frac{15}{4} =$$

$$\frac{30}{4} = \qquad \frac{26}{8} = \qquad \frac{42}{9} =$$

Change these mixed numbers to improper fractions.

$$4\frac{3}{4} = \qquad 9\frac{1}{2} = \qquad 12\frac{1}{4} =$$

$$3\frac{2}{3} = \qquad 6\frac{3}{4} = \qquad 3\frac{9}{10} =$$

$$5\frac{1}{8} = \qquad 3\frac{2}{5} = \qquad 2\frac{5}{6} =$$

$$5\frac{1}{4} = \qquad 3\frac{3}{8} = \qquad 2\frac{11}{12} =$$

$$2\frac{7}{10} = \qquad 4\frac{3}{10} = \qquad 4\frac{1}{8} =$$

$$7\frac{3}{4} = \qquad 8\frac{1}{2} = \qquad 1\frac{5}{12} =$$

Rounding decimals

Write these decimals to the nearest tenth.

6.23 is 6.2   6.27 is 6.3

If the second decimal place is a 5, we round up the first decimal place to the next larger number.

6.25 is 6.3

Write these decimals to the nearest tenth.

9.21 is	4.38 is	2.47 is
3.48 is	8.17 is	6.28 is
7.14 is	3.91 is	2.56 is
8.41 is	2.36 is	1.53 is

Write these decimals to the nearest tenth.

9.35 is	8.71 is	6.05 is
1.19 is	3.65 is	4.21 is
8.55 is	7.35 is	9.14 is
6.83 is	2.15 is	6.34 is

Write these decimals to the nearest tenth.

25.61 is	14.35 is	11.24 is
16.85 is	24.34 is	71.36 is
26.85 is	11.54 is	37.25 is
92.42 is	95.65 is	27.36 is
45.17 is	36.75 is	22.05 is

Adding with different numbers of digits

Find the total for each problem.

$$432 + 43 = 475$$

$$\overset{11}{176} + 97 = 273$$

Remember to regroup if you need to.

Find the total for each problem.

$$148 + 31$$

$$271 + 17$$

$$371 + 24$$

$$938 + 31$$

$$942 + 26$$

$$747 + 34$$

$$633 + 43$$

$$101 + 75$$

Write the answer in the box.

$$47 + 320 = $$

$$26 + 251 = $$

$$273 + 97 = $$

$$849 + 38 = $$

Write in the missing numbers in these problems.

$$2\,4\,2 + 2\,7 = 2\,\_\,9$$

$$9\,3\_ + 3\,8 = 9\,7\,7$$

$$8\,\_\,5 + 1\,2 = 8\,3\,7$$

$$6\,\_\,4 + 6\,3 = 6\,8\,7$$

Find the answer to these problems. Use the space for working them out.

Tommy has saved $238. For his birthday he is given another $52. How much does he have now?

A circus sells 208 adult tickets and 86 children's tickets. How many tickets are sold altogether?

Adding with different numbers of digits

Work out the answer to each problem.

$$\begin{array}{r} {}^{1}\ {}^{1}{}^{1}\ \\ 987 \\ +\ 423,123 \\ \hline 424,110 \end{array}$$

$$\begin{array}{r} {}^{1}\ {}^{1}{}^{1}\ \\ 2,767 \\ +\ 12,844 \\ \hline 15,611 \end{array}$$

Remember to regroup if you need to.

Work out the answer to each problem.

$$\begin{array}{r} 3,587 \\ +\ 17,628 \\ \hline \end{array}$$

$$\begin{array}{r} 8,537,227 \\ +\ 86,518 \\ \hline \end{array}$$

$$\begin{array}{r} 27 \\ +\ 9,964 \\ \hline \end{array}$$

$$\begin{array}{r} 436 \\ +\ 12,844 \\ \hline \end{array}$$

$$\begin{array}{r} 387,177 \\ +\ 8,381 \\ \hline \end{array}$$

$$\begin{array}{r} 6,770 \\ +\ 772,142 \\ \hline \end{array}$$

Write the answer in the box.

$$6,437,501 + 913,548 =$$

$$101,876 + 62,725 =$$

Write in the missing numbers in these sums.

$$\begin{array}{r} 5,\ \ 8\ \ \\ +\ \ \ \ 849 \\ \hline 6,236 \end{array}$$

$$\begin{array}{r} 2\ 1\ \ \\ +8,1\ 8\ 9 \\ \hline 8,5\ 1\ \ \end{array}$$

$$\begin{array}{r} 6,7\ 5\ \ \\ +\ \ \ 9\ 0\ 9 \\ \hline 7,6\ 6\ 1 \end{array}$$

Work out the answer to the problem. Use the space for working it out.

Jennifer has 1,342 stamps in her collection. Dennis has 742.
How many do they have altogether?

Subtracting one number from another

Find the difference for each problem.

$$\begin{array}{r} {}^{7\,13}\\ 8\cancel{3}4 \\ -\ \ 44 \\ \hline 790 \end{array}$$
$$\begin{array}{r} {}^{3\,12\,11}\\ \cancel{4}\cancel{3}\cancel{1} \\ -\ \ 84 \\ \hline 347 \end{array}$$

Find the difference for each problem.

$$\begin{array}{r} 835 \\ -\ 23 \\ \hline \end{array}$$
$$\begin{array}{r} 490 \\ -\ 70 \\ \hline \end{array}$$
$$\begin{array}{r} 175 \\ -\ 54 \\ \hline \end{array}$$
$$\begin{array}{r} 428 \\ -\ 67 \\ \hline \end{array}$$

$$\begin{array}{r} 587 \\ -\ 43 \\ \hline \end{array}$$
$$\begin{array}{r} 674 \\ -\ 62 \\ \hline \end{array}$$
$$\begin{array}{r} 389 \\ -\ 58 \\ \hline \end{array}$$
$$\begin{array}{r} 270 \\ -\ 30 \\ \hline \end{array}$$

$$\begin{array}{r} 483 \\ -\ 35 \\ \hline \end{array}$$
$$\begin{array}{r} 951 \\ -\ 28 \\ \hline \end{array}$$
$$\begin{array}{r} 746 \\ -\ 17 \\ \hline \end{array}$$
$$\begin{array}{r} 234 \\ -\ 16 \\ \hline \end{array}$$

Write the answer in the box.

$491 - 31 =$

$654 - 22 =$

$874 - 63 =$

$577 - 26 =$

Find the difference for each problem.

There are 565 children in a school. If 36 children are on a field trip, how many children are still at school?

A hardware store has 247 cans of paint. If they sell 29 cans, how many will they have left?

Subtracting one number from another

Work out the answer to each problem.

$$
\begin{array}{r}
{\scriptstyle 1\ 16\ 16\ 7\ 15} \\
27{,}6\cancel{8}\cancel{5} \\
-\ 8{,}726 \\
\hline
18{,}959
\end{array}
\qquad
\begin{array}{r}
{\scriptstyle 1\ 10\ 14\quad 3\ 12} \\
2{,}1\cancel{4}7{,}4\cancel{2}3 \\
-\ 165{,}351 \\
\hline
1{,}982{,}072
\end{array}
$$

Work out the answer to each problem.

$$
\begin{array}{r}
568{,}231 \\
-\ \ \ 3{,}846 \\
\hline
\end{array}
\qquad
\begin{array}{r}
6{,}262{,}411 \\
-\ \ 347{,}566 \\
\hline
\end{array}
\qquad
\begin{array}{r}
11{,}684 \\
-\ 2{,}845 \\
\hline
\end{array}
\qquad
\begin{array}{r}
337{,}481 \\
-\ 19{,}804 \\
\hline
\end{array}
$$

$$
\begin{array}{r}
6{,}157{,}965 \\
-3{,}633{,}976 \\
\hline
\end{array}
\qquad
\begin{array}{r}
892{,}112 \\
-\ 746{,}489 \\
\hline
\end{array}
\qquad
\begin{array}{r}
67{,}444 \\
-\ 29{,}545 \\
\hline
\end{array}
\qquad
\begin{array}{r}
82{,}818 \\
-\ 7{,}465 \\
\hline
\end{array}
$$

$$
\begin{array}{r}
952{,}812 \\
-\ 387{,}341 \\
\hline
\end{array}
\qquad
\begin{array}{r}
3{,}732{,}522 \\
-\ \ \ \ \ 3{,}176 \\
\hline
\end{array}
\qquad
\begin{array}{r}
38{,}529 \\
-25{,}892 \\
\hline
\end{array}
\qquad
\begin{array}{r}
116{,}387 \\
-\ \ 2{,}798 \\
\hline
\end{array}
$$

Write the answer in the box.

$4{,}555{,}562 - 1{,}624{,}871 =$

$962{,}118 \quad - \quad 8{,}467 =$

Work out the answer to the problem. Use the space for working it out.

2,826 people went to see a rock concert. 135 had to leave early to catch their train. How many were left at the end?

Real-life problems

Toby has $525.95 in the bank and he spends $146.37 on his vacation. How much does he have left?

Toby has $379.58 left.

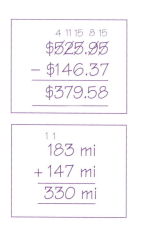

```
   4 11 15  8 15
   $5̶2̶5̶.9̶5̶
 − $146.37
   $379.58
```

A rally driver drives 183 mi on the first day of a race and 147 mi on the second day. How many miles does he travel in the two days?

He drives 330 miles.

```
   1 1
   183 mi
 + 147 mi
   330 mi
```

Mia spends $1,525 on a new computer and $146 on a printer. How much does she spend altogether?

Derek has a board that is 3.46 m long to make a shelf to fit an alcove 2.63 m long. How much must he cut off his board in order for it to fit?

A family is on a vacation. If they travel 358 mi in the first week and 388 mi in the second week, how many miles have they traveled altogether?

If their car had already gone 17,028 mi before the vacation, how many miles will it have gone by the end?

Two boxers are weighed before a boxing match. If the first weighs $186\frac{1}{2}$ lb and the second weighs 184 lb, what is the difference between their weights?

Everyday problems

An electrician buys 415 ft of cable. If he uses 234 ft, how much does he have left?

He has 181 ft of cable left.

$$\begin{array}{r} {}^{3}{}^{11} \\ \cancel{4}\cancel{1}5 \text{ ft} \\ -\ 234 \text{ ft} \\ \hline 181 \text{ ft} \end{array}$$

Simon travels by train for 110 mi, by bus for 56 mi and then walks the final 5 mi. How far does he travel?

Simon travels 171 mi.

$$\begin{array}{r} {}^{1} \\ 110 \text{ mi} \\ 56 \text{ mi} \\ +\ \ \ 5 \text{ mi} \\ \hline 171 \text{ mi} \end{array}$$

Mr. Hindley works 185 hours a month. His wife works 73 hours a month. How many hours do they work altogether in a month?

A school collects money for the local shelter. If the pupils collect $275 in the first month, $210 in the second month, and $136 in the third month, how much do they collect altogether?

Danny's car finishes the race in 12.75 seconds, Rachelle's car finishes in 14.83 seconds. Whose car won the race?

How much faster was the winning car?

A builder buys 8,755 lb of sand, but uses only 6,916 lb. How much does he have left?

Everyday problems

Rudy, Andrew, and Rachelle want to put their money together to buy a present for their brother. If Rudy gives $12.50, Andrew gives $14.75, and Rachelle gives $15.25, how much will they have to spend?

$$\begin{array}{r} {}^{11}\ {}^{1}\ \\ \$12.50 \\ \$14.75 \\ +\ \$15.25 \\ \hline \$42.50 \end{array}$$

They will have $42.50 to spend.

A store has 130 lb of potatoes and sells 80 lb. How much does it have left?

$$\begin{array}{r} {}^{13}\ \\ 1\cancel{3}0\ lb \\ -\ \ 80\ lb \\ \hline 50\ lb \end{array}$$

The store has 50 lb left.

A bakery orders 145 lb of sugar, 565 lb of salt, and 926 lb of butter. What is the total weight of the order?

Mr. Jean-Paul traveled in a limo to the airport. After he paid a fare of $65, he had $125 left. How much money did he start with?

A vacation in Florida costs $394. A vacation in Majorca costs $876. How much cheaper is the Florida vacation?

Chamique is saving up to buy a guitar that costs $159.99. If she already has $65.37, how much more does she need?

Mr. Lorenzo's garden is 10 ft long and 8 ft wide. How much fence does he need to surround all four sides?

Decimal addition

Write the answer to each problem.

$$\begin{array}{r} 53.72 \\ +77.92 \\ \hline \end{array} \qquad \begin{array}{r} 84.17 \\ +68.21 \\ \hline \end{array} \qquad \begin{array}{r} 29.36 \\ +66.84 \\ \hline \end{array} \qquad \begin{array}{r} 23.56 \\ +79.14 \\ \hline \end{array} \qquad \begin{array}{r} 62.49 \\ +18.75 \\ \hline \end{array}$$

$$\begin{array}{r} 35.67 \\ +12.99 \\ \hline \end{array} \qquad \begin{array}{r} 29.88 \\ +43.02 \\ \hline \end{array} \qquad \begin{array}{r} 67.39 \\ +81.70 \\ \hline \end{array} \qquad \begin{array}{r} 49.32 \\ +14.95 \\ \hline \end{array} \qquad \begin{array}{r} 27.22 \\ +38.84 \\ \hline \end{array}$$

Write the answer to each problem.

$$\begin{array}{r} 76.30 \\ +22.97 \\ \hline \end{array} \qquad \begin{array}{r} 44.29 \\ +11.04 \\ \hline \end{array} \qquad \begin{array}{r} 81.97 \\ +69.14 \\ \hline \end{array} \qquad \begin{array}{r} 29.86 \\ +76.33 \\ \hline \end{array} \qquad \begin{array}{r} 68.25 \\ +84.36 \\ \hline \end{array}$$

$$\begin{array}{r} 83.90 \\ +30.24 \\ \hline \end{array} \qquad \begin{array}{r} 45.83 \\ +45.71 \\ \hline \end{array} \qquad \begin{array}{r} 52.17 \\ +90.21 \\ \hline \end{array} \qquad \begin{array}{r} 84.93 \\ +29.37 \\ \hline \end{array} \qquad \begin{array}{r} 72.83 \\ +41.16 \\ \hline \end{array}$$

Write the answer to each problem.

$37.89 + 82.15 =$ \qquad $32.44 + 21.88 =$ \qquad $37.19 + 28.24 =$

$68.67 + 29.82 =$ \qquad $21.99 + 79.32 =$ \qquad $52.45 + 34.58 =$

$84.77 + 39.12 =$ \qquad $63.84 + 29.81 =$ \qquad $34.43 + 25.64 =$

$33.97 + 24.62 =$ \qquad $76.39 + 43.78 =$ \qquad $52.38 + 38.43 =$

Decimal addition

Write the sum for each problem.

$$\begin{array}{r}\overset{1}{2}9\overset{1}{6}.48 \\ +\ 131.70 \\ \hline 428.18 \end{array}$$

$$\begin{array}{r}\overset{1}{7}\overset{1}{3}.00 \\ +\ 269.23 \\ \hline 342.23 \end{array}$$

Write the sum for each problem.

$$\begin{array}{r}491.83 \\ +\ 37.84 \\ \hline \end{array}$$
$$\begin{array}{r}964.71 \\ +\ 321.2 \\ \hline \end{array}$$
$$\begin{array}{r}32.045 \\ +\ 204.99 \\ \hline \end{array}$$
$$\begin{array}{r}306 \\ +\ 844.24 \\ \hline \end{array}$$

$$\begin{array}{r}471.932 \\ +\ 755.26 \\ \hline \end{array}$$
$$\begin{array}{r}842.01 \\ +\ 11.842 \\ \hline \end{array}$$
$$\begin{array}{r}675.82 \\ +\ 105 \\ \hline \end{array}$$
$$\begin{array}{r}37.82 \\ +\ 399.71 \\ \hline \end{array}$$

$$\begin{array}{r}65.24 \\ +\ 605.27 \\ \hline \end{array}$$
$$\begin{array}{r}178.935 \\ +\ 599.41 \\ \hline \end{array}$$
$$\begin{array}{r}184.70 \\ +\ 372.81 \\ \hline \end{array}$$
$$\begin{array}{r}443.27 \\ +\ 75 \\ \hline \end{array}$$

$$\begin{array}{r}563 \\ +\ 413.98 \\ \hline \end{array}$$
$$\begin{array}{r}703.95 \\ +\ 85.11 \\ \hline \end{array}$$
$$\begin{array}{r}825.36 \\ +\ 249.857 \\ \hline \end{array}$$
$$\begin{array}{r}529.3 \\ +\ 482.56 \\ \hline \end{array}$$

Write the sum for each problem.

$421 + 136.25 =$

$92.31 + 241.73 =$

$501.8 + 361.93 =$

$558.32 + 137.945 =$

$27 + 142.07 =$

$75.31 + 293.33 =$

$153.3 + 182.02 =$

$491.445 + 105.37 =$

$253.71 + 62 =$

$829.2 + 63.74 =$

Decimal subtraction

Write the difference for each problem.

$$\begin{array}{r} {}^{6}5\overset{6}{9}.\overset{16}{7}6 \\ -\ 21.47 \\ \hline 38.29 \end{array} \qquad \begin{array}{r} 5\overset{0}{7}.\overset{18}{1}8 \\ -\ 22.09 \\ \hline 35.09 \end{array}$$

Write the difference for each problem.

$$\begin{array}{r} 64.92 \\ -\ 26.35 \\ \hline \end{array} \qquad \begin{array}{r} 64.21 \\ -\ 16.02 \\ \hline \end{array} \qquad \begin{array}{r} 73.71 \\ -\ 19.24 \\ \hline \end{array} \qquad \begin{array}{r} 92.63 \\ -\ 67.14 \\ \hline \end{array}$$

$$\begin{array}{r} 45.76 \\ -\ 16.18 \\ \hline \end{array} \qquad \begin{array}{r} 73.52 \\ -\ 39.27 \\ \hline \end{array} \qquad \begin{array}{r} 98.98 \\ -\ 39.19 \\ \hline \end{array} \qquad \begin{array}{r} 53.58 \\ -\ 14.39 \\ \hline \end{array}$$

$$\begin{array}{r} 94.87 \\ -\ 65.28 \\ \hline \end{array} \qquad \begin{array}{r} 21.74 \\ -\ 12.1 \\ \hline \end{array} \qquad \begin{array}{r} 62.35 \\ -\ 13.16 \\ \hline \end{array} \qquad \begin{array}{r} 81.94 \\ -\ 28.15 \\ \hline \end{array}$$

$$\begin{array}{r} 62.95 \\ -\ 33.37 \\ \hline \end{array} \qquad \begin{array}{r} 81.42 \\ -\ 25.04 \\ \hline \end{array} \qquad \begin{array}{r} 48.52 \\ -\ 14.49 \\ \hline \end{array} \qquad \begin{array}{r} 61.55 \\ -\ 13.26 \\ \hline \end{array}$$

Write the difference for each problem.

$51.52 - 12.13 =$ $\qquad$ $72.41 - 23.18 =$

$91.91 - 22.22 =$ $\qquad$ $53.84 - 19.65 =$

$41.82 - 18.13 =$ $\qquad$ $51.61 - 23.14 =$

$83.91 - 14.73 =$ $\qquad$ $64.65 - 37.26 =$

$53.21 - 35.12 =$ $\qquad$ $77.31 - 28.15 =$

Decimal subtraction

Write the difference for each problem.

$$
\begin{array}{r}
\overset{7\ 11}{68.\cancel{1}7} \\
-11.40 \\
\hline
56.77
\end{array}
\qquad
\begin{array}{r}
\overset{1\ 10}{39.2\cancel{0}} \\
-13.15 \\
\hline
26.05
\end{array}
$$

Work out the difference for each problem.

$$
\begin{array}{r}
87.23 \\
-\ 24.4 \\
\hline
\end{array}
\qquad
\begin{array}{r}
95.15 \\
-\ 31.356 \\
\hline
\end{array}
\qquad
\begin{array}{r}
66.37 \\
-\ 21.9 \\
\hline
\end{array}
\qquad
\begin{array}{r}
85 \\
-\ 26.32 \\
\hline
\end{array}
$$

$$
\begin{array}{r}
72.28 \\
-\ 1.3 \\
\hline
\end{array}
\qquad
\begin{array}{r}
63.14 \\
-\ 32 \\
\hline
\end{array}
\qquad
\begin{array}{r}
99.235 \\
-\ 33.70 \\
\hline
\end{array}
\qquad
\begin{array}{r}
62.1 \\
-\ 29.34 \\
\hline
\end{array}
$$

$$
\begin{array}{r}
77.3 \\
-\ 24.42 \\
\hline
\end{array}
\qquad
\begin{array}{r}
55.492 \\
-\ 27.66 \\
\hline
\end{array}
\qquad
\begin{array}{r}
68 \\
-\ 31.5 \\
\hline
\end{array}
\qquad
\begin{array}{r}
35.612 \\
-\ 13.207 \\
\hline
\end{array}
$$

$$
\begin{array}{r}
82.35 \\
-\ 23.40 \\
\hline
\end{array}
\qquad
\begin{array}{r}
63.20 \\
-\ 15.36 \\
\hline
\end{array}
\qquad
\begin{array}{r}
53.64 \\
-\ 23 \\
\hline
\end{array}
\qquad
\begin{array}{r}
35.612 \\
-\ 26.19 \\
\hline
\end{array}
$$

Write the difference for each problem.

$63.4 - 24.51 =$ $92.197 - 63.28 =$

$91.3 - 33 =$ $41.24 - 14.306 =$

$52.251 - 22.42 =$ $72.6 - 53.71 =$

$92.84 - 23 =$ $61.16 - 24.4 =$

$81.815 - 55.90 =$ $94.31 - 27.406 =$

Multiplying larger numbers by ones

Write the product for each problem.

```
    1 3              1 31
   529            1,273
x     4          x     5
─────────        ─────────
 2,116            6,365
```

Write the product for each problem.

```
   724            831            126            455
x    2          x   3          x   3          x   4
─────           ─────          ─────          ─────
```

```
   161            282            349            253
x    4          x   5          x   5          x   6
─────           ─────          ─────          ─────
```

```
   328            465            105            562
x    6          x   6          x   4          x   4
─────           ─────          ─────          ─────
```

Write the product for each problem.

```
 4,261          1,582          3,612          4,284
x    3          x   3          x   4          x   4
─────           ─────          ─────          ─────
```

```
 5,907          1,263          1,303          1,467
x    5          x   5          x   6          x   6
─────           ─────          ─────          ─────
```

```
 6,521          8,436          1,599          3,761
x    6          x   6          x   6          x   6
─────           ─────          ─────          ─────
```

```
 5,837          6,394          8,124          3,914
x    4          x   5          x   6          x   6
─────           ─────          ─────          ─────
```

Multiplying larger numbers by ones

Write the answer to each problem.

```
     1 4              1 7 4
    417              2,185
 x     7          x        9
   2,919             19,665
```

Write the answer to each problem.

```
    419              604              715              327
 x     7          x     7          x     8          x     7
 _____          _____          _____          _____


    425              171              682              246
 x     8          x     9          x     8          x     8
 _____          _____          _____          _____


    436              999              319              581
 x     8          x     9          x     9          x     9
 _____          _____          _____          _____
```

Work out the answer to each problem.

```
  4,331            2,816            1,439            2,617
 x     7          x     7          x     8          x     8
 _____          _____          _____          _____


  3,104            4,022            3,212            2,591
 x     8          x     8          x     9          x     9
 _____          _____          _____          _____


  1,710            3,002            2,468            1,514
 x     9          x     8          x     7          x     8
 _____          _____          _____          _____


  4,624            2,993            3,894            4,361
 x     7          x     8          x     8          x     9
 _____          _____          _____          _____
```

Real-life multiplication problems

There are 157 apples in a box.
How many will there be in three boxes?

471 apples

$$
\begin{array}{r}
\,^{1}\!^{2}157 \\
\times \quad 3 \\
\hline
471
\end{array}
$$

A stamp album can hold 550 stamps.
How many stamps will 5 albums hold?

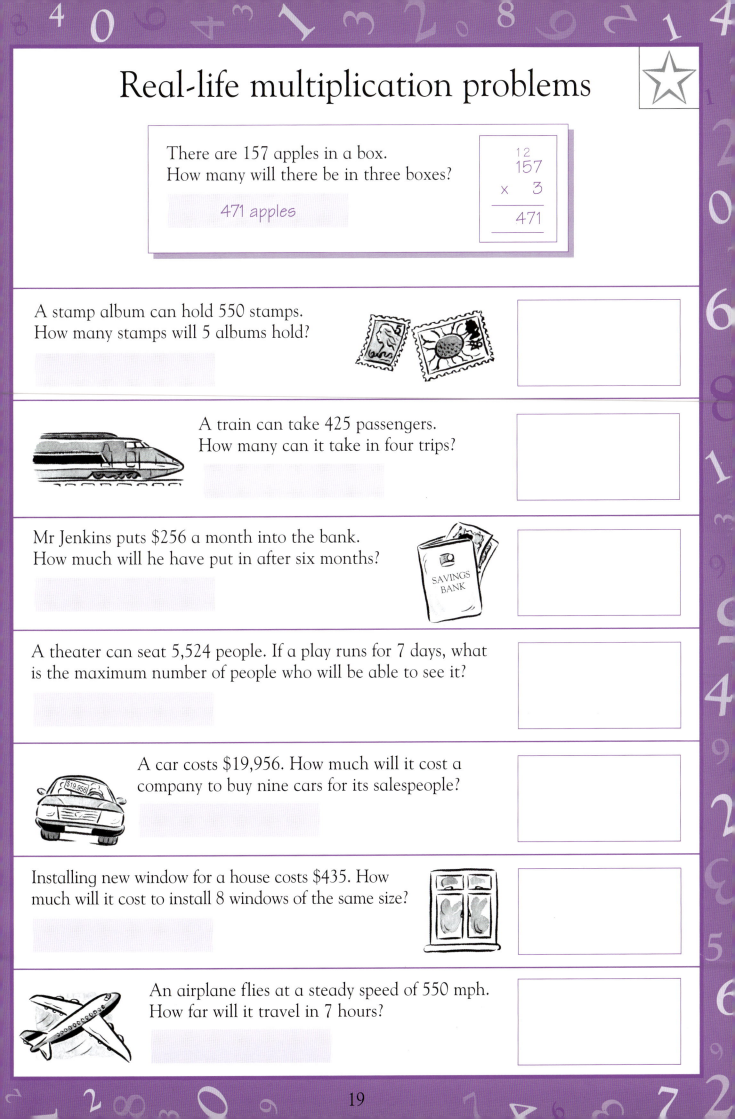

A train can take 425 passengers.
How many can it take in four trips?

Mr Jenkins puts $256 a month into the bank.
How much will he have put in after six months?

A theater can seat 5,524 people. If a play runs for 7 days, what is the maximum number of people who will be able to see it?

A car costs $19,956. How much will it cost a company to buy nine cars for its salespeople?

Installing new window for a house costs $435. How much will it cost to install 8 windows of the same size?

An airplane flies at a steady speed of 550 mph.
How far will it travel in 7 hours?

Comparing and ordering decimals

Compare the decimals. Which decimal is greater?

2.2 and 3.1   0.45 and 0.6

Line them up vertically.

2.2   0.45
3.1   0.60

3>2, so 3.1>2.2   6>4, so 0.6>0.45

Compare the decimals. Which decimal is greater?

7.9 and 8.1   0.5 and 0.62   3.6 and 0.94   0.4 and 0.67

1.6 and 1.9   0.31 and 3.10   8.5 and 6.9   6.75 and 6.71

Find the greatest decimal.

2.9 and 2.75 and 2.6   0.97 and 1.09 and 1.3   4.9 and 3.87 and 4.75

Write the decimals in order from greatest to least.

0.33   3.1   0.3   24.95   23.9   24.5   7.5   6.95   7.58

Find the answer to each problem.

The Weather Bureau reported 5.18 inches of rain in March, 6.74 inches in April, and 5.23 inches in May. Which month had the least rainfall?

A postal worker walked 4.5 miles on Wednesday, 3.75 miles on Thursday, and 4.25 miles on Friday. Which day did she walk the farthest?

Converting units of measure

Convert 25 centimeters to millimeters.   Convert 200¢ to dollars.

25 x 10 = 250 mm   200 ÷ 100 = $2

Convert these centimeters to millimeters.

40 cm		15 cm		9 cm	
12 cm		34 cm		62 cm	
43 cm		96 cm		105 cm	
92 cm		20 cm		426 cm	

Convert these millimeters to centimeters.

30 mm		100 mm		120 mm	
60 mm		90 mm		200 mm	
130 mm		10 mm		400 mm	

Convert these dollars to cents.

$35		$600		$15	
$12		$36		$95	
$72		$4		$250	

Convert these cents to dollars.

450¢		900¢		6 000¢	
250¢		400¢		150¢	
100¢		300¢		750¢	

Converting units of measure

Convert these centimetres to metres.

500 cm	900 cm	400 cm
8,000 cm	3,000 cm	4,000 cm
9,800 cm	8,300 cm	6,200 cm
36,800 cm	94,200 cm	73,500 cm

Convert these meters to centimeters.

47 m	29 m	84 m
69 m	24 m	38 m
146 m	237 m	921 m

Convert these meters to kilometers.

5,000 m	6,000 m	9,000 m
15,000 m	27,000 m	71,000 m
19,000 m	86,000 m	42,000 m

Convert these kilometers to meters.

7 km	9 km	4 km
23 km	46 km	87 km
12 km	96 km	39 km

Area of rectangles and squares

Find the area of this rectangle

To find the area of a rectangle or square, we multiply length (l) by width (w).

Area = 800 in.²

(w)   25 in.

(l)

32 in.

$$\begin{array}{r} \overset{1}{32} \\ \times\ 25 \\ \hline \overset{1}{160} \\ +640 \\ \hline 800\ \text{in.}^2 \end{array}$$

Find the area of these rectangles and squares.
You may need to do your work on a separate sheet.

42 in.

21 in.

_____ in.²

84 in.

84 in.

_____ in.²

95 ft

36 ft

_____ ft²

41 ft

87 ft

_____ ft²

68 mm

49 mm

_____ mm²

77 mm

83 mm

_____ mm²

99 in.

99 in.

_____ in.²

39 in.

85 in.

_____ in.²

69 in.

83 in.

_____ in.²

Perimeter of shapes

Find the perimeter of this rectangle.

To find the perimeter of a rectangle or square, we add the two lengths and the two widths together.

12.4 in.

27.3 in.

```
 1  1
  27.3 in.
  27.3 in.
  12.4 in.
+ 12.4 in.
  79.4 in.
```

79.4 in.

Find the perimeter of these rectangles and squares.
You may need to do your work on a separate sheet.

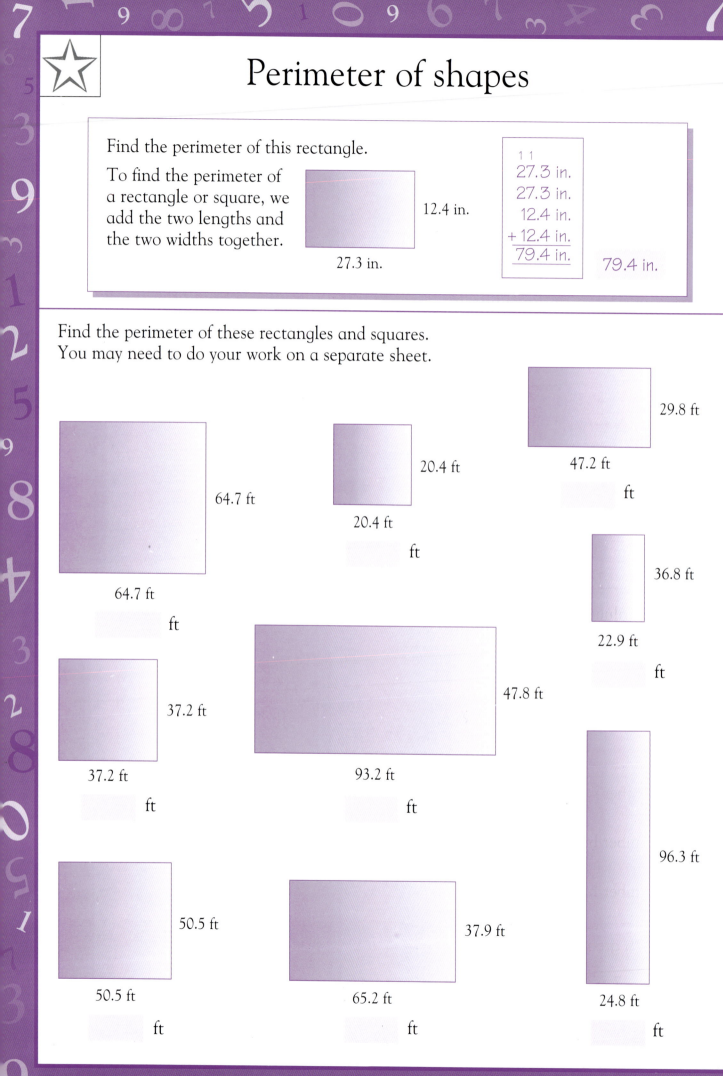

64.7 ft

64.7 ft

_____ ft

20.4 ft

20.4 ft

_____ ft

29.8 ft

47.2 ft

_____ ft

37.2 ft

37.2 ft

_____ ft

47.8 ft

93.2 ft

_____ ft

36.8 ft

22.9 ft

_____ ft

50.5 ft

50.5 ft

_____ ft

37.9 ft

65.2 ft

_____ ft

96.3 ft

24.8 ft

_____ ft

24

Decimal place value

Work out the answer to the problem.

2.385
What is the value of the digit 8?

Ones	Tenths	Hundredths	Thousandths	Ten-thousandths
2.	3	8	5	0

2.3850
8 is in the hundredths place, so, its value is 8 hundredths.

Name the place of the digit 8 in each of the problems.

0.387	3.0738	4.82	1.118

Name the value of the highlighted digit.

6.5937	5.371	7.4032	0.4215

8.246	3.611	1.062

Which number has a digit with the value 6 tenths?

Which number has a digit with the value 6 hundredths?

Which number has a digit with the value 6 thousandths?

How much greater is the second decimal than the first?

7.46 7.56	3.272 3.273	0.821 0.831
one tenth more		

Speed problems

How long will it take a bike rider to travel 36 mi at a constant speed of 9 miles per hour?

Time = Distance ÷ Speed

If a car traveled 150 mi at a constant speed in 5 hours, at what speed was it traveling?

30 mph

5⟌150

Speed = Distance ÷ Time

If a bus travels for 5 hours at 40 mph, how far does it travel?

5 × 40 = 200 mi

Distance = Speed × Time

A car travels along a road at a steady speed of 60 mph. How far will it travel in 6 hours?

A train covers a distance of 480 mi in 8 hours. If it travels at a constant speed, how fast is it traveling?

John walks at a steady speed of 3 mph. How long will it take him to travel 24 miles?

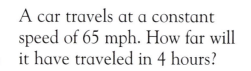

A car travels at a constant speed of 65 mph. How far will it have traveled in 4 hours?

Melanie completes a long distance run at an average speed of 6 mph. If it takes her 3 hours, how far did she run?

Sarah cycles 30 mi to her grandmother's house at a steady speed of 10 mph. If she leaves home at 2:00 P.M., what time will she arrive?

Conversion table

This is part of a conversion table that shows how to change dollars to francs when 10 French francs (10F) equal $1.

U.S. Dollars	French Francs
1	10
2	20
3	30

How many francs would you get for $2?   20F

How much is 25F worth in dollars? $2.50

How many dollars would you get for 40F?

How many dollars would you get for 85F?

How much is 1F worth?

Change $65 into francs.

What is $3.50 in francs?

Change 250F into dollars.

How many francs could you get for $0.40?

U.S. Dollars	French Francs
1	10
2	20
3	30
4	40
5	50
6	60
7	70
8	80
9	90
10	100

The rate then changes to 8F to the dollar.
The conversion chart now looks like the one shown here.

How many francs are worth $4?

How many dollars can you get for 56F?

How many francs are worth $9.50?

How many francs can you get for $20?

How many dollars would you get for 120F?

What is the value of 4F?

U.S. Dollars	French Francs
1	8
2	16
3	24
4	32
5	40
6	48
7	56
8	64
9	72
10	80

Interpreting circle graphs

32 children voted for their favorite ice-cream flavors.
How many children voted for chocolate?

$\frac{3}{8}$ of 32 is 12

12 children voted for chocolate.

12 children

How many children voted for fudge?

$\frac{1}{8}$ of 32 is 4

4 children voted for fudge.

4 children

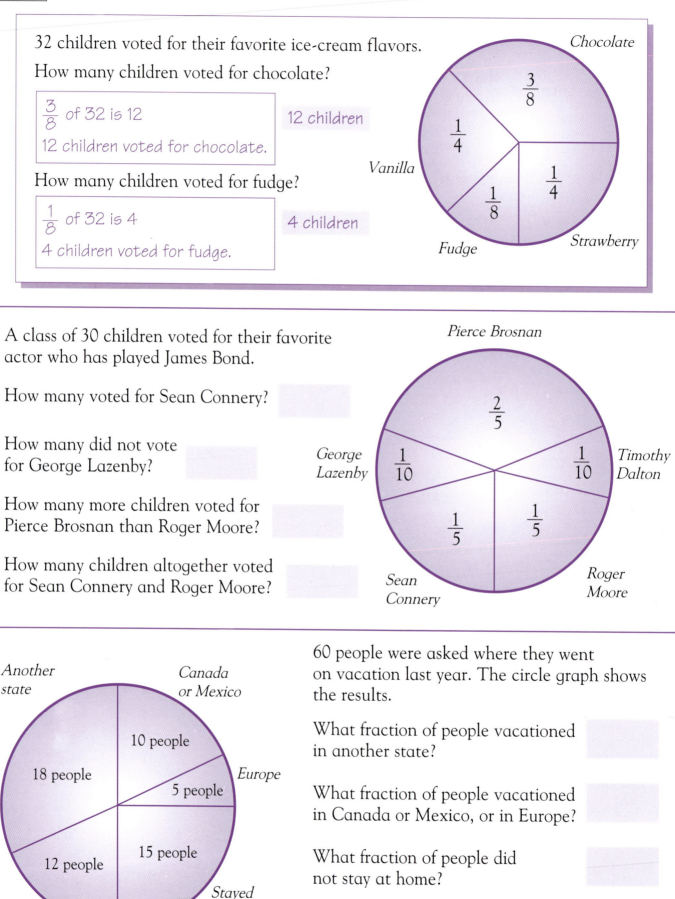

A class of 30 children voted for their favorite actor who has played James Bond.

How many voted for Sean Connery?

How many did not vote for George Lazenby?

How many more children voted for Pierce Brosnan than Roger Moore?

How many children altogether voted for Sean Connery and Roger Moore?

60 people were asked where they went on vacation last year. The circle graph shows the results.

What fraction of people vacationed in another state?

What fraction of people vacationed in Canada or Mexico, or in Europe?

What fraction of people did not stay at home?

What fraction of people vacationed in their state or another state?

Probability scale 0 to 1

Look at this probability line.

Impossible = 0
Poor chance = 0.25
Fair = 0.5
Good chance = 0.75
Certain = 1

Write each letter in the correct place on the probability line.

a. It will be daylight in New Orleans at midnight.
b. The sun will come up tomorrow.
c. If I toss a coin it will come down heads.

a ↓   c ↓   b ↓

0   0.25   0.5   0.75   1

---

0   0.25   0.5   0.75   1

Write each letter in the correct place on the probability line.

a. If I cut a pack of cards I will get a red card.

b. If I cut a pack of cards I will get a diamond.

c. If I cut a pack of cards I will get a diamond, a spade, or a club.

d. If I cut a pack of cards I will get a diamond, a spade, a club, or a heart.

e. If I cut a pack of cards it will be a 15.

---

0   0.25   0.5   0.75   1

Write each letter in the correct place on the probability line.

a. Next week, Wednesday will be the day after Tuesday.

b. There will be 33 days in February next year.

c. It will snow in Miami in May.

d. It will snow in Chicago in January.

e. The next person to knock on the door will be a woman.

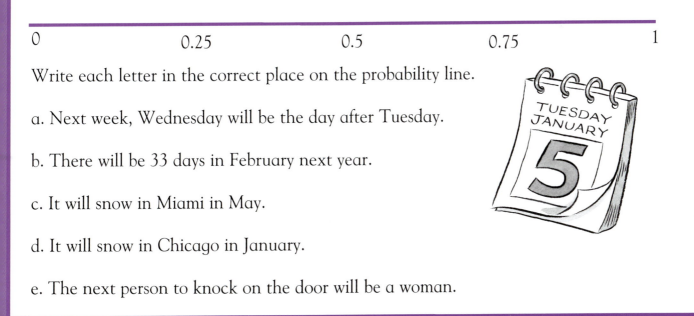

Likely outcomes

Throw one coin 20 times.
Keep a tally.

H	ⵏⵯⵏ ‖‖
T	ⵏⵯⵏ ⵏⵯⵏ ‖

Put your results on a bar graph.

Number of throws

20
15
10
5

H   T

What do you notice?

Heads and tails come up roughly the same number of times because there are only two possible outcomes and they are equally likely.

Predict what you think the outcome will be if you tossed two coins 48 times.

2 heads _____ times   2 tails _____ times   1 of each _____ times

Now actually throw two coins 48 times and record your results on this tally chart.

2 Heads	
2 Tails	
1 of each	

Draw a bar graph to show your results.

Number of throws

50
45
40
35
30
25
20
15
10
5
0

Heads   Tails   1 of each

Which result comes up the most often?

Can you explain why some results
are more probable than others?

30

Naming quadrilaterals

Name this shape.

Rhombus

Name these shapes.

Sketch these shapes.

Parallelogram   Rectangle

Rhombus   Trapezoid

Speed trials

Write the answers as fast as you can, but get them right!

$4 \times 10 = 40$ $8 \times 2 = 16$ $6 \times 5 = 30$

Write the answers as fast as you can, but get them right!

$3 \times 2 =$	$0 \times 5 =$	$3 \times 10 =$	$0 \times 3 =$
$5 \times 2 =$	$10 \times 5 =$	$5 \times 10 =$	$10 \times 3 =$
$1 \times 2 =$	$8 \times 5 =$	$1 \times 10 =$	$8 \times 3 =$
$4 \times 2 =$	$6 \times 5 =$	$4 \times 10 =$	$6 \times 3 =$
$7 \times 2 =$	$2 \times 5 =$	$7 \times 10 =$	$2 \times 3 =$
$2 \times 2 =$	$7 \times 5 =$	$2 \times 10 =$	$7 \times 3 =$
$6 \times 2 =$	$4 \times 5 =$	$6 \times 10 =$	$4 \times 3 =$
$8 \times 2 =$	$1 \times 5 =$	$8 \times 10 =$	$1 \times 3 =$
$10 \times 2 =$	$5 \times 5 =$	$10 \times 10 =$	$5 \times 3 =$
$0 \times 2 =$	$3 \times 5 =$	$0 \times 10 =$	$3 \times 3 =$
$9 \times 2 =$	$5 \times 3 =$	$9 \times 10 =$	$6 \times 4 =$
$2 \times 7 =$	$5 \times 8 =$	$10 \times 7 =$	$3 \times 4 =$
$2 \times 1 =$	$5 \times 6 =$	$10 \times 1 =$	$7 \times 4 =$
$2 \times 4 =$	$5 \times 9 =$	$10 \times 4 =$	$4 \times 4 =$
$3 \times 7 =$	$5 \times 7 =$	$10 \times 7 =$	$10 \times 4 =$
$2 \times 5 =$	$5 \times 4 =$	$10 \times 5 =$	$8 \times 4 =$
$2 \times 9 =$	$5 \times 1 =$	$10 \times 9 =$	$0 \times 4 =$
$2 \times 6 =$	$4 \times 7 =$	$10 \times 6 =$	$9 \times 4 =$
$2 \times 8 =$	$5 \times 10 =$	$10 \times 8 =$	$5 \times 4 =$
$2 \times 3 =$	$5 \times 2 =$	$10 \times 3 =$	$2 \times 4 =$

All the 3s

You will need to know these:

$1 \times 3 = 3$ $2 \times 3 = 6$ $3 \times 3 = 9$ $4 \times 3 = 12$ $5 \times 3 = 15$ $10 \times 3 = 30$

How many altogether?

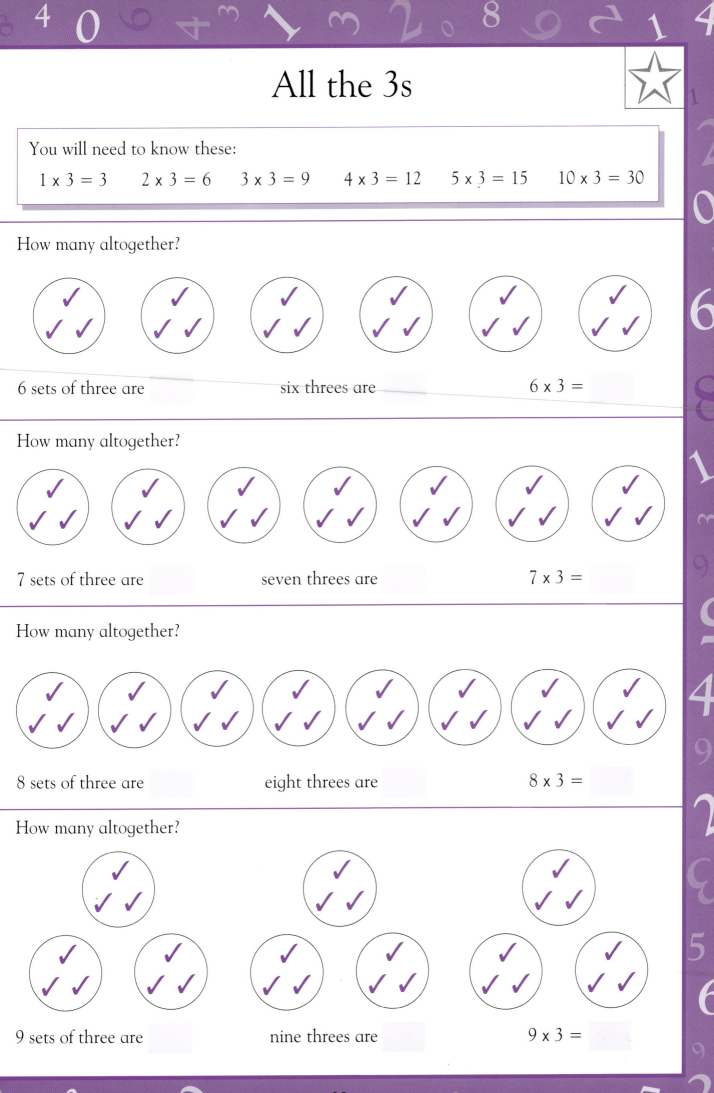

6 sets of three are   six threes are $6 \times 3 =$

How many altogether?

7 sets of three are   seven threes are $7 \times 3 =$

How many altogether?

8 sets of three are   eight threes are $8 \times 3 =$

How many altogether?

9 sets of three are   nine threes are $9 \times 3 =$

All the 3s again

You should know all of the three times table by now.

1 x 3 = 3	2 x 3 = 6	3 x 3 = 9	4 x 3 = 12	5 x 3 = 15
6 x 3 = 18	7 x 3 = 21	8 x 3 = 24	9 x 3 = 27	10 x 3 = 30

Say these to yourself a few times.

Cover the three times table with a sheet of paper so you can't see the numbers. Write the answers. Be as fast as you can, but get them right!

1 x 3 =	5 x 3 =	6 x 3 =
2 x 3 =	7 x 3 =	9 x 3 =
3 x 3 =	9 x 3 =	4 x 3 =
4 x 3 =	4 x 3 =	5 x 3 =
5 x 3 =	6 x 3 =	3 x 7 =
6 x 3 =	8 x 3 =	3 x 4 =
7 x 3 =	10 x 3 =	2 x 3 =
8 x 3 =	1 x 3 =	10 x 3 =
9 x 3 =	3 x 3 =	3 x 9 =
10 x 3 =	2 x 3 =	3 x 6 =
3 x 1 =	3 x 5 =	3 x 5 =
3 x 2 =	3 x 7 =	3 x 8 =
3 x 3 =	3 x 9 =	7 x 3 =
3 x 4 =	3 x 4 =	3 x 2 =
3 x 5 =	3 x 6 =	3 x 10 =
3 x 6 =	3 x 8 =	8 x 3 =
3 x 7 =	3 x 10 =	3 x 0 =
3 x 8 =	3 x 1 =	1 x 3 =
3 x 9 =	3 x 0 =	3 x 3 =
3 x 10 =	3 x 2 =	3 x 9 =

All the 4s

How many altogether?

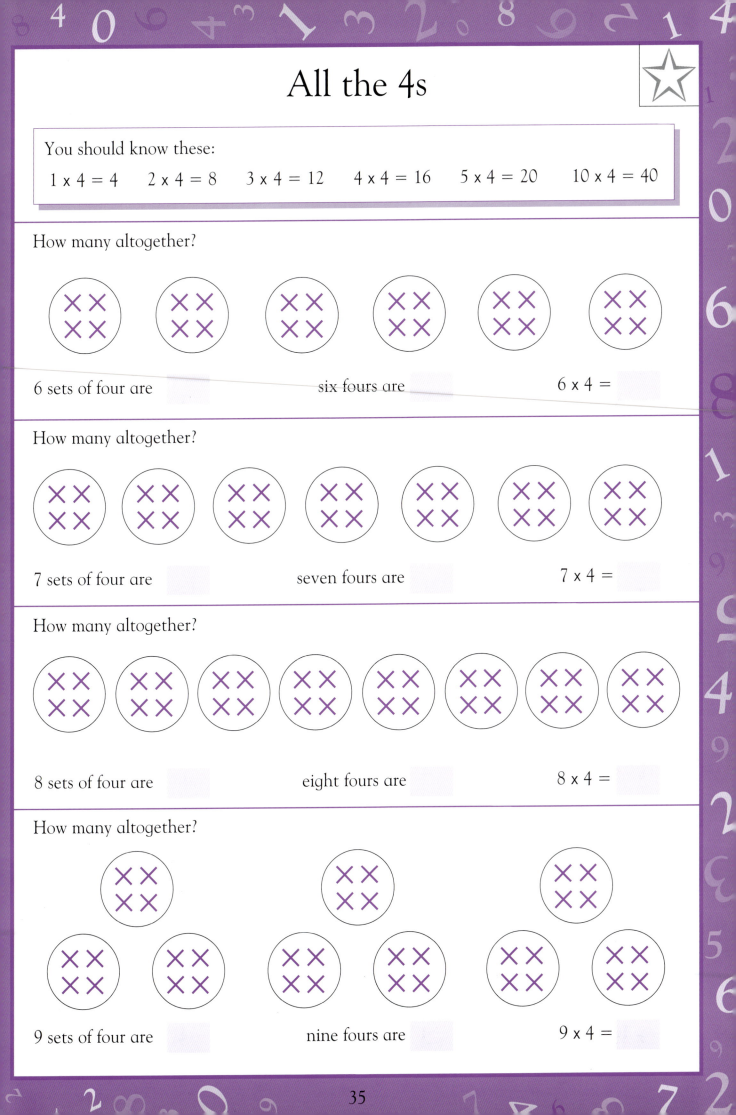

6 sets of four are   six fours are   6 x 4 =

How many altogether?

7 sets of four are   seven fours are   7 x 4 =

How many altogether?

8 sets of four are   eight fours are   8 x 4 =

How many altogether?

9 sets of four are   nine fours are   9 x 4 =

All the 4s again

Cover the four times table with a sheet of paper so you can't see the numbers.
Write the answers. Be as fast as you can, but get them right!

1 x 4 =	5 x 4 =	6 x 4 =
2 x 4 =	7 x 4 =	9 x 4 =
3 x 4 =	9 x 4 =	4 x 1 =
4 x 4 =	3 x 4 =	5 x 4 =
5 x 4 =	6 x 4 =	4 x 7 =
6 x 4 =	8 x 4 =	3 x 4 =
7 x 4 =	10 x 4 =	2 x 4 =
8 x 4 =	1 x 4 =	10 x 4 =
9 x 4 =	4 x 4 =	4 x 3 =
10 x 4 =	2 x 4 =	4 x 6 =
4 x 1 =	4 x 5 =	4 x 5 =
4 x 2 =	4 x 7 =	4 x 8 =
4 x 3 =	4 x 9 =	7 x 4 =
4 x 4 =	4 x 4 =	4 x 2 =
4 x 5 =	4 x 6 =	4 x 10 =
4 x 6 =	4 x 8 =	8 x 4 =
4 x 7 =	4 x 10 =	4 x 0 =
4 x 8 =	4 x 1 =	1 x 4 =
4 x 9 =	4 x 0 =	4 x 4 =
4 x 10 =	4 x 2 =	4 x 9 =

Speed trials

You should know all of the 1, 2, 3, 4, 5, and 10 times tables by now, but how quickly can you do them?
Ask someone to time you as you do this page.
Remember, you must be fast but also correct.

4 x 2 =	6 x 3 =	9 x 5 =
8 x 3 =	3 x 4 =	8 x 10 =
7 x 4 =	7 x 5 =	7 x 2 =
6 x 5 =	3 x 10 =	6 x 3 =
8 x 10 =	1 x 2 =	5 x 4 =
8 x 2 =	7 x 3 =	4 x 5 =
5 x 3 =	4 x 4 =	3 x 10 =
9 x 4 =	6 x 5 =	2 x 2 =
5 x 5 =	4 x 10 =	1 x 3 =
7 x 10 =	6 x 2 =	0 x 4 =
0 x 2 =	5 x 3 =	10 x 5 =
4 x 3 =	8 x 4 =	9 x 2 =
6 x 4 =	0 x 5 =	8 x 3 =
3 x 5 =	2 x 10 =	7 x 4 =
4 x 10 =	7 x 2 =	6 x 5 =
7 x 2 =	8 x 3 =	5 x 10 =
3 x 3 =	9 x 4 =	4 x 0 =
2 x 4 =	5 x 5 =	3 x 2 =
7 x 5 =	7 x 10 =	2 x 8 =
9 x 10 =	5 x 2 =	1 x 9 =

Some of the 6s

You should already know parts of the 6 times table because they are parts of the 1, 2, 3, 4, 5, and 10 times tables.

$1 \times 6 = 6$ $2 \times 6 = 12$ $3 \times 6 = 18$

$4 \times 6 = 24$ $5 \times 6 = 30$ $10 \times 6 = 60$

Find out if you can remember them quickly and correctly.

Cover the six times table with paper so you can't see the numbers.
Write the answers as quickly as you can.

What is three sixes?   What is ten sixes?

What is two sixes?   What is four sixes?

What is one six?   What is five sixes?

Write the answers as quickly as you can.

How many sixes make 12?   How many sixes make 6?

How many sixes make 30?   How many sixes make 18?

How many sixes make 24?   How many sixes make 60?

Write the answers as quickly as you can.

Multiply six by three.   Multiply six by ten.

Multiply six by two.   Multiply six by five.

Multiply six by one.   Multiply six by four.

Write the answers as quickly as you can.

$4 \times 6 =$ $2 \times 6 =$ $10 \times 6 =$

$5 \times 6 =$ $1 \times 6 =$ $3 \times 6 =$

Write the answers as quickly as you can.

A box contains six eggs. A man buys five boxes. How many eggs does he have?

A pack contains six sticks of gum.
How many sticks will there be in 10 packs?

The rest of the 6s

This work will help you remember the 6 times table.

Complete these sequences.

| 6 | 12 | 18 | 24 | 30 | | | | | |

5 x 6 = 30   so   6 x 6 = 30 plus another 6 =

| 18 | 24 | 30 | | | | | |

6 x 6 = 36   so   7 x 6 = 36 plus another 6 =

| 6 | 12 | 18 | | | | 48 | | 60 |

7 x 6 = 42   so   8 x 6 = 42 plus another 6 =

| 6 | | 18 | 24 | 30 | | | | |

8 x 6 = 48   so   9 x 6 = 48 plus another 6 =

| | | | 24 | | | 42 | | | 60 |

Test yourself on the rest of the 6 times table.
Cover the above part of the page with a sheet of paper.

What is six sixes?   What is seven sixes?

What is eight sixes?   What is nine sixes?

8 x 6 =   7 x 6 =   6 x 6 =   9 x 6 =

Practice the 6s

You should know all of the 6 times table now, but how quickly can you remember it?
Ask someone to time you as you do this page.
Remember, you must be fast but also correct.

$1 \times 6 =$ $2 \times 6 =$ $7 \times 6 =$

$2 \times 6 =$ $4 \times 6 =$ $3 \times 6 =$

$3 \times 6 =$ $6 \times 6 =$ $9 \times 6 =$

$4 \times 6 =$ $8 \times 6 =$ $6 \times 4 =$

$5 \times 6 =$ $10 \times 6 =$ $1 \times 6 =$

$6 \times 6 =$ $1 \times 6 =$ $6 \times 2 =$

$7 \times 6 =$ $3 \times 6 =$ $6 \times 8 =$

$8 \times 6 =$ $5 \times 6 =$ $0 \times 6 =$

$9 \times 6 =$ $7 \times 6 =$ $6 \times 3 =$

$10 \times 6 =$ $9 \times 6 =$ $5 \times 6 =$

$6 \times 1 =$ $6 \times 3 =$ $6 \times 7 =$

$6 \times 2 =$ $6 \times 5 =$ $2 \times 6 =$

$6 \times 3 =$ $6 \times 7 =$ $6 \times 9 =$

$6 \times 4 =$ $6 \times 9 =$ $4 \times 6 =$

$6 \times 5 =$ $6 \times 2 =$ $8 \times 6 =$

$6 \times 6 =$ $6 \times 4 =$ $10 \times 6 =$

$6 \times 7 =$ $6 \times 6 =$ $6 \times 5 =$

$6 \times 8 =$ $6 \times 8 =$ $6 \times 0 =$

$6 \times 9 =$ $6 \times 10 =$ $6 \times 1 =$

$6 \times 10 =$ $6 \times 0 =$ $6 \times 6 =$

Speed trials

You should know all of the 1, 2, 3, 4, 5, 6, and 10 times tables by now,
but how quickly can you remember them?
Ask someone to time you as you do this page.
Remember, you must be fast but also correct.

4 x 6 =	6 x 3 =	9 x 6 =
5 x 3 =	8 x 6 =	8 x 6 =
7 x 3 =	6 x 6 =	7 x 3 =
6 x 5 =	3 x 10 =	6 x 6 =
6 x 10 =	6 x 2 =	5 x 4 =
8 x 2 =	7 x 3 =	4 x 6 =
5 x 3 =	4 x 6 =	3 x 6 =
9 x 6 =	6 x 5 =	2 x 6 =
5 x 5 =	6 x 10 =	6 x 3 =
7 x 6 =	6 x 2 =	0 x 6 =
0 x 2 =	5 x 3 =	10 x 5 =
6 x 3 =	8 x 4 =	6 x 2 =
6 x 6 =	0 x 6 =	8 x 3 =
3 x 5 =	5 x 10 =	7 x 6 =
4 x 10 =	7 x 6 =	6 x 5 =
7 x 10 =	8 x 3 =	5 x 10 =
3 x 6 =	9 x 6 =	6 x 0 =
2 x 4 =	5 x 5 =	3 x 10 =
6 x 9 =	7 x 10 =	2 x 8 =
9 x 10 =	5 x 6 =	1 x 8 =

Some of the 7s

You should already know parts of the 7 times table because they are parts of the 1, 2, 3, 4, 5, 6 and 10 times tables.

1 x 7 = 7   2 x 7 = 14   3 x 7 = 21   4 x 7 = 28
5 x 7 = 35   6 x 7 = 42   10 x 7 = 70

Find out if you can remember them quickly and correctly.

Cover the seven times table with paper and write the answers to these questions as quickly as you can.

What is three sevens?   What is ten sevens?

What is two sevens?   What is four sevens?

What is six sevens?   What is five sevens?

Write the answers as quickly as you can.

How many sevens make 14?   How many sevens make 42?

How many sevens make 35?   How many sevens make 21?

How many sevens make 28?   How many sevens make 70?

Write the answers as quickly as you can.

Multiply seven by three.   Multiply seven by ten.

Multiply seven by two.   Multiply seven by five.

Multiply seven by six.   Multiply seven by four.

Write the answers as quickly as you can.

4 x 7 =   2 x 7 =   10 x 7 =

5 x 7 =   1 x 7 =   3 x 7 =

Write the answers as quickly as you can.

A bag has seven candies. Ann buys five bags. How many candies does she have?

How many days are there in six weeks?

The rest of the 7s

You should now know all of the 1, 2, 3, 4, 5, 6, and 10 times tables.
You need to learn only these parts of the seven times table.
7 x 7 = 49   8 x 7 = 56   9 x 7 = 63

This work will help you remember the 7 times table.

Complete these sequences.

7   14   21   28   35   42

6 x 7 = 42   so   7 x 7 = 42 plus another 7 =

21   28   35

7 x 7 = 49   so   8 x 7 = 49 plus another 7 =

7   14   21   56   70

8 x 7 = 56   so   9 x 7 = 56 plus another 7 =

7   21   28   35

Test yourself on the rest of the 7 times table.
Cover the section above with a sheet of paper.

What is seven sevens?   What is eight sevens?

What is nine sevens?   What is ten sevens?

8 x 7 =   7 x 7 =   9 x 7 =   10 x 7 =

How many days are there in eight weeks?

A package contains seven pens.
How many pens will there be in nine packets?

How many sevens make 56?

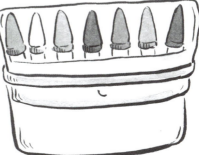

43

Practice the 7s

You should know all of the 7 times table now, but how quickly can you remember it?
Ask someone to time you as you do this page.
Remember, you must be fast but also correct.

1 x 7 =	2 x 7 =	7 x 6 =
2 x 7 =	4 x 7 =	3 x 7 =
3 x 7 =	6 x 7 =	9 x 7 =
4 x 7 =	8 x 7 =	7 x 4 =
5 x 7 =	10 x 7 =	1 x 7 =
6 x 7 =	1 x 7 =	7 x 2 =
7 x 7 =	3 x 7 =	7 x 8 =
8 x 7 =	5 x 7 =	0 x 7 =
9 x 7 =	7 x 7 =	7 x 3 =
10 x 7 =	9 x 7 =	5 x 7 =
7 x 1 =	7 x 3 =	7 x 7 =
7 x 2 =	7 x 5 =	2 x 7 =
7 x 3 =	7 x 7 =	7 x 9 =
7 x 4 =	7 x 9 =	4 x 7 =
7 x 5 =	7 x 2 =	8 x 7 =
7 x 6 =	7 x 4 =	10 x 7 =
7 x 7 =	7 x 6 =	7 x 5 =
7 x 8 =	7 x 8 =	7 x 0 =
7 x 9 =	7 x 10 =	7 x 1 =
7 x 10 =	7 x 0 =	6 x 7 =

Speed trials

You should know all of the 1, 2, 3, 4, 5, 6, 7, and 10 times tables by now, but how quickly can you remember them?
Ask someone to time you as you do this page.
Remember, you must be fast but also correct.

$4 \times 7 =$	$7 \times 3 =$	$9 \times 7 =$
$5 \times 10 =$	$8 \times 7 =$	$7 \times 6 =$
$7 \times 5 =$	$6 \times 6 =$	$8 \times 3 =$
$6 \times 5 =$	$5 \times 10 =$	$6 \times 6 =$
$6 \times 10 =$	$6 \times 3 =$	$7 \times 4 =$
$8 \times 7 =$	$7 \times 5 =$	$4 \times 6 =$
$5 \times 8 =$	$4 \times 6 =$	$3 \times 7 =$
$9 \times 6 =$	$6 \times 5 =$	$2 \times 8 =$
$5 \times 7 =$	$7 \times 10 =$	$7 \times 3 =$
$7 \times 6 =$	$6 \times 7 =$	$0 \times 6 =$
$0 \times 5 =$	$5 \times 7 =$	$10 \times 7 =$
$6 \times 3 =$	$8 \times 4 =$	$6 \times 2 =$
$6 \times 7 =$	$0 \times 7 =$	$8 \times 7 =$
$3 \times 5 =$	$5 \times 8 =$	$7 \times 7 =$
$4 \times 7 =$	$7 \times 6 =$	$6 \times 5 =$
$7 \times 10 =$	$8 \times 3 =$	$5 \times 10 =$
$7 \times 8 =$	$9 \times 6 =$	$7 \times 0 =$
$2 \times 7 =$	$7 \times 7 =$	$3 \times 10 =$
$4 \times 9 =$	$9 \times 10 =$	$2 \times 7 =$
$9 \times 10 =$	$5 \times 6 =$	$7 \times 8 =$

Some of the 8s

You should already know some of the 8 times table because it is part of the 1, 2, 3, 4, 5, 6, 7, and 10 times tables.

1 x 8 = 8	2 x 8 = 16	3 x 8 = 24	4 x 8 = 32
5 x 8 = 40	6 x 8 = 48	7 x 8 = 56	10 x 8 = 80

Find out if you can remember them quickly and correctly.

Cover the 8 times table with paper so you can't see the numbers.
Write the answers as quickly as you can.

What is three eights?   What is ten eights?

What is two eights?   What is four eights?

What is six eights?   What is five eights?

Write the answers as quickly as you can.

How many eights equal 16?   How many eights equal 40?

How many eights equal 32?   How many eights equal 24?

How many eights equal 56?   How many eights equal 48?

Write the answers as quickly as you can.

Multiply eight by three.   Multiply eight by ten.

Multiply eight by two.   Multiply eight by five.

Multiply eight by six.   Multiply eight by four.

Write the answers as quickly as you can.

6 x 8 =   2 x 8 =   10 x 8 =

5 x 8 =   7 x 8 =   3 x 8 =

Write the answers as quickly as you can.

A pizza has eight slices. John buys six pizzas.

How many slices does he have?

Which number multiplied by 8 gives the answer 56?

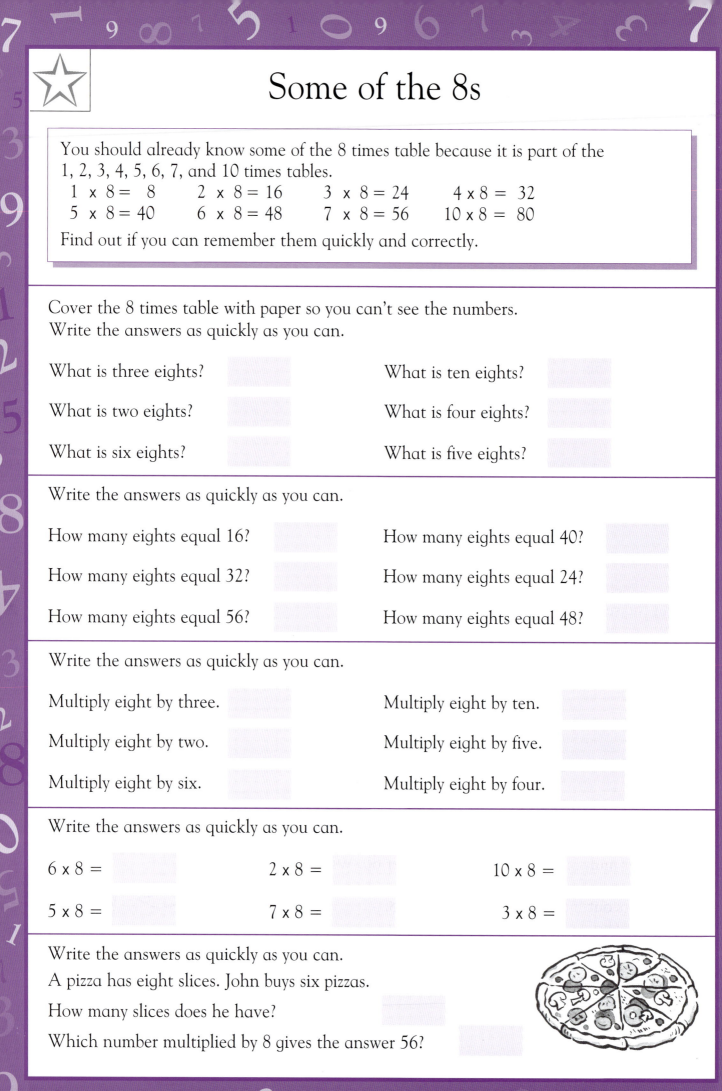

The rest of the 8s

You need to learn only these parts of the eight times table.
8 x 8 = 64   9 x 8 = 72

This work will help you remember the 8 times table.

Complete these sequences.

8   16   24   32   40   48

7 x 8 = 56   so   8 x 8 = 56 plus another 8 =

24   32   40

8 x 8 = 64   so   9 x 8 = 64 plus another 8 =

8   16   24   64   80

8   24   40

Test yourself on the rest of the 8 times table.
Cover the section above with a sheet of paper.

What is seven eights?   What is eight eights?

What is nine eights?   What is eight nines?

8 x 8 =   9 x 8 =   8 x 9 =   10 x 8 =

What number multiplied by 8 gives the answer 72?

A number multiplied by 8 gives the answer 80. What is the number?

David puts out building bricks in piles of 8.
How many bricks will there be in 10 piles?

What number multiplied by 5 gives the answer 40?

How many 8s make 72?

Practice the 8s

You should know all of the 8 times table now, but how quickly can you remember it?
Ask someone to time you as you do this page.
Be fast but also correct.

1 x 8 =	2 x 8 =	8 x 6 =
2 x 8 =	4 x 8 =	3 x 8 =
3 x 8 =	6 x 8 =	9 x 8 =
4 x 8 =	8 x 8 =	8 x 4 =
5 x 8 =	10 x 8 =	1 x 8 =
6 x 8 =	1 x 8 =	8 x 2 =
7 x 8 =	3 x 8 =	7 x 8 =
8 x 8 =	5 x 8 =	0 x 8 =
9 x 8 =	7 x 8 =	8 x 3 =
10 x 8 =	9 x 8 =	5 x 8 =
8 x 1 =	8 x 3 =	8 x 8 =
8 x 2 =	8 x 5 =	2 x 8 =
8 x 3 =	8 x 8 =	8 x 9 =
8 x 4 =	8 x 9 =	4 x 8 =
8 x 5 =	8 x 2 =	8 x 6 =
8 x 6 =	8 x 4 =	10 x 8 =
8 x 7 =	8 x 6 =	8 x 5 =
8 x 8 =	8 x 8 =	8 x 0 =
8 x 9 =	8 x 10 =	8 x 1 =
8 x 10 =	8 x 0 =	6 x 8 =

Speed trials

4 x 8 =	7 x 8 =	9 x 8 =
5 x 10 =	8 x 7 =	7 x 6 =
7 x 8 =	6 x 8 =	8 x 3 =
8 x 5 =	8 x 10 =	8 x 8 =
6 x 10 =	6 x 3 =	7 x 4 =
8 x 7 =	7 x 7 =	4 x 8 =
5 x 8 =	5 x 6 =	3 x 7 =
9 x 8 =	6 x 7 =	2 x 8 =
8 x 8 =	7 x 10 =	7 x 3 =
7 x 6 =	6 x 9 =	0 x 8 =
7 x 5 =	5 x 8 =	10 x 8 =
6 x 8 =	8 x 4 =	6 x 2 =
6 x 7 =	0 x 8 =	8 x 6 =
5 x 7 =	5 x 9 =	7 x 8 =
8 x 4 =	7 x 6 =	6 x 5 =
7 x 10 =	8 x 3 =	8 x 10 =
2 x 8 =	9 x 6 =	8 x 7 =
4 x 7 =	8 x 6 =	5 x 10 =
6 x 9 =	9 x 10 =	8 x 2 =
9 x 10 =	6 x 6 =	8 x 9 =

Some of the 9s

You should already know nearly all of the 9 times table because it is part of the 1, 2, 3, 4, 5, 6, 7, 8, and 10 times tables.

$1 \times 9 = 9$	$2 \times 9 = 18$	$3 \times 9 = 27$	$4 \times 9 = 36$	$5 \times 9 = 45$
$6 \times 9 = 54$	$7 \times 9 = 63$	$8 \times 9 = 72$	$10 \times 9 = 90$	

Find out if you can remember them quickly and correctly.

Cover the nine times table so you can't see the numbers.
Write the answers as quickly as you can.

What is three nines?   What is ten nines?

What is two nines?   What is four nines?

What is six nines?   What is five nines?

What is seven nines?   What is eight nines?

Write the answers as quickly as you can.

How many nines equal 18?   How many nines equal 54?

How many nines equal 90?   How many nines equal 27?

How many nines equal 72?   How many nines equal 36?

How many nines equal 45?   How many nines equal 63?

Write the answers as quickly as you can.

Multiply nine by seven.   Multiply nine by ten.

Multiply nine by two.   Multiply nine by five.

Multiply nine by six.   Multiply nine by four.

Multiply nine by three.   Multiply nine by eight.

Write the answers as quickly as you can.

$6 \times 9 =$	$2 \times 9 =$	$10 \times 9 =$
$5 \times 9 =$	$3 \times 9 =$	$8 \times 9 =$
$0 \times 9 =$	$7 \times 9 =$	$4 \times 9 =$

The rest of the 9s

You need to learn only this part of the nine times table.

9 x 9 = 81

This work will help you remember the 9 times table.

Complete these sequences.

| 9 | 18 | 27 | 36 | 45 | 54 | | | | |

8 x 9 = 72   so   9 x 9 = 72 plus another 9 =

| 27 | 36 | 45 | | | | | | | |

| 9 | 18 | 27 | | | | 72 | | 90 |

| 9 | | 27 | | 45 | | | | | |

Look for a pattern in the nine times table.

1	x	9	=	09
2	x	9	=	18
3	x	9	=	27
4	x	9	=	36
5	x	9	=	45
6	x	9	=	54
7	x	9	=	63
8	x	9	=	72
9	x	9	=	81
10	x	9	=	90

Write down any patterns you can see. (There is more than one.)

_____

_____

_____

_____

_____

_____

_____

Practice the 9s

You should know all of the 9 times table now, but how quickly can you remember it?
Ask someone to time you as you do this page.
Be fast and correct.

1 x 9 =	2 x 9 =	9 x 6 =
2 x 9 =	4 x 9 =	3 x 9 =
3 x 9 =	6 x 9 =	9 x 9 =
4 x 9 =	9 x 7 =	9 x 4 =
5 x 9 =	10 x 9 =	1 x 9 =
6 x 9 =	1 x 9 =	9 x 2 =
7 x 9 =	3 x 9 =	7 x 9 =
8 x 9 =	5 x 9 =	0 x 9 =
9 x 9 =	7 x 9 =	9 x 3 =
10 x 9 =	9 x 9 =	5 x 9 =
9 x 1 =	9 x 3 =	9 x 9 =
9 x 2 =	9 x 5 =	2 x 9 =
9 x 3 =	0 x 9 =	8 x 9 =
9 x 4 =	9 x 1 =	4 x 9 =
9 x 5 =	9 x 2 =	9 x 7 =
9 x 6 =	9 x 4 =	10 x 9 =
9 x 7 =	9 x 6 =	9 x 5 =
9 x 8 =	9 x 8 =	9 x 0 =
9 x 9 =	9 x 10 =	9 x 1 =
9 x 10 =	9 x 0 =	6 x 9 =

Speed trials

You should know all of the times tables by now, but how quickly can you remember them?
Ask someone to time you as you do this page.
Be fast and correct.

$6 \times 8 =$	$4 \times 8 =$	$8 \times 10 =$
$9 \times 10 =$	$9 \times 8 =$	$7 \times 9 =$
$5 \times 8 =$	$6 \times 6 =$	$8 \times 5 =$
$7 \times 5 =$	$8 \times 9 =$	$8 \times 7 =$
$6 \times 4 =$	$6 \times 4 =$	$7 \times 4 =$
$8 \times 8 =$	$7 \times 3 =$	$4 \times 9 =$
$5 \times 10 =$	$5 \times 9 =$	$6 \times 7 =$
$9 \times 8 =$	$6 \times 8 =$	$4 \times 6 =$
$8 \times 3 =$	$7 \times 7 =$	$7 \times 8 =$
$7 \times 7 =$	$6 \times 9 =$	$6 \times 9 =$
$9 \times 5 =$	$7 \times 8 =$	$10 \times 8 =$
$4 \times 8 =$	$8 \times 4 =$	$6 \times 5 =$
$6 \times 7 =$	$0 \times 9 =$	$8 \times 8 =$
$2 \times 9 =$	$10 \times 10 =$	$7 \times 6 =$
$8 \times 4 =$	$7 \times 6 =$	$6 \times 8 =$
$7 \times 10 =$	$8 \times 7 =$	$9 \times 10 =$
$2 \times 8 =$	$9 \times 6 =$	$8 \times 4 =$
$4 \times 7 =$	$8 \times 6 =$	$7 \times 10 =$
$6 \times 9 =$	$9 \times 9 =$	$5 \times 8 =$
$9 \times 9 =$	$6 \times 7 =$	$8 \times 9 =$

Times tables for division

Knowing the times tables can also help with division problems. Look at these examples.

$3 \times 6 = 18$ which means that $18 \div 3 = 6$ and that $18 \div 6 = 3$
$4 \times 5 = 20$ which means that $20 \div 4 = 5$ and that $20 \div 5 = 4$
$9 \times 3 = 27$ which means that $27 \div 3 = 9$ and that $27 \div 9 = 3$

Use your knowledge of the times tables to work these division problems.

$3 \times 8 = 24$ which means that $24 \div 3 =$ and that $24 \div 8 =$

$4 \times 7 = 28$ which means that $28 \div 4 =$ and that $28 \div 7 =$

$3 \times 5 = 15$ which means that $15 \div 3 =$ and that $15 \div 5 =$

$4 \times 3 = 12$ which means that $12 \div 3 =$ and that $12 \div 4 =$

$3 \times 10 = 30$ which means that $30 \div 3 =$ and that $30 \div 10 =$

$4 \times 8 = 32$ which means that $32 \div 4 =$ and that $32 \div 8 =$

$3 \times 9 = 27$ which means that $27 \div 3 =$ and that $27 \div 9 =$

$4 \times 10 = 40$ which means that $40 \div 4 =$ and that $40 \div 10 =$

These division problems help practice the 3 and 4 times tables.

$20 \div 4 =$	$15 \div 3 =$	$16 \div 4 =$
$24 \div 4 =$	$27 \div 3 =$	$30 \div 3 =$
$12 \div 3 =$	$18 \div 3 =$	$28 \div 4 =$
$24 \div 3 =$	$32 \div 4 =$	$21 \div 3 =$

How many fours in 36?	Divide 27 by three.
Divide 28 by 4.	How many threes in 21?
How many fives in 35?	Divide 40 by 5.
Divide 15 by 3.	How many eights in 48?

Times tables for division

$20 \div 5 = \quad 4 \qquad 18 \div 3 = \quad 6 \qquad 60 \div 10 = \quad 6$

Complete the problems.

$40 \div 10 =$	$14 \div 2 =$	$32 \div 4 =$
$25 \div 5 =$	$21 \div 3 =$	$16 \div 4 =$
$24 \div 4 =$	$28 \div 4 =$	$12 \div 2 =$
$45 \div 5 =$	$35 \div 5 =$	$12 \div 3 =$
$10 \div 2 =$	$40 \div 10 =$	$12 \div 4 =$
$20 \div 10 =$	$20 \div 2 =$	$20 \div 2 =$
$6 \div 2 =$	$18 \div 3 =$	$20 \div 4 =$
$24 \div 3 =$	$32 \div 4 =$	$20 \div 5 =$
$30 \div 5 =$	$40 \div 5 =$	$20 \div 10 =$
$30 \div 10 =$	$80 \div 10 =$	$18 \div 2 =$
$40 \div 5 =$	$6 \div 2 =$	$18 \div 3 =$
$21 \div 3 =$	$15 \div 3 =$	$15 \div 3 =$
$14 \div 2 =$	$24 \div 4 =$	$15 \div 5 =$
$27 \div 3 =$	$15 \div 5 =$	$24 \div 3 =$
$90 \div 10 =$	$10 \div 10 =$	$24 \div 4 =$
$15 \div 5 =$	$4 \div 2 =$	$50 \div 5 =$
$15 \div 3 =$	$9 \div 3 =$	$50 \div 10 =$
$20 \div 5 =$	$4 \div 4 =$	$30 \div 3 =$
$20 \div 4 =$	$10 \div 5 =$	$30 \div 5 =$
$16 \div 2 =$	$100 \div 10 =$	$30 \div 10 =$

Times tables for division

This page will help you remember times tables by dividing by 2, 3, 4, 5, 6, and 10.

$30 \div 6 =$ 5 $12 \div 6 =$ 2 $60 \div 10 =$ 6

Complete the problems.

$18 \div 6 =$	$27 \div 3 =$	$48 \div 6 =$
$30 \div 10 =$	$18 \div 6 =$	$35 \div 5 =$
$14 \div 2 =$	$20 \div 2 =$	$36 \div 4 =$
$18 \div 3 =$	$24 \div 6 =$	$24 \div 3 =$
$20 \div 4 =$	$24 \div 3 =$	$20 \div 2 =$
$15 \div 5 =$	$24 \div 4 =$	$30 \div 6 =$
$36 \div 6 =$	$30 \div 10 =$	$25 \div 5 =$
$50 \div 10 =$	$18 \div 2 =$	$32 \div 4 =$
$8 \div 2 =$	$18 \div 3 =$	$27 \div 3 =$
$15 \div 3 =$	$36 \div 4 =$	$16 \div 2 =$
$16 \div 4 =$	$36 \div 6 =$	$42 \div 6 =$
$25 \div 5 =$	$40 \div 5 =$	$5 \div 5 =$
$6 \div 6 =$	$100 \div 10 =$	$4 \div 4 =$
$10 \div 10 =$	$16 \div 4 =$	$28 \div 4 =$
$42 \div 6 =$	$42 \div 6 =$	$14 \div 2 =$
$24 \div 4 =$	$48 \div 6 =$	$24 \div 6 =$
$54 \div 6 =$	$54 \div 6 =$	$18 \div 6 =$
$90 \div 10 =$	$60 \div 6 =$	$54 \div 6 =$
$30 \div 6 =$	$60 \div 10 =$	$60 \div 6 =$
$30 \div 5 =$	$30 \div 6 =$	$40 \div 5 =$

Times tables for division

This page will help you remember times tables by dividing by 2, 3, 4, 5, 6, and 7.

$14 \div 7 =$ 2 $28 \div 7 =$ 4 $70 \div 7 =$ 10

Complete the problems.

$21 \div 7 =$	$18 \div 6 =$	$49 \div 7 =$
$35 \div 5 =$	$28 \div 7 =$	$35 \div 5 =$
$14 \div 2 =$	$24 \div 6 =$	$35 \div 7 =$
$18 \div 6 =$	$24 \div 4 =$	$24 \div 6 =$
$20 \div 5 =$	$24 \div 2 =$	$21 \div 3 =$
$15 \div 3 =$	$21 \div 7 =$	$70 \div 7 =$
$36 \div 4 =$	$42 \div 7 =$	$42 \div 7 =$
$56 \div 7 =$	$18 \div 3 =$	$32 \div 4 =$
$18 \div 2 =$	$49 \div 7 =$	$27 \div 3 =$
$15 \div 5 =$	$36 \div 4 =$	$16 \div 4 =$
$49 \div 7 =$	$36 \div 6 =$	$42 \div 6 =$
$25 \div 5 =$	$40 \div 5 =$	$45 \div 5 =$
$7 \div 7 =$	$70 \div 7 =$	$40 \div 4 =$
$63 \div 7 =$	$24 \div 3 =$	$24 \div 3 =$
$42 \div 7 =$	$42 \div 6 =$	$14 \div 7 =$
$24 \div 6 =$	$48 \div 6 =$	$24 \div 4 =$
$54 \div 6 =$	$54 \div 6 =$	$18 \div 3 =$
$28 \div 7 =$	$60 \div 6 =$	$56 \div 7 =$
$30 \div 6 =$	$63 \div 7 =$	$63 \div 7 =$
$35 \div 7 =$	$25 \div 5 =$	$48 \div 6 =$

Times tables for division

This page will help you remember times tables by dividing by 2, 3, 4, 5, 6, 7, 8, and 9.

$16 \div 8 =$ 2 $35 \div 7 =$ 5 $27 \div 9 =$ 3

Complete the problems.

$42 \div 6 =$ $81 \div 9 =$ $56 \div 7 =$

$32 \div 8 =$ $56 \div 7 =$ $45 \div 5 =$

$14 \div 7 =$ $72 \div 9 =$ $35 \div 7 =$

$18 \div 9 =$ $24 \div 8 =$ $18 \div 9 =$

$63 \div 7 =$ $27 \div 9 =$ $21 \div 3 =$

$72 \div 9 =$ $72 \div 9 =$ $28 \div 7 =$

$72 \div 8 =$ $42 \div 6 =$ $64 \div 8 =$

$56 \div 7 =$ $27 \div 3 =$ $32 \div 8 =$

$18 \div 6 =$ $14 \div 7 =$ $27 \div 9 =$

$81 \div 9 =$ $36 \div 4 =$ $16 \div 8 =$

$63 \div 9 =$ $36 \div 6 =$ $42 \div 6 =$

$45 \div 5 =$ $48 \div 8 =$ $45 \div 9 =$

$54 \div 9 =$ $21 \div 7 =$ $40 \div 4 =$

$70 \div 7 =$ $24 \div 3 =$ $24 \div 8 =$

$42 \div 7 =$ $40 \div 8 =$ $63 \div 7 =$

$30 \div 5 =$ $45 \div 9 =$ $24 \div 6 =$

$54 \div 6 =$ $54 \div 6 =$ $18 \div 6 =$

$56 \div 8 =$ $42 \div 7 =$ $56 \div 8 =$

$30 \div 5 =$ $63 \div 9 =$ $63 \div 9 =$

$35 \div 7 =$ $50 \div 5 =$ $48 \div 8 =$

Times tables practice grids

This is a times tables grid.

X	3	4	5
7	21	28	35
8	24	32	40

Complete each times tables grid.

X	1	3	5	7	9
2					
3					

X	4	6
6		
7		
8		

X	6	7	8	9	10
3					
4					
5					

X	10	7	8	4
3				
5				
7				

X	6	2	4	7
5				
10				

X	8	7	9	6
9				
7				

59

Times tables practice grids

Here are more times tables grids.

X	2	4	6
5			
7			

X	8	3	9	2
5				
6				
7				

X	2	3	4	5
8				
9				

X	10	9	8	7
6				
5				
4				

X	3	8
2		
3		
4		
5		
6		
7		

X	2	4	6	8
1				
3				
5				
7				
9				
0				

Times tables practice grids

Here are some other times tables grids.

X	8	9
7		
8		

X	9	8	7	6	5	4
9						
8						
7						

X	2	5	9
4			
7			
8			

X	2	3	4	5	7
4					
6					
8					

X	3	5	7
2			
8			
6			
0			
4			
7			

X	8	7	9	6
7				
9				
0				
10				
8				
6				

Speed trials

Try this final test.

27 ÷ 3 =	4 x 9 =	14 ÷ 2 =
7 x 9 =	18 ÷ 2 =	9 x 9 =
64 ÷ 8 =	6 x 8 =	15 ÷ 3 =
90 ÷ 10 =	21 ÷ 3 =	8 x 8 =
6 x 8 =	9 x 7 =	24 ÷ 4 =
45 ÷ 9 =	36 ÷ 4 =	7 x 8 =
3 x 7 =	4 x 6 =	30 ÷ 5 =
9 x 5 =	45 ÷ 5 =	6 x 6 =
48 ÷ 6 =	8 x 5 =	42 ÷ 6 =
7 x 7 =	42 ÷ 6 =	9 x 5 =
3 x 9 =	7 x 4 =	49 ÷ 7 =
56 ÷ 8 =	35 ÷ 7 =	8 x 6 =
36 ÷ 4 =	9 x 3 =	72 ÷ 8 =
24 ÷ 3 =	24 ÷ 8 =	9 x 7 =
36 ÷ 9 =	8 x 2 =	54 ÷ 9 =
6 x 7 =	36 ÷ 9 =	7 x 6 =
4 x 4 =	6 x 10 =	10 ÷ 10 =
32 ÷ 8 =	80 ÷ 10 =	7 x 7 =
49 ÷ 7 =	6 x 9 =	16 ÷ 8 =
25 ÷ 5 =	16 ÷ 2 =	7 x 9 =
56 ÷ 7 =	54 ÷ 9 =	63 ÷ 7 =

Line of symmetry

If a plane figure is cut into two equal parts, the line of the cut is called a line of symmetry.

Draw as many lines of symmetry as you can find on each of these shapes.

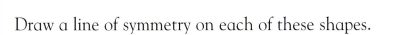
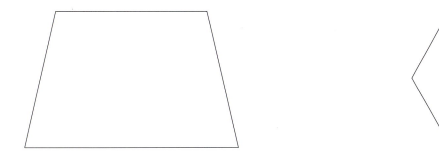

Draw a line of symmetry on each of these shapes.

Draw as many lines of symmetry on as you can find on these shapes.

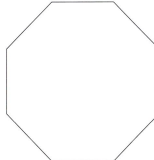

Ordering large numbers

Write these numbers in order, starting with the least.

256	9,654,327	39,214	147,243	9,631
256	9,631	39,214	147,243	9,654,327

Write these numbers in order, starting with the least.

72,463	8,730,241	261	5,247	643,292

9,641,471	260,453	59,372	657,473	4,290

327,914	3,647,212	47,900	3,825	416

593,103	761	374,239	91,761	1,425

5,600,200	500,200	5,200	50,200	52,000

6,437	643	64,370	6,430	643,000

9,900	999	900,200	920,200	9,200,000

In a country's election
O'Neil got 900,550 votes,
Schneider got 840,690 votes,
Rojas got 8,406,900 votes,
Marsalis got 7,964,201 votes and
Samperi got 859,999 votes.

Place the candidates in order.

1st _____

2nd _____

3rd _____

4th _____

5th _____

Rounding whole numbers

Write these numbers to the nearest hundred.

529   *500*   1687   *1,700*

If the place to the right of the place we are roundng is 5, round to the number above.

652   *700*

Round to the nearest hundred.

873	295	7,348	3,561
16,537	4,855	569	1,200
22,851	227	782	452

Round to the nearest ten-thousand.

23,478	418,700	58,397	351,899
109,544	31,059	67,414	33,500
89,388	801,821	134,800	45,010

Round to the nearest ten.

87	397	52	65
1,392	15	12,489	2,861
75	715	34	18,149

Round to the nearest thousand.

3,284	112,810	10,518	83,477
8,499	225,500	4,500	6,112
1,059	93,606	6,752	2,550

Choosing units of measure

Circle the units that are the closest estimate.

The amount of orange juice in a full glass.

(6 fluid ounces)   4 pints   2 gallons

Circle the units that are the closest estimate.

The weight of a box
of cereal

The length of a
football field

The area of a rug

The amount of cough
medicine in a bottle

The distance from home
plate to first base

The weight of a
package of sugar

The length of an
airport runway

The amount of water
in a full pail

The area of a place
mat

Comparing fractions

Which is greater, $\frac{2}{3}$ or $\frac{3}{4}$?　　$\frac{3}{4}$

The common denominator of 3 and 4 is 12.

So $\frac{2}{3} = \frac{8}{12}$　and　$\frac{3}{4} = \frac{9}{12}$

$\frac{3}{4}$ is greater.

Which is greater?

$\frac{1}{4}$ or $\frac{1}{3}$　　　$\frac{5}{6}$ or $\frac{7}{9}$　　　$\frac{1}{2}$ or $\frac{5}{8}$　　　$\frac{4}{9}$ or $\frac{1}{3}$

$\frac{2}{5}$ or $\frac{3}{8}$　　　$\frac{7}{10}$ or $\frac{8}{9}$　　　$\frac{8}{10}$ or $\frac{7}{8}$　　　$\frac{7}{12}$ or $\frac{2}{3}$

$\frac{2}{3}$ or $\frac{5}{8}$　　　$\frac{4}{15}$ or $\frac{1}{3}$　　　$\frac{3}{5}$ or $\frac{2}{3}$　　　$\frac{3}{8}$ or $\frac{1}{4}$

Which two fractions in each row are equal?

$\frac{1}{4}$	$\frac{3}{8}$	$\frac{4}{12}$	$\frac{3}{12}$	$\frac{7}{8}$	$\frac{5}{8}$	
$\frac{5}{8}$	$\frac{6}{9}$	$\frac{7}{10}$	$\frac{8}{12}$	$\frac{1}{2}$	$\frac{3}{4}$	
$\frac{7}{12}$	$\frac{6}{14}$	$\frac{7}{14}$	$\frac{3}{8}$	$\frac{4}{8}$	$\frac{9}{12}$	
$\frac{3}{8}$	$\frac{3}{9}$	$\frac{2}{6}$	$\frac{4}{7}$	$\frac{9}{10}$	$\frac{6}{7}$	
$\frac{3}{10}$	$\frac{5}{15}$	$\frac{2}{10}$	$\frac{3}{15}$	$\frac{4}{10}$	$\frac{7}{15}$	

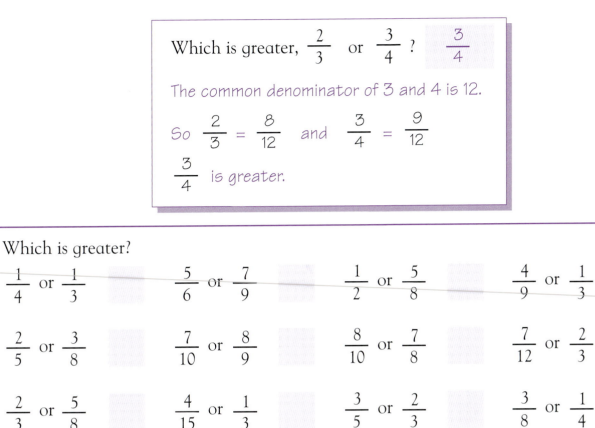

Put these fractions in order starting with the least.

$\frac{1}{2}$　$\frac{5}{6}$　$\frac{2}{3}$

$\frac{5}{8}$　$\frac{3}{4}$　$\frac{11}{12}$

$\frac{2}{3}$　$\frac{8}{15}$　$\frac{3}{5}$

Converting fractions to decimals

Convert these fractions to decimals.

$$\frac{3}{10} = \boxed{0.3}$$

(because the three goes in the tenths column)

$$\frac{7}{100} = \boxed{0.07}$$

(because the seven goes in the hundredths column)

Convert these fractions to decimals.

$\frac{6}{10} =$ $\frac{9}{100} =$ $\frac{4}{100} =$ $\frac{6}{100} =$

$\frac{4}{10} =$ $\frac{2}{10} =$ $\frac{1}{10} =$ $\frac{7}{100} =$

$\frac{8}{100} =$ $\frac{5}{10} =$ $\frac{7}{10} =$ $\frac{8}{10} =$

$\frac{2}{100} =$ $\frac{5}{100} =$ $\frac{1}{100} =$ $\frac{3}{10} =$

Convert $\frac{1}{4}$ to a decimal.

To do this we have to divide the bottom number into the top.

When we run out of numbers we put in the
decimal point and enough zeros to finish the sum.
Be careful to keep the decimal point in your answer
above the decimal point in the sum.

$$
\begin{array}{r}
0.25 \\
4\overline{)1.00} \\
8 \\
\hline
20 \\
20 \\
\hline
0
\end{array}
$$

Convert these fractions to decimals.

$\frac{1}{2} =$ $\frac{3}{4} =$ $\frac{2}{5} =$ $\frac{1}{5} =$

$\frac{4}{5} =$ $\frac{3}{8} =$ $\frac{3}{5} =$ $\frac{1}{4} =$

Adding fractions

Work out the answer to the problem.

$$\frac{1}{5} + \frac{3}{5} = \boxed{\frac{4}{5}}$$

$$\frac{4}{9} + \frac{2}{9} = \frac{\cancel{6}^{2}}{\cancel{9}_{3}} = \frac{2}{3}$$

Remember to reduce to simplest form if you need to.

Work out the answer to each sum. Reduce to simplest form if you need to.

$$\frac{2}{7} + \frac{3}{7} = \frac{}{7}$$
$$\frac{2}{9} + \frac{5}{9} = \frac{}{9}$$
$$\frac{1}{3} + \frac{1}{3} = \frac{}{3}$$

$$\frac{3}{10} + \frac{4}{10} = \frac{}{10}$$
$$\frac{1}{8} + \frac{2}{8} = \frac{}{8}$$
$$\frac{2}{9} + \frac{3}{9} = \frac{}{9}$$

$$\frac{2}{5} + \frac{1}{5} = \frac{}{}$$
$$\frac{1}{7} + \frac{5}{7} = \frac{}{}$$
$$\frac{4}{9} + \frac{1}{9} = \frac{}{9}$$

$$\frac{3}{20} + \frac{4}{20} = \frac{}{}$$
$$\frac{3}{100} + \frac{8}{100} = \frac{}{}$$
$$\frac{7}{10} + \frac{2}{10} = \frac{}{}$$

$$\frac{1}{6} + \frac{2}{6} = \frac{}{} = \frac{}{}$$
$$\frac{31}{100} + \frac{19}{100} = \frac{}{} = \frac{}{}$$
$$\frac{11}{20} + \frac{4}{20} = \frac{}{} = \frac{}{}$$

$$\frac{3}{10} + \frac{3}{10} = \frac{}{} = \frac{}{}$$
$$\frac{1}{12} + \frac{5}{12} = \frac{}{} = \frac{}{}$$
$$\frac{2}{6} + \frac{2}{6} = \frac{}{} = \frac{}{}$$

$$\frac{3}{8} + \frac{3}{8} = \frac{}{} = \frac{}{}$$
$$\frac{3}{8} + \frac{1}{8} = \frac{}{} = \frac{}{}$$
$$\frac{5}{12} + \frac{3}{12} = \frac{}{} = \frac{}{}$$

$$\frac{1}{4} + \frac{1}{4} = \frac{}{} = \frac{}{}$$
$$\frac{3}{20} + \frac{2}{20} = \frac{}{} = \frac{}{}$$
$$\frac{2}{6} + \frac{2}{6} = \frac{}{} = \frac{}{}$$

$$\frac{2}{7} + \frac{4}{7} = \frac{}{}$$
$$\frac{2}{9} + \frac{2}{9} = \frac{}{}$$
$$\frac{13}{20} + \frac{5}{20} = \frac{}{} = \frac{}{}$$

$$\frac{81}{100} + \frac{9}{100} = \frac{}{} = \frac{}{}$$
$$\frac{7}{20} + \frac{6}{20} = \frac{}{}$$
$$\frac{3}{8} + \frac{2}{8} = \frac{}{}$$

$$\frac{6}{10} + \frac{2}{10} = \frac{}{} = \frac{}{}$$
$$\frac{29}{100} + \frac{46}{100} = \frac{}{} = \frac{}{}$$
$$\frac{73}{100} + \frac{17}{100} = \frac{}{} = \frac{}{}$$

Subtracting fractions

Write the answer to each problem.

$$\frac{4}{5} - \frac{2}{5} = \frac{2}{5}$$

$$\frac{8}{9} - \frac{5}{9} = \frac{3}{9_3} = \frac{1}{3}$$

Reduce to simplest form if you need to.

Write the answer to each problem. Reduce to simplest form if you need to.

$$\frac{3}{5} - \frac{1}{5} = \frac{}{5}$$

$$\frac{6}{7} - \frac{3}{7} = \frac{}{7}$$

$$\frac{9}{10} - \frac{6}{10} = \frac{}{10}$$

$$\frac{7}{10} - \frac{4}{10} = \frac{}{}$$

$$\frac{5}{9} - \frac{4}{9} = \frac{}{}$$

$$\frac{2}{3} - \frac{1}{3} = \frac{}{}$$

$$\frac{7}{8} - \frac{3}{8} = \frac{}{} = \frac{}{}$$

$$\frac{14}{20} - \frac{10}{20} = \frac{}{} = \frac{}{}$$

$$\frac{5}{6} - \frac{1}{6} = \frac{}{} = \frac{}{}$$

$$\frac{11}{12} - \frac{5}{12} = \frac{}{} = \frac{}{}$$

$$\frac{17}{20} - \frac{12}{20} = \frac{}{} = \frac{}{}$$

$$\frac{9}{12} - \frac{3}{12} = \frac{}{} = \frac{}{}$$

$$\frac{8}{10} - \frac{6}{10} = \frac{}{} = \frac{}{}$$

$$\frac{12}{12} - \frac{2}{12} = \frac{}{} = \frac{}{}$$

$$\frac{9}{10} - \frac{3}{10} = \frac{}{} = \frac{}{}$$

$$\frac{8}{9} - \frac{2}{9} = \frac{}{} = \frac{}{}$$

$$\frac{7}{8} - \frac{1}{8} = \frac{}{} = \frac{}{}$$

$$\frac{9}{12} - \frac{5}{12} = \frac{}{} = \frac{}{}$$

$$\frac{3}{4} - \frac{2}{4} = \frac{}{}$$

$$\frac{6}{8} - \frac{3}{8} = \frac{}{}$$

$$\frac{18}{20} - \frac{8}{20} = \frac{}{} = \frac{}{}$$

$$\frac{4}{6} - \frac{2}{6} = \frac{}{} = \frac{}{}$$

$$\frac{5}{12} - \frac{4}{12} = \frac{}{}$$

$$\frac{3}{8} - \frac{2}{8} = \frac{}{}$$

$$\frac{5}{7} - \frac{1}{7} = \frac{}{}$$

$$\frac{5}{16} - \frac{1}{16} = \frac{}{} = \frac{}{}$$

$$\frac{90}{100} - \frac{80}{100} = \frac{}{} = \frac{}{}$$

Adding fractions

Write the answer to each problem.

$$\frac{3}{8} + \frac{5}{8} = \frac{8}{8} = 1 \qquad \frac{3}{4} + \frac{3}{4} = \frac{36}{42} = \frac{3}{2} = 1\frac{1}{2}$$

Write the answer to each problem.

$$\frac{7}{10} + \frac{6}{10} = \frac{}{10} = 1\frac{}{10} \qquad \frac{6}{7} + \frac{5}{7} = \frac{}{7} = 1\frac{}{7} \qquad \frac{2}{3} + \frac{2}{3} = \frac{}{3} = 1\frac{}{3}$$

$$\frac{5}{10} + \frac{6}{10} = \frac{}{} = \frac{}{} \qquad \frac{8}{13} + \frac{5}{13} = \frac{}{} = \qquad \frac{7}{8} + \frac{4}{8} = \frac{}{} = \frac{}{}$$

$$\frac{7}{8} + \frac{5}{8} = \frac{}{} = \frac{}{} = \frac{}{} \qquad \frac{2}{5} + \frac{3}{5} = \frac{}{} = \qquad \frac{5}{8} + \frac{5}{8} = \frac{}{} = \frac{}{} = \frac{}{}$$

$$\frac{10}{20} + \frac{15}{20} = \frac{}{} = \frac{}{} = \frac{}{} \qquad \frac{2}{3} + \frac{1}{3} = \frac{}{} = \qquad \frac{5}{6} + \frac{5}{6} = \frac{}{} = \frac{}{} = \frac{}{}$$

$$\frac{5}{6} + \frac{3}{6} = \frac{}{} = \frac{}{} = \frac{}{} \qquad \frac{6}{12} + \frac{7}{12} = \frac{}{} = \frac{}{} \qquad \frac{8}{10} + \frac{6}{10} = \frac{}{} = \frac{}{} = \frac{}{}$$

$$\frac{12}{20} + \frac{10}{20} = \frac{}{} = \frac{}{} = \frac{}{} \qquad \frac{3}{10} + \frac{7}{10} = \frac{}{} = \qquad \frac{75}{100} + \frac{75}{100} = \frac{}{} = \frac{}{} = \frac{}{}$$

$$\frac{10}{20} + \frac{16}{20} = \frac{}{} = \frac{}{} = \frac{}{} \qquad \frac{4}{5} + \frac{4}{5} = \frac{}{} = \frac{}{} \qquad \frac{11}{21} + \frac{17}{21} = \frac{}{} = \frac{}{} = \frac{}{}$$

Adding fractions

Write the answer to each problem.

$$\frac{2}{3} + \frac{1}{6} = \frac{4}{6} + \frac{1}{6} = \frac{5}{6}$$

$$\frac{3}{4} + \frac{5}{6} = \frac{9}{12} + \frac{10}{12} = \frac{19}{12} = 1\frac{7}{12}$$

Work out the answer to each problem. Rename as a mixed number if you need to.

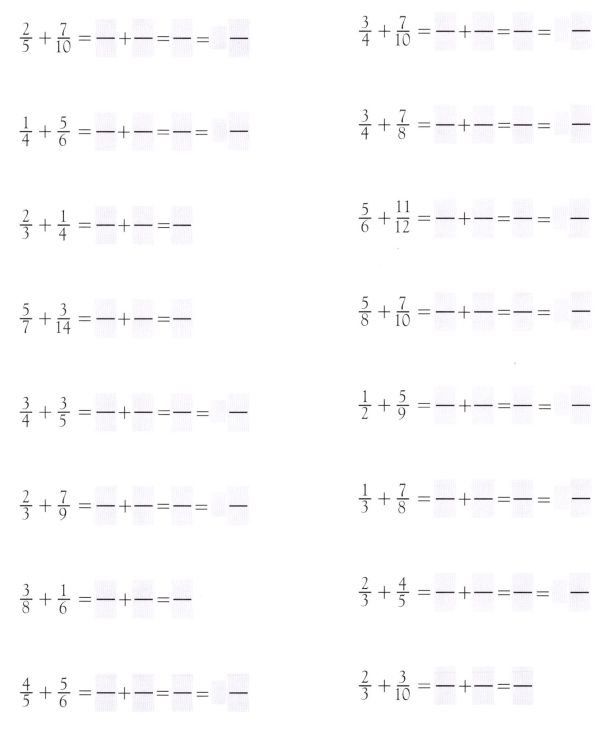

$$\frac{2}{5} + \frac{7}{10} = \frac{}{} + \frac{}{} = \frac{}{} = \frac{}{}$$

$$\frac{3}{4} + \frac{7}{10} = \frac{}{} + \frac{}{} = \frac{}{} = \frac{}{}$$

$$\frac{1}{4} + \frac{5}{6} = \frac{}{} + \frac{}{} = \frac{}{} = \frac{}{}$$

$$\frac{3}{4} + \frac{7}{8} = \frac{}{} + \frac{}{} = \frac{}{} = \frac{}{}$$

$$\frac{2}{3} + \frac{1}{4} = \frac{}{} + \frac{}{} = \frac{}{}$$

$$\frac{5}{6} + \frac{11}{12} = \frac{}{} + \frac{}{} = \frac{}{} = \frac{}{}$$

$$\frac{5}{7} + \frac{3}{14} = \frac{}{} + \frac{}{} = \frac{}{}$$

$$\frac{5}{8} + \frac{7}{10} = \frac{}{} + \frac{}{} = \frac{}{} = \frac{}{}$$

$$\frac{3}{4} + \frac{3}{5} = \frac{}{} + \frac{}{} = \frac{}{} = \frac{}{}$$

$$\frac{1}{2} + \frac{5}{9} = \frac{}{} + \frac{}{} = \frac{}{} = \frac{}{}$$

$$\frac{2}{3} + \frac{7}{9} = \frac{}{} + \frac{}{} = \frac{}{} = \frac{}{}$$

$$\frac{1}{3} + \frac{7}{8} = \frac{}{} + \frac{}{} = \frac{}{} = \frac{}{}$$

$$\frac{3}{8} + \frac{1}{6} = \frac{}{} + \frac{}{} = \frac{}{}$$

$$\frac{2}{3} + \frac{4}{5} = \frac{}{} + \frac{}{} = \frac{}{} = \frac{}{}$$

$$\frac{4}{5} + \frac{5}{6} = \frac{}{} + \frac{}{} = \frac{}{} = \frac{}{}$$

$$\frac{2}{3} + \frac{3}{10} = \frac{}{} + \frac{}{} = \frac{}{}$$

Subtracting fractions

Work out the answer to the problems.

$$\frac{7}{9} - \frac{1}{3} = \frac{7}{9} - \frac{3}{9} = \frac{4}{9}$$

$$\frac{7}{10} - \frac{3}{8} = \frac{28}{40} - \frac{15}{40} = \frac{13}{40}$$

Work out the answer to each problem. Reduce to the simplest form if you need to.

$$\frac{5}{8} - \frac{1}{2} = \underline{} - \underline{} = \underline{}$$

$$\frac{5}{6} - \frac{1}{4} = \underline{} - \underline{} = \underline{}$$

$$\frac{9}{10} - \frac{3}{8} = \underline{} - \underline{} = \underline{}$$

$$\frac{9}{10} - \frac{5}{8} = \underline{} - \underline{} = \underline{}$$

$$\frac{6}{7} - \frac{2}{5} = \underline{} - \underline{} = \underline{}$$

$$\frac{11}{12} - \frac{1}{6} = \underline{} - \underline{} = \underline{} = \underline{}$$

$$\frac{7}{12} - \frac{1}{6} = \underline{} - \underline{} = \underline{}$$

$$\frac{7}{10} - \frac{1}{4} = \underline{} - \underline{} = \underline{} = \underline{}$$

$$\frac{5}{9} - \frac{1}{3} = \underline{} - \underline{} = \underline{}$$

$$\frac{7}{9} - \frac{1}{4} = \underline{} - \underline{} = \underline{}$$

$$\frac{7}{16} - \frac{1}{8} = \underline{} - \underline{} = \underline{}$$

$$\frac{3}{7} - \frac{1}{5} = \underline{} - \underline{} = \underline{}$$

$$\frac{3}{8} - \frac{1}{6} = \underline{} - \underline{} = \underline{}$$

$$\frac{3}{5} - \frac{1}{4} = \underline{} - \underline{} = \underline{}$$

$$\frac{2}{3} - \frac{1}{2} = \underline{} - \underline{} = \underline{}$$

$$\frac{4}{5} - \frac{1}{4} = \underline{} - \underline{} = \underline{}$$

Adding mixed numbers

Work out the answer to each problem.

$$8\frac{10}{30} + 1\frac{3}{30} = 9\frac{13}{30} = 9\frac{13}{30}$$

$$3\frac{1}{4} + 1\frac{1}{6} = 3\frac{3}{12} = 1\frac{1}{12} = 4\frac{5}{12}$$

Work out the answer to each problem.

$$2\frac{1}{8} + 3\frac{3}{8} = \boxed{} = \boxed{}$$

$$3\frac{5}{6} + 1\frac{1}{8} = \boxed{} + \boxed{} = \boxed{}$$

$$3\frac{3}{4} + 2\frac{1}{16} = \boxed{} + \boxed{} = \boxed{}$$

$$1\frac{2}{3} + 3\frac{2}{7} = \boxed{} + \boxed{} = \boxed{}$$

$$4\frac{1}{4} + 2\frac{1}{6} = \boxed{} + \boxed{} = \boxed{}$$

$$6\frac{1}{6} + 3\frac{2}{9} = \boxed{} + \boxed{} = \boxed{}$$

$$7\frac{5}{6} + 2\frac{1}{10} = \boxed{} + \boxed{} = \boxed{} = \boxed{}$$

$$1\frac{7}{12} + 4\frac{1}{12} = \boxed{} = \boxed{}$$

$$5\frac{1}{4} + 3\frac{2}{5} = \boxed{} + \boxed{} = \boxed{} = \boxed{}$$

$$3\frac{3}{8} + 1\frac{1}{4} = \boxed{} + \boxed{} = \boxed{}$$

$$6\frac{1}{4} + 2\frac{1}{4} = \boxed{} = \boxed{}$$

$$6\frac{2}{3} + 3\frac{1}{10} = \boxed{} + \boxed{} = \boxed{}$$

$$7\frac{1}{3} + 1\frac{2}{9} = \boxed{} + \boxed{} = \boxed{}$$

$$2\frac{2}{5} + 1\frac{3}{10} = \boxed{} + \boxed{} = \boxed{}$$

Subtracting mixed numbers

Work out the answer to the problems.

$$2\frac{7}{8} - 1\frac{5}{8} = 1\frac{2}{8} = 1\frac{1}{4} \qquad\qquad 9\frac{9}{10} - 6\frac{5}{8} = 9\frac{36}{40} - 6\frac{25}{40} = 3\frac{11}{40}$$

Work out the answer to each problem.

$$7\frac{3}{8} - 3\frac{1}{8} = \boxed{} = \boxed{} \qquad\qquad 2\frac{14}{15} - 1\frac{4}{9} = \boxed{} - \boxed{} = \boxed{}$$

$$2\frac{2}{3} - 1\frac{1}{6} = \boxed{} - \boxed{} = \boxed{} = \boxed{} \qquad\qquad 6\frac{4}{5} - 2\frac{1}{2} = \boxed{} - \boxed{} = \boxed{}$$

$$5\frac{11}{20} - 2\frac{1}{8} = \boxed{} - \boxed{} = \boxed{} \qquad\qquad 8\frac{11}{12} - 5\frac{5}{12} = \boxed{} = \boxed{}$$

$$9\frac{7}{9} - 3\frac{4}{6} = \boxed{} - \boxed{} = \boxed{} = \boxed{} \qquad\qquad 4\frac{7}{8} - 2\frac{1}{4} = \boxed{} - \boxed{} = \boxed{}$$

$$8\frac{2}{5} - 4\frac{1}{4} = \boxed{} - \boxed{} = \boxed{} \qquad\qquad 4\frac{5}{6} - 3\frac{1}{4} = \boxed{} - \boxed{} = \boxed{}$$

$$4\frac{2}{3} - 1\frac{2}{3} = \boxed{} = \boxed{} \qquad\qquad 9\frac{8}{9} - 3\frac{3}{4} = \boxed{} - \boxed{} = \boxed{}$$

$$3\frac{8}{15} - 2\frac{2}{5} = \boxed{} - \boxed{} = \boxed{} \qquad\qquad 2\frac{7}{9} - 1\frac{1}{5} = \boxed{} - \boxed{} = \boxed{}$$

Adding mixed numbers and fractions

Work out the answer to the problems.

$$4\frac{3}{4} + \frac{3}{4} = \boxed{4\frac{6}{4}} = \boxed{5\frac{2}{4}} = \boxed{5\frac{1}{2}}$$

$$3\frac{1}{2} + \frac{2}{3} = \boxed{3\frac{3}{6}} + \boxed{\frac{4}{6}} = \boxed{3\frac{7}{6}} = \boxed{4\frac{1}{6}}$$

Work out the answer to each problem.

$$6\frac{2}{3} + \frac{2}{3} = \boxed{} = \boxed{}$$

$$4\frac{1}{4} + \frac{7}{8} = \boxed{} + \boxed{} = \boxed{} = \boxed{}$$

$$4\frac{5}{8} + \frac{7}{8} = \boxed{} = \boxed{}$$

$$3\frac{7}{10} + \frac{1}{2} = \boxed{} + \boxed{} = \boxed{} = \boxed{}$$

$$2\frac{3}{7} + \frac{8}{7} = \boxed{} = \boxed{}$$

$$1\frac{1}{2} + \frac{3}{4} = \boxed{} + \boxed{} = \boxed{} = \boxed{}$$

$$3\frac{5}{6} + \frac{2}{3} = \boxed{} + \boxed{} = \boxed{} = \boxed{}$$

$$5\frac{3}{4} + \frac{4}{5} = \boxed{} + \boxed{} = \boxed{} = \boxed{}$$

$$3\frac{7}{8} + \frac{1}{4} = \boxed{} + \boxed{} = \boxed{} = \boxed{}$$

$$3\frac{6}{7} + \frac{3}{4} = \boxed{} + \boxed{} = \boxed{} = \boxed{}$$

$$7\frac{7}{8} + \frac{1}{4} = \boxed{} + \boxed{} = \boxed{} = \boxed{}$$

$$4\frac{2}{3} + \frac{5}{8} = \boxed{} + \boxed{} = \boxed{} = \boxed{}$$

$$1\frac{9}{10} + \frac{2}{5} = \boxed{} + \boxed{} = \boxed{} = \boxed{}$$

$$8\frac{5}{6} + \frac{3}{5} = \boxed{} + \boxed{} = \boxed{} = \boxed{}$$

Simple use of parentheses

Work out these problems.

$(4 + 6) - (2 + 1) =$ 10 − 3 = 7

$(2 \times 5) + (10 - 4) =$ 10 + 6 = 16

Remember to work out the parentheses first.

Work out these problems.

$(5 + 3) + (6 - 2) =$ $(3 - 1) + (12 - 1) =$

$(6 - 1) - (1 + 2) =$ $(9 + 5) - (3 + 6) =$

$(8 + 3) + (12 - 2) =$ $(14 + 12) - (9 + 4) =$

$(7 - 2) + (4 + 5) =$ $(9 - 3) - (4 + 2) =$

Now try these longer problems.

$(5 + 9) + (12 - 2) - (4 + 3) =$

$(10 + 5) - (2 + 4) + (9 + 6) =$

$(19 + 4) - (3 + 2) - (2 + 1) =$

$(24 - 5) - (3 + 7) - (5 - 2) =$

$(15 + 3) + (7 - 2) - (5 + 7) =$

(2+3)
=
(4−1)
=

Now try these. Be careful, the parentheses now have multiplication problems.

$(2 \times 3) + (5 \times 2) =$ $(3 \times 4) - (2 \times 2) =$

$(7 \times 2) + (3 \times 3) =$ $(5 \times 4) - (3 \times 2) =$

$(6 \times 4) - (4 \times 3) =$ $(9 \times 5) - (4 \times 6) =$

$(12 \times 4) - (8 \times 3) =$ $(7 \times 4) - (8 \times 2) =$

If the answer is 24, which of these problems gives the correct answer? Write the correct letter.

a $(3 + 5) + (3 \times 1)$ c $(3 \times 5) + (3 \times 3)$ e $(5 \times 7) - (2 \times 5)$

b $(3 \times 5) + (3 \times 2)$ d $(2 \times 5) + (2 \times 6)$ f $(6 + 7) + (12 - 2)$

Simple use of parentheses

Work out these problems.

$(3 + 2) \times (4 + 1) =$ $5 \times 5 = 25$

$(10 \times 5) \div (10 - 5) =$ $50 \div 5 = 10$

Remember to work out the parentheses first.

Work out these problems.

$(7 + 3) \quad \times \quad (8 - 4) =$ $(5 - 2) \quad \times \quad (8 - 1) =$

$(9 + 5) \quad \div \quad (1 + 6) =$ $(14 - 6) \quad \times \quad (4 + 3) =$

$(14 + 4) \div (12 - 6) =$ $(9 + 21) \div (8 - 5) =$

$(11 - 5) \quad \times \quad (7 + 5) =$ $(8 + 20) \div (12 - 10) =$

$(6 + 9) \quad \div \quad (8 - 3) =$ $(14 - 3) \quad \times \quad (6 + 1) =$

$(10 + 10) \div (2 + 3) =$ $(9 + 3) \quad \times \quad (2 + 4) =$

Now try these.

$(4 \times 3) \quad \div \quad (1 \times 2) =$ $(5 \times 4) \quad \div \quad (2 \times 2) =$

$(8 \times 5) \quad \div \quad (4 \times 1) =$ $(6 \times 4) \quad \div \quad (3 \times 4) =$

$(2 \times 4) \quad \times \quad (2 \times 3) =$ $(3 \times 5) \quad \times \quad (1 \times 2) =$

$(8 \times 4) \quad \div \quad (2 \times 2) =$ $(6 \times 4) \quad \div \quad (4 \times 2) =$

If the answer is 30, which of these problems gives the correct answer?

a $(3 \times 5) \times (2 \times 2)$ d $(20 \div 2) \times (12 \div 3)$

b $(4 \times 5) \times (5 \times 2)$ e $(5 \times 12) \div (2 \times 5)$

c $(12 \times 5) \div (8 \div 4)$ f $(9 \times 5) \div (10 \div 2)$

If the answer is 8, which of these problems gives the correct answer?

a $(16 \div 2) \div (2 \times 1)$ d $(24 \div 6) \times (8 \div 4)$

b $(9 \div 3) \times (3 \times 2)$ e $(8 \div 4) \times (8 \div 1)$

c $(12 \times 4) \div (6 \times 2)$ f $(16 \div 4) \times (20 \div 4)$

Simple use of parentheses

Work out these problems.

$(5 + 3) + (9 - 2) =$ $8 + 7 = 15$

$(5 + 2) - (4 - 1) =$ $7 - 3 = 4$

$(4 + 2) \times (3 + 1) =$ $6 \times 4 = 24$

$(3 \times 5) \div (9 - 6) =$ $15 \div 3 = 5$

Remember to work out the parentheses first.

Work out these problems.

$(5 + 4) + (7 - 3) =$ _____ $(9 - 2) + (6 + 4) =$ _____

$(7 + 3) - (9 - 7) =$ _____ $(15 - 5) + (2 + 3) =$ _____

$(11 \times 2) - (3 \times 2) =$ _____ $(15 \div 3) + (9 \times 2) =$ _____

$(12 \times 2) - (3 \times 3) =$ _____ $(6 \div 2) + (8 \times 2) =$ _____

$(9 \times 3) - (7 \times 3) =$ _____ $(15 \div 5) + (3 \times 4) =$ _____

$(20 \div 5) - (8 \div 2) =$ _____ $(5 \times 10) - (12 \times 4) =$ _____

Now try these.

$(4 + 8) \div (3 \times 2) =$ _____ $(6 \times 4) \div (3 \times 2) =$ _____

$(9 + 5) \div (2 \times 1) =$ _____ $(7 \times 4) \div (3 + 4) =$ _____

$(3 + 6) \times (3 \times 3) =$ _____ $(5 \times 5) \div (10 \div 2) =$ _____

$(24 \div 2) \times (3 \times 2) =$ _____ $(8 \times 6) \div (2 \times 12) =$ _____

Write down the letters of all the problems that make 25.

a $(2 \times 5) \times (3 \times 2)$ d $(40 \div 2) + (10 \div 2)$

b $(5 \times 5) + (7 - 2)$ e $(10 \times 5) - (5 \times 5)$

c $(6 \times 5) - (10 \div 2)$ f $(10 \times 10) \div (10 - 6)$

Write down the letters of all the problems that make 20.

a $(10 \div 2) \times (4 \div 4)$ d $(20 \div 4) \times (8 + 2)$

b $(7 \times 3) - (3 \div 3)$ e $(10 \div 2) + (20 \div 2)$

c $(8 \times 4) - (6 \times 2)$ f $(14 \div 2) + (2 \times 7)$

Multiplying decimals

Work out these problems.

1		4		3	
4.6		3.9		8.4	
x 3		x 5		x 8	
13.8		**19.5**		**67.2**	

Work out these problems.

4.7	9.1	5.8	1.7	5.1
x 3	x 3	x 3	x 2	x 2

7.4	3.6	6.5	4.2	3.8
x 2	x 4	x 4	x 2	x 2

4.2	4.7	1.8	3.4	3.7
x 4	x 4	x 5	x 5	x 5

2.5	2.4	5.3	7.2	5.1
x 5	x 6	x 7	x 8	x 9

7.9	8.6	8.8	7.5	9.9
x 9	x 9	x 8	x 8	x 6

6.8	5.7	6.9	7.5	8.4
x 7	x 6	x 7	x 9	x 9

7.3	2.8	3.8	7.7	9.4
x 8	x 7	x 8	x 7	x 9

Multiplying decimals

Work out these problems.

$$
\begin{array}{r}
\scriptstyle 1\ 1 \\
37.5 \\
\times\ \ \ \ 2 \\
\hline
75.0
\end{array}
\qquad
\begin{array}{r}
\scriptstyle 3\ 1 \\
26.2 \\
\times\ \ \ \ 5 \\
\hline
131.0
\end{array}
\qquad
\begin{array}{r}
\scriptstyle 4\ 2 \\
65.3 \\
\times\ \ \ \ 9 \\
\hline
587.7
\end{array}
$$

Work out these problems.

53.3 × 2	93.2 × 2	51.4 × 2	34.6 × 3	35.2 × 3
46.5 × 4	25.8 × 4	16.4 × 3	47.1 × 5	37.4 × 5
12.4 × 5	46.3 × 5	17.5 × 6	36.5 × 6	72.4 × 7
37.5 × 7	20.3 × 7	73.4 × 7	92.6 × 6	47.9 × 6
53.9 × 8	75.6 × 8	28.8 × 8	79.4 × 8	99.9 × 9
37.9 × 9	14.8 × 9	35.4 × 9	46.8 × 8	27.2 × 7
39.5 × 6	84.2 × 9	68.5 × 8	73.2 × 9	47.6 × 6

Real-life problems

Carlos earns $3.50 a day on his paper route. How much does he earn per week?

$24.50

$$\begin{array}{r} 3 \\ \$3.50 \\ \times \quad 7 \\ \hline \$24.50 \end{array}$$

When Chanté subtracts the width of her closet from the length of her bedroom wall she finds she has 3.65 m of wall space left. If the closet is 0.87 m wide, what is the length of her bedroom wall?

4.52 m

$$\begin{array}{r} 1 \ 1 \\ 3.65 \\ + \ 0.87 \\ \hline 4.52 \end{array}$$

Sophie buys her mother a bunch of flowers for $12.95 and her brothers some candy for $2.76. If she has $7.83 left, how much did she start with?

If Pedro were 7.5 cm taller, he would be twice as tall as Ian. Ian is 74.25 cm tall, so how tall is Pedro?

Sasha is making some shelves which are 75.5 cm long. If the wood she is using is 180 cm long, how many pieces will she need to make six shelves?

A café uses 27.5 quarts of milk a day. If they have a weekly delivery of 180 quarts, how much will they have left after six days?

Charles has 12.5 m of railway track. Gavin has 8.6 m and Kristy has 4.8 m. If they put their track together how long will their layout be?

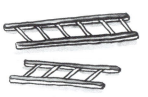

Real-life problems

A novelist writes 9.5 pages of his book a day.
How many pages will he write in nine days?

85.5 pages

$$
\begin{array}{r}
^{4}\ 9.5 \\
\times\ \ \ 9 \\
\hline
85.5
\end{array}
$$

After driving 147.7 mi a driver stops at a service
station. If he has another 115.4 mi to go, how long
will his trip be?

263.1 mi

$$
\begin{array}{r}
^{1\ 1}\ 147.7 \\
+\ 115.4 \\
\hline
263.1
\end{array}
$$

Mr. Mayfield divides his money equally
among four separate banks. If he has $98.65
in each bank, what is the total of his savings?

Mrs. Eldon buys two bottles of perfume; one contains
48.5 ml and the other contains 150.5 ml. How much
more perfume is in the larger of the two bottles?

A teacher spends 5.75 minutes grading
each story. How long would it take to
grade eight stories?

Eight tiles, each 15.75 cm wide, fit exactly
across the width of the bathroom wall. How
wide is the bathroom wall?

Terry has $8.50. If he spends $1.05 a day
over the next seven days, how much will he
have left at the end of the seven days?

A shop sells 427.56 kg of loose peanuts the
first week and 246.94 kg the second week.
How much did they sell over the two weeks?

Real-life problems

In a class of 30 children, 6 children are painting. What percent of children are painting?

$\frac{6}{30}$ of the children are painting and to change a fraction to a percent we multiply by 100.

20%

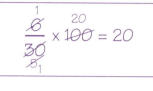
$\frac{\cancel{6}^{1}}{\cancel{30}_{1}} \times \cancel{100}^{20} = 20$

40% of a class is made up of girls. If there are 12 girls, how many children are in the class?

If 12 girls are 40% of the class, we divide 12 by 40 to find 1%. Then we multiply by 100 to find 100%.

30 children

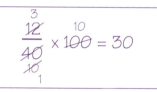
$\frac{\cancel{12}^{3}}{\cancel{40}_{10}} \times \cancel{100}^{10} = 30$

A shop has 60 books by a new author. If the shop sells 45 books, what percent does it sell?

A school disco sells 65% of its tickets. If it had 120 tickets to start with, how many has it sold?

200 people go on a school trip. If 14% are adults, how many children go on the trip?

A shop sells 150 T-shirts but 12 are returned because they are faulty. What percent of the T-shirts was faulty?

A group of 120 children are asked their favorite colors.

15% like red. How many children like red?

20% like green. How many children like green?

30% like yellow. How many children like yellow?

35% like blue. How many children like blue?

Conversions: length

Units of length	
12 inches	1 foot
3 feet	1 yard
5,280 feet	1 mile
1,760 yards	1 mile

This conversion table shows how to convert inches, feet, yards, and miles.

Brian's rope is 60 inches long. How many feet long is it?

60 ÷ 12 = 5   5 feet long

Neilika's rope is 3 yards long. How many inches long is it?

3 x 3 = 9   9 feet long
9 x 12 = 108   108 inches long

Convert each measurement to feet.

36 inches	12 inches	48 inches	72 inches

Convert each measurement to yards.

6 feet	12 feet	27 feet	36 feet

Convert each measurement to inches.

4 feet	12 feet	8 feet	5 feet

Convert each measurement to feet.

6 yards	2 yards	7 yards	5 yards

Convert each measurement.

4 yards	5 yards	4 miles	1 mile
inches	inches	feet	inches

15,840 feet	31,680 feet	1,760 yards	3,520 yards
miles	miles	mile	miles

Conversions: capacity

Units of capacity	
8 fluid ounces	1 cup
2 cups	1 pint
2 pints	1 quart
4 quarts	1 gallon

This conversion table shows how to convert ounces, cups pints, quarts, and gallons.

Katya's thermos holds 8 pints. How many cups does it hold?

8 x 2 = 16   16 cups

Hannah's thermos holds 6 cups. How many pints does it hold?

6 ÷ 2 = 3   3 pints

Convert each measurement to cups.

32 fluid ounces	16 fluid ounces	96 fluid ounces	80 fluid ounces

Convert each measurement to pints.

6 cups	12 cups	36 cups	50 cups

4 quarts	12 quarts	30 quarts	6 quarts

Convert each measurement to gallons.

16 quarts	32 quarts	100 quarts	20 quarts

Convert each measurement.

3 gallons	5 quarts	36 cups	72 pints
pints	cups	quarts	gallons

1 quart	240 fluid ounces	7 quarts	11 gallons
fluid ounces	pints	cups	pints

Fraction of a number

Work out to find the fraction of the number. Write the answer in the box.

$\frac{1}{6}$ of 42

$\frac{1}{6}$ x 42 = $\frac{42}{6}$ = 7

1 x 7 = 7

So, $\frac{1}{6}$ of 42 = 7

$\frac{1}{4}$ of 100 = $\frac{100}{4}$ = 25

$\frac{3}{5}$ of 35

$\frac{1}{5}$ x 35 = $\frac{35}{5}$ = 7

3 x 7 = 21

So, $\frac{3}{5}$ of 35 = 21

$\frac{1}{3}$ of 69 = $\frac{69}{3}$ = 23

Work out to find the fraction of the number. Write the answer in the box.

$\frac{1}{8}$ of 72

$\frac{1}{9}$ of 54

$\frac{1}{4}$ of 52

$\frac{1}{5}$ of 175

$\frac{1}{6}$ of 300

$\frac{1}{10}$ of 100

$\frac{3}{4}$ of 100

$\frac{2}{5}$ of 25

$\frac{5}{9}$ of 36

$\frac{3}{4}$ of 56

$\frac{4}{5}$ of 100

$\frac{2}{3}$ of 210

$\frac{1}{5}$ of 250

$\frac{1}{2}$ of 84

$\frac{1}{7}$ of 140

$\frac{1}{8}$ of 64

$\frac{1}{9}$ of 81

$\frac{1}{5}$ of 55

$\frac{2}{3}$ of 75

$\frac{5}{8}$ of 40

$\frac{2}{3}$ of 225

$\frac{5}{7}$ of 133

$\frac{2}{10}$ of 100

$\frac{4}{9}$ of 90

$\frac{1}{2}$ of 38

$\frac{1}{6}$ of 72

$\frac{1}{3}$ of 36

$\frac{1}{4}$ of 100

$\frac{1}{2}$ of 114

$\frac{1}{7}$ of 140

$\frac{4}{7}$ of 42

$\frac{2}{3}$ of 27

$\frac{5}{6}$ of 120

$\frac{2}{3}$ of 180

$\frac{3}{8}$ of 64

$\frac{7}{8}$ of 72

Showing decimals

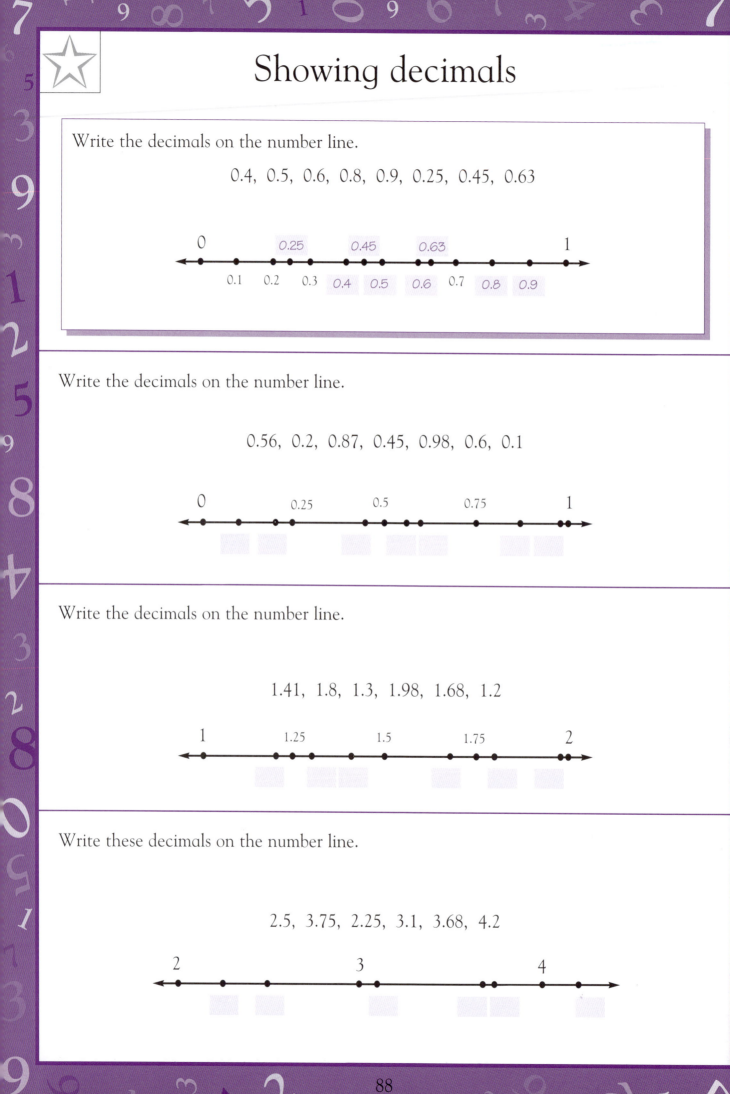

Write the decimals on the number line.

0.4, 0.5, 0.6, 0.8, 0.9, 0.25, 0.45, 0.63

Write the decimals on the number line.

0.56, 0.2, 0.87, 0.45, 0.98, 0.6, 0.1

Write the decimals on the number line.

1.41, 1.8, 1.3, 1.98, 1.68, 1.2

Write these decimals on the number line.

2.5, 3.75, 2.25, 3.1, 3.68, 4.2

Area of right-angled triangles

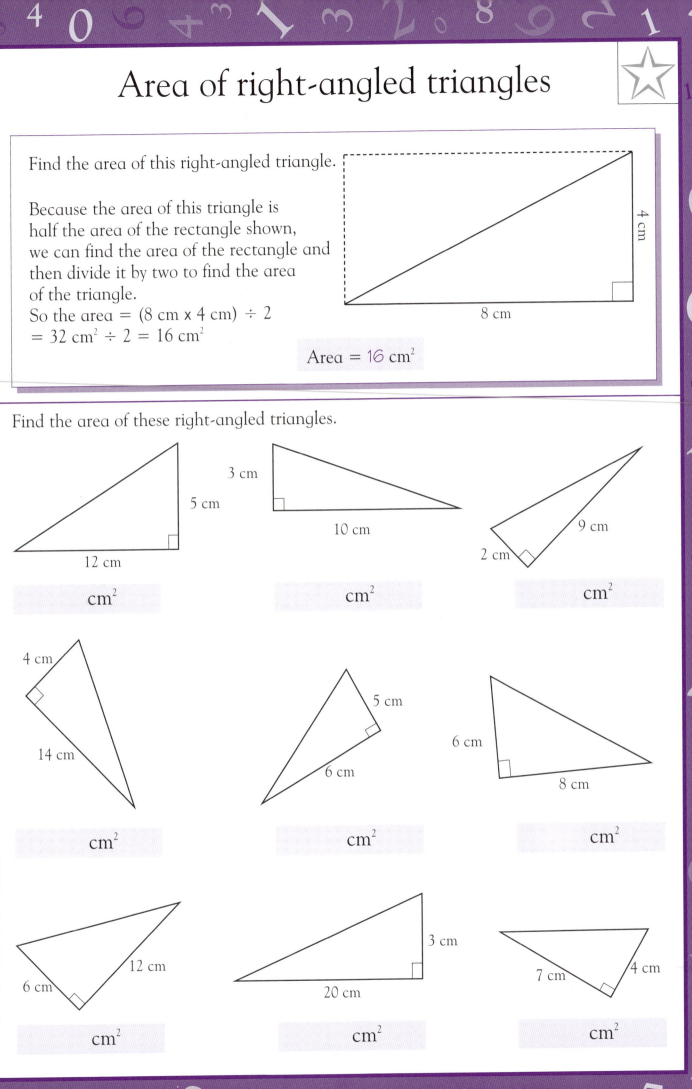

Find the area of this right-angled triangle.

Because the area of this triangle is
half the area of the rectangle shown,
we can find the area of the rectangle and
then divide it by two to find the area
of the triangle.
So the area = (8 cm x 4 cm) ÷ 2
= 32 cm² ÷ 2 = 16 cm²

4 cm

8 cm

Area = 16 cm²

Find the area of these right-angled triangles.

3 cm
5 cm
12 cm

cm²

10 cm

cm²

9 cm
2 cm

cm²

4 cm
14 cm

cm²

5 cm
6 cm

cm²

6 cm
8 cm

cm²

12 cm
6 cm

cm²

20 cm

cm²

3 cm
7 cm
4 cm

cm²

Speed problems

How long would it take to travel
120 mi at 8 mph?
(Time = Distance ÷ Speed)

15 hours

$$\begin{array}{r} 15 \\ 8)\overline{120} \end{array}$$

If a bus takes 3 hours to travel 150 mi,
how fast is it going?
(Speed = Distance ÷ Time)

50 mph

$$\begin{array}{r} 50 \\ 3)\overline{150} \end{array}$$

If a car travels at 60 mph for 2 hours,
how far has it gone?
(Distance = Speed × Time)

120 mi

$$\begin{array}{r} 60 \\ \times\, 2 \\ \hline 120 \end{array}$$

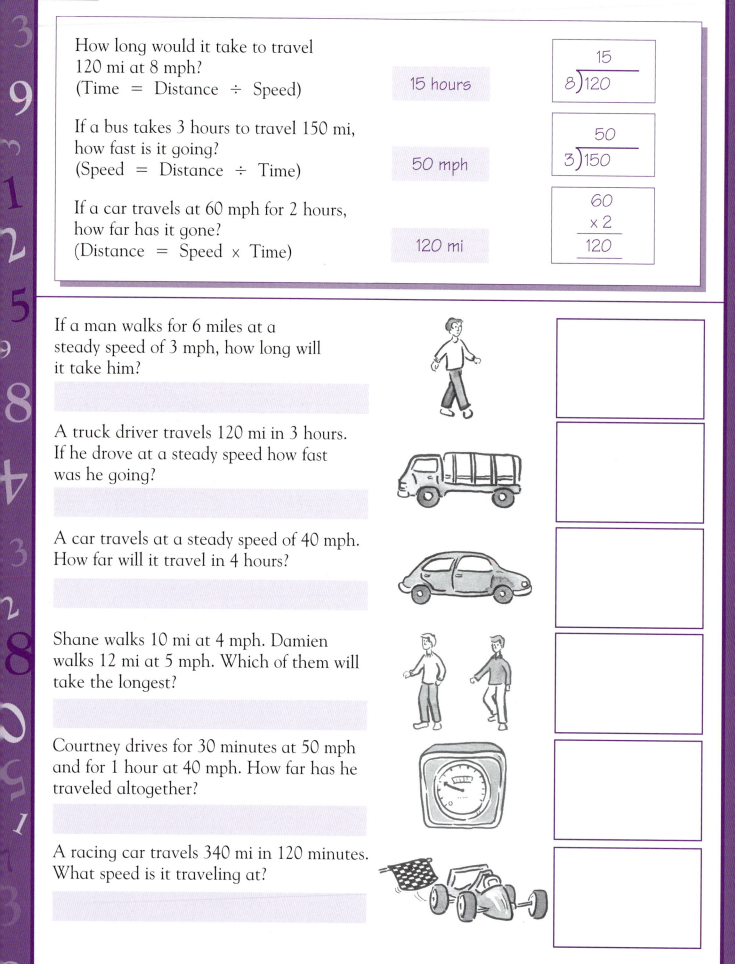

If a man walks for 6 miles at a
steady speed of 3 mph, how long will
it take him?

A truck driver travels 120 mi in 3 hours.
If he drove at a steady speed how fast
was he going?

A car travels at a steady speed of 40 mph.
How far will it travel in 4 hours?

Shane walks 10 mi at 4 mph. Damien
walks 12 mi at 5 mph. Which of them will
take the longest?

Courtney drives for 30 minutes at 50 mph
and for 1 hour at 40 mph. How far has he
traveled altogether?

A racing car travels 340 mi in 120 minutes.
What speed is it traveling at?

Conversion tables

Draw a table to convert dollars to cents.

$	cents
1	100
2	200
3	300

Complete the conversion chart below.

Weeks	Days
1	7
2	
	28
10	70

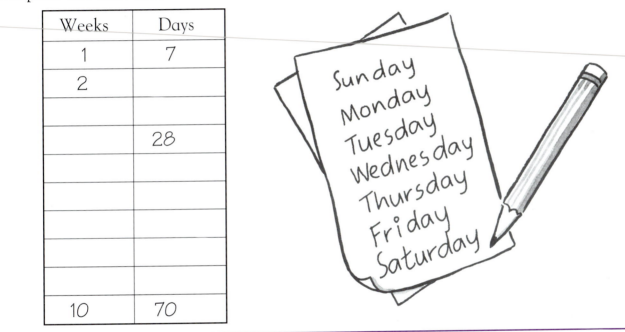

If there are 60 minutes in 1 hour, make a conversion chart for up to 10 hours.

Hours	Minutes

Reading bar graphs

Look at this graph.

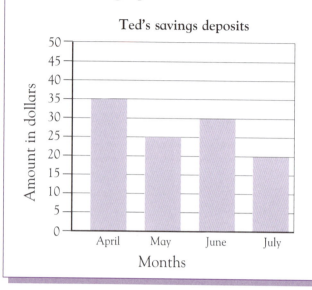

Ted's savings deposits

In which month did Ted save $25?

May

How much more money did Ted save in June than in July?

$10

Look at this graph.

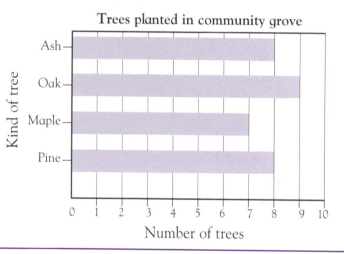

Trees planted in community grove

How many maple trees were planted?

The same number of ash trees were planted as what other kind of tree?

How many more oak trees were planted than maple trees?

Look at this graph.

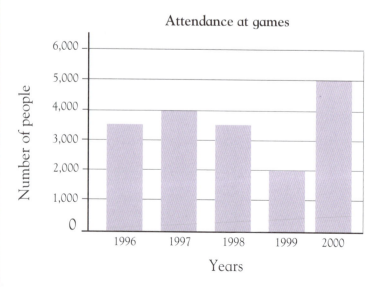

Attendance at games

In which year did 4,000 people attend the games?

How many more people attend the games in 2000 than on 1997?

The biggest increase in attendance was between which years?

Expanded form

What is the value of 3 in 2,308?   300

Write 32,084 in expanded form.   30,000 + 2,000 + 80 + 4

What is the value of 6 in these numbers?

26		162		36,904	
12,612		6,130		567,902	
13,036		9,764		17,632	

What is the value of 4 in these numbers?

14,300		942		8,764	
10,408		1,043		45,987	
6,045		804,001		694	

Circle the numbers that have a 7 with the value of seventy thousand.

457,682	67,924	870,234	372,987
171,345	767,707	79,835	16,757

Write the numbers in expanded form.

34,897

508,061

50,810

8,945

60,098

Cubes of small numbers

What is 2^3?

$2 \times 2 \times 2 = 8$

2 in.

What is the volume of this cube?

$2 \text{ in.} \times 2 \text{ in.} \times 2 \text{ in.} = 8 \text{ in.}^3$

You find the volume of a cube in the same way you work out the cube of a number.

Use extra paper here if you need to. What is...

3^3

4^3

6^3

5^3

1^3

2^3

What are the volumes of these cubes?

7 in.

in.^{3}

8 in.

in.^{3}

9 in.

in.^{3}

10 in.

in.^{3}

Multiplying fractions

Write the product.

$$\frac{3}{\overset{1}{8}} \times \frac{\overset{1}{4}}{7} = \boxed{\frac{3}{14}}$$

$$\overset{1}{\cancel{5}} \times \frac{3}{\underset{2}{10}} = \boxed{\frac{3}{2} = 1\frac{1}{2}}$$

Write the product.

$$\frac{1}{4} \times \frac{1}{4} = \boxed{}$$

$$\frac{3}{10} \times \frac{2}{6} = \boxed{}$$

$$6 \times \frac{3}{4} = \boxed{} = \boxed{}$$

$$8 \times \frac{1}{4} = \boxed{}$$

$$\frac{2}{5} \times \frac{5}{7} = \boxed{}$$

$$\frac{2}{5} \times \frac{5}{6} = \boxed{}$$

$$\frac{2}{5} \times \frac{2}{3} = \boxed{}$$

$$4 \times \frac{3}{16} = \boxed{}$$

$$\frac{3}{8} \times 10 = \boxed{} = \boxed{}$$

$$\frac{1}{3} \times 15 = \boxed{}$$

$$\frac{5}{9} \times \frac{1}{5} = \boxed{}$$

$$\frac{3}{4} \times \frac{4}{9} = \boxed{}$$

$$\frac{1}{4} \times \frac{2}{7} = \boxed{}$$

$$\frac{2}{9} \times \frac{3}{4} = \boxed{}$$

$$12 \times \frac{3}{10} = \boxed{} = \boxed{}$$

$$\frac{2}{3} \times \frac{1}{3} = \boxed{}$$

$$\frac{1}{12} \times 2 = \boxed{}$$

$$\frac{3}{4} \times \frac{1}{4} = \boxed{}$$

$$\frac{5}{6} \times 8 = \boxed{} = \boxed{}$$

$$7 \times \frac{1}{8} = \boxed{}$$

$$\frac{1}{6} \times \frac{5}{6} = \boxed{}$$

$$\frac{1}{2} \times 25 = \boxed{} = \boxed{}$$

$$\frac{7}{10} \times \frac{5}{7} = \boxed{}$$

$$4 \times \frac{3}{4} = \boxed{}$$

More complex fraction problems

Find $\frac{3}{5}$ of $30.00.

> Find $\frac{1}{5}$: $30 ÷ 5 = $6
>
> $6 × 3 = $18
>
> So, $\frac{3}{5}$ of $30 is $18

Find $\frac{7}{10}$ of 60 in.

> Find $\frac{1}{10}$: 60 in. ÷ 10 = 6 in.
>
> 6 in. × 7 = 42 in.
>
> So, $\frac{7}{10}$ of 60 in. is 42 in.

Find $\frac{3}{5}$ of these amounts.

40 in.

$50

$10.50

80 yd

75 oz

45 lb

Find $\frac{7}{10}$ of these amounts.

48 yd

$98.00

75 mi

Find $\frac{2}{3}$ of these amounts.

48 in.

120 lb

$24.00

Finding percentages

Find 30% of 140.

$$\frac{14\cancel{0}}{10\cancel{0}} \times 3\cancel{0} = 42$$

(Divide by 100 to find 1% and then multiply by 30 to find 30%.)

Find 12% of 75.

$$\frac{\cancel{75}^{\,3}}{\cancel{100}_{\,4\,1}} \times \cancel{12}^{\,3} = 9$$

(Divide by 100 to find 1% and then multiply by 12 to find 12%.)

Find 30% of these numbers.

620   240

80   160

Find 60% of these numbers.

60   100

160   580

Find 45% of these numbers.

80 oz   40 in.

240 fl oz   600 mi

Find 12% of these numbers.

$150 $600

125 ft   775 ft

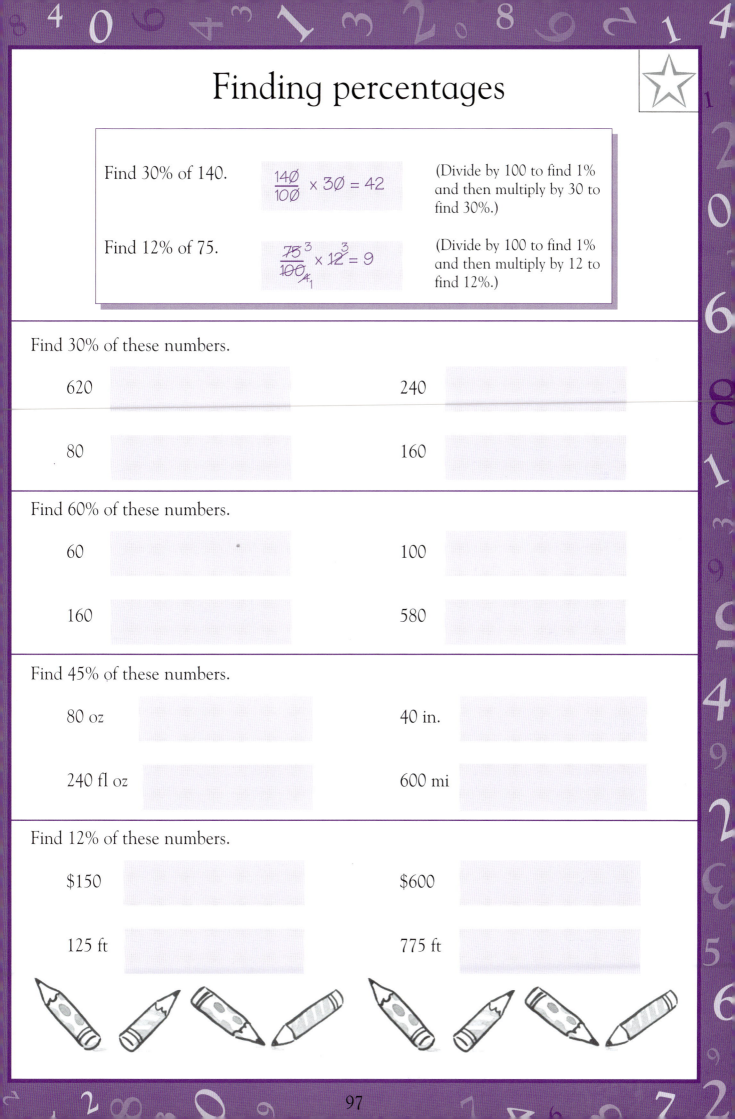

Addition

Find each sum.

```
  5,831        3,724        9,994          524
  8,375        9,942        7,358        7,034
+   219      +   623      +   471      +    95
  _____       _____       _____       _____
```

```
  7,341        9,328        7,159          208
    299          347           39        4,943
+ 5,143      + 8,222      +   748      +    55
  _____       _____       _____       _____
```

Find each sum.

```
  8,594        7,362        3,041        7,641
    629          843          571           93
  9,878        4,732        5,210        8,521
+    96      +    53      +    71      +   843
  _____       _____       _____       _____
```

```
  8,795        6,043           27          146
    659            4          153        3,714
  3,212          147        8,612           26
+   961      + 8,948      +   127      + 5,003
  _____       _____       _____       _____
```

More addition

Find each sum.

```
  17,203          29,521          65,214          25,046
    112            6,211            973              15
+ 5,608          +    58          + 1,291          +   263
-------          -------          -------          -------
```

```
   6,958          73,009          11,536          87,019
     71                3             48             127
+ 16,911          +   581          + 2,435          + 5,652
-------          -------          -------          -------
```

Find each sum.

```
  79,622          64,599           6,940          72,148
   8,011            122             936             999
  47,391          6,375          58,274           7,481
+      7          +    91          +    36          + 21,685
-------          -------          -------          -------
```

```
  58,975          36,403              8              23
    858             73            22,849          99,951
  8,423            712              502             358
+    27          + 6,229          + 4,034          + 6,231
-------          -------          -------          -------
```

99

Dividing by ones

$477 \div 2$ can be written in two ways:

$$238\frac{1}{2}$$

or

$$238 \text{ r } 1$$

$2\overline{)477}$

$2\overline{)477}$

Work out the answers to these problems. Use fraction remainders.

$2\overline{)479}$ $\qquad$ $4\overline{)863}$ $\qquad$ $5\overline{)579}$ $\qquad$ $7\overline{)860}$

$2\overline{)175}$ $\qquad$ $3\overline{)167}$ $\qquad$ $9\overline{)457}$ $\qquad$ $3\overline{)293}$

Work out the answers to these problems. Use unit remainders.

$2\overline{)705}$ $\qquad$ $5\overline{)637}$ $\qquad$ $4\overline{)330}$ $\qquad$ $7\overline{)921}$

Dividing by tens

$361 \div 20$ can be written in two ways:

$$18\frac{1}{20} \qquad\qquad 18 \text{ r } 1$$

$$20\overline{)361} \qquad \text{or} \qquad 20\overline{)361}$$

Work out the answers to these problems. Use fraction remainders.

$40\overline{)320}$ $\qquad$ $70\overline{)490}$ $\qquad$ $80\overline{)349}$ $\qquad$ $90\overline{)547}$

$10\overline{)807}$ $\qquad$ $20\overline{)437}$ $\qquad$ $10\overline{)943}$ $\qquad$ $30\overline{)361}$

Work out the answers to these problems. Use unit remainders.

$50\overline{)417}$ $\qquad$ $90\overline{)810}$ $\qquad$ $30\overline{)303}$ $\qquad$ $40\overline{)366}$

$20\overline{)768}$ $\qquad$ $70\overline{)980}$ $\qquad$ $60\overline{)787}$ $\qquad$ $10\overline{)297}$

Dividing by larger numbers

589 ÷ 15 can be written in two ways:

$39\frac{4}{15}$ or   39 r 4

15)589   15)589

Work out the answers to these problems. Use fractions remainders.

48)435   21)359   57)452   72)792

30)937   65)799   17)289   51)854

Work out the answers to these problems. Use unit remainders.

79)653   24)545   68)952   36)411

12)876   96)797   17)742   45)582

Everyday problems

A plumber has 6 m of copper tubing. If he uses 2.36 m, how much will he have left?

3.64 m

```
        9
     5 1̸0 1̸0
     6̸.0̸0̸
    − 2.36
     3.64
```

If he buys another 4.5 m of copper tubing, how much will he now have?

8.14 m

```
      1
     3.64
   + 4.50
     8.14
```

A man spends $35.65, $102.43, $68.99 and $36.50 in 4 different stores. How much money did he spend altogether?

A gas station has 10,400 gallons of gasoline delivered on Monday, 13,350 gal on Tuesday, 14,755 gal on Wednesday, 9,656 gal on Thursday, and 15,975 gal on Friday. How much did they have delivered from Monday through Friday?

If they sold 59,248 gallons that week, how much gasoline did they have left?

Daniel runs 22.56 km in a charity fun run. Sandra runs 8,420 m less. How far does Sandra run?

What is the combined distance run by Daniel and Sandra?

Dianne is 4 ft 10 in. tall. Tania is 5 ft 1 in. tall. How much taller is Tania?

Real-life problems

A man walks 18.34 km on Saturday and 16.57 km on Sunday.
How far did he walk that weekend?

34.91 km

How much farther did he walk on Saturday?

1.77 km

$$\begin{array}{r} \overset{1}{1}\overset{1}{8}.34 \\ +\ 16.57 \\ \hline 34.91 \end{array}$$

$$\begin{array}{r} 7\ \overset{12}{\cancel{2}}14 \\ 1\cancel{8}.\cancel{3}4 \\ -\ 16.57 \\ \hline 1\ .77 \end{array}$$

A rectangular field measures 103.7 m by 96.5 m. What is the perimeter of the field?

When Joe and Kerry stand on a scale it reads $236\frac{1}{2}$ lb.
When Joe steps off, it reads $68\frac{1}{4}$ lb.
How much does Joe weigh?

A rectangular room has an area of 32.58 m². When a carpet is put down there is still 7.99 m² of floor showing. What is the area of the carpet?

A brother's and sister's combined height is $108\frac{3}{4}$ in. If the sister is $51\frac{1}{2}$ in. tall, how tall is the brother?

A state has 4 highways: Rte 1, which is 1,246 mi long;
Rte 2 which is 339 mi long; Rte 3 which is 1,573 mi long; and
Rte 4 which is 48 mi long. How much highway does the state have in total?

Jenny's aquarium holds $25\frac{1}{2}$ quarts of water. She buys a new one that holds 32 quarts. How much extra water do her fish have?

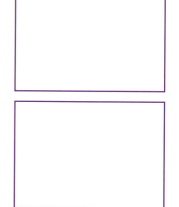

104

Real-life problems

Deborah's school bag weighs $14\frac{1}{2}$ lb.
Asha's weighs $12\frac{1}{2}$ lb. How much more does
Deborah's weigh than Asha's?

2 lb

What is the total weight of the two bags?

27 lb

$$14\frac{1}{2}$$
$$-12\frac{1}{2}$$
$$\overline{2}$$

$$14\frac{1}{2}$$
$$+12\frac{1}{2}$$
$$\overline{26\frac{2}{2}} = 27$$

Mr Shaw needs to put weather stripping around four sides of his front door. The door is 80 in. high and 36 in. wide. How many inches of weather stripping does he needs?

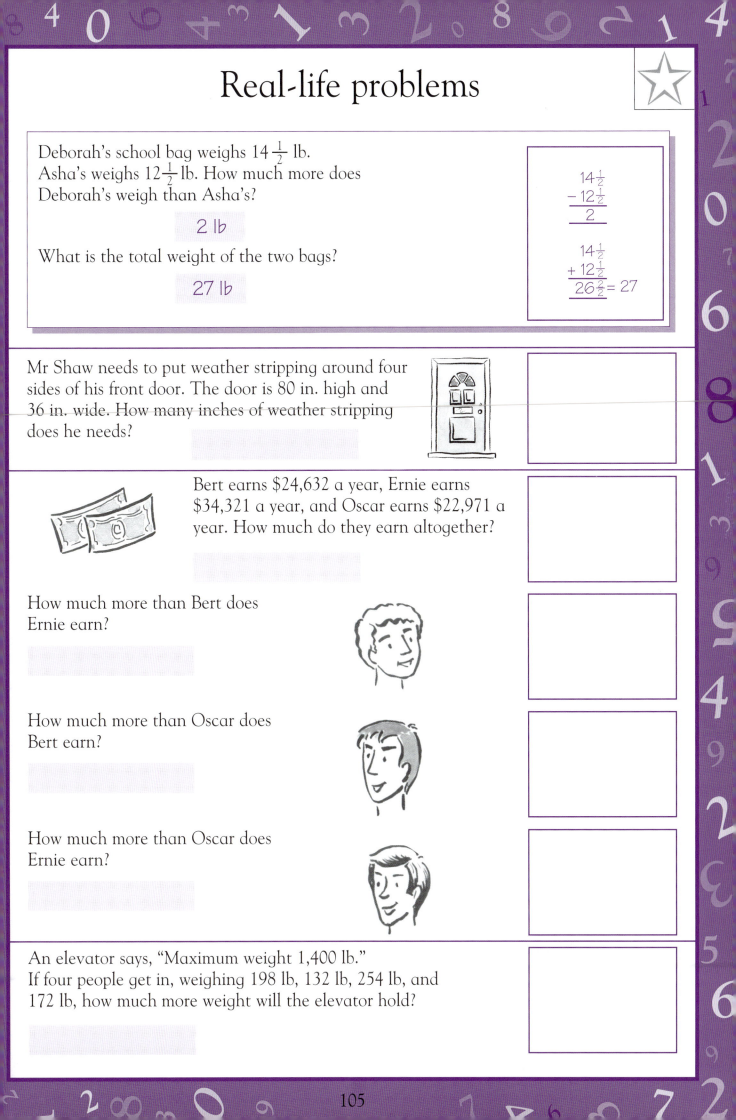

Bert earns $24,632 a year, Ernie earns $34,321 a year, and Oscar earns $22,971 a year. How much do they earn altogether?

How much more than Bert does Ernie earn?

How much more than Oscar does Bert earn?

How much more than Oscar does Ernie earn?

An elevator says, "Maximum weight 1,400 lb."
If four people get in, weighing 198 lb, 132 lb, 254 lb, and 172 lb, how much more weight will the elevator hold?

Multiplication by 2-digit numbers

Work out the answer to each problem.

```
    527              834
  x  76            x  58
  -----            -----
  3,162           41,700
 36,890            6,672
 ------           ------
 40,052           48,372
```

Work out the answer to each problem.

```
    426              895              632              778
  x  84            x  65            x  39            x  49
```

```
    597              994              632              747
  x  46            x  37            x  64            x  75
```

```
    428              147              236              145
  x  95            x  62            x  87            x  33
```

```
    346              529              485              763
  x  85            x  72            x  29            x  84
```

Division by ones

$47 \div 2$ can be written in two ways:

$$\begin{array}{r} 23 \\ 2\overline{)47} \\ \underline{4} \\ 7 \\ \underline{6} \\ 1 \end{array}$$ $23\frac{1}{2}$ or $$\begin{array}{r} 23 \\ 2\overline{)47} \\ \underline{4} \\ 7 \\ \underline{6} \\ 1 \end{array}$$ $23\ r\ 1$

Write the quotients for these problems with fraction remainders.

$2\overline{)17}$ $4\overline{)19}$ $3\overline{)16}$ $4\overline{)37}$

$3\overline{)29}$ $2\overline{)45}$ $5\overline{)87}$ $5\overline{)49}$

Write the quotients for these problems with unit remainders.

$2\overline{)73}$ $2\overline{)85}$ $2\overline{)39}$ $4\overline{)59}$

$4\overline{)71}$ $4\overline{)83}$ $5\overline{)29}$ $5\overline{)47}$

Dividing larger numbers

$645 \div 13$ can be written in two ways:

$49\frac{8}{13}$ or $49 \text{ r } 8$

$13\overline{)645}$ $13\overline{)645}$

Work out the answer to each problem. Use fraction remainders.

$43\overline{)377}$ $21\overline{)169}$ $17\overline{)158}$ $41\overline{)368}$

$50\overline{)197}$ $91\overline{)636}$ $12\overline{)325}$ $14\overline{)787}$

Work out the answer to each problem. Use unit remainders.

$52\overline{)947}$ $35\overline{)731}$ $57\overline{)878}$ $11\overline{)875}$

$70\overline{)495}$ $84\overline{)735}$ $44\overline{)387}$ $62\overline{)489}$

Division of 3-digit decimal numbers

Work out these division sums.

```
     0.89              0.74
 3)2.67            4)2.96
   24                28
   27                16
   27                16
    0    0.89         0    0.74
```

Work out these division problems.

2)2.94   4)7.32   4)6.12   2)3.24

2)9.98   3)9.72   4)6.24   4)7.48

4)2.24   3)2.22   3)2.25   3)2.61

Division of 3-digit decimal numbers

Work out these division problems.

```
      1.99                    1.61
  5)9.95                  6)9.66
    5                       6
    49                      36
    45                      36
    45                       6
    45                       6
     0                       0
```

1.99   1.61

Work out these division problems.

5)8.15   5)9.25   5)6.35   6)9.12

6)2.16   7)8.82   7)4.83   8)5.92

8)8.72   9)8.19   9)5.67   6)6.36

Real-life problems

A builder uses 1,600 lb of sand a day.
How much will he use in 5 days?

8,000 lb

$$\begin{array}{r} \overset{3}{1,600} \\ \times\ \ \ 5 \\ \hline 8,000 \end{array}$$

If he uses 9,500 lb the next week,
how much more has he used than
the week before?

1,500 lb

$$\begin{array}{r} 9,500 \\ -\ 8,000 \\ \hline 1,500 \end{array}$$

An electrician uses 184 ft of cable while
working on four houses. If he uses the same
amount on each house, how much does
he use on one house?

A family looks at vacations in two different resorts.
The first one costs $846.95. The second costs $932.
How much will the family save if they choose
the cheaper resort?

Doris has 5 sections of fence, each 36 in.
wide. If she puts them together, how much
of her yard can she fence off?

Shula goes on a sponsored walk and collects
$15.95 from her mother, $8.36 from her uncle,
$4.65 from her brother, and $2.75 from her aunt.
How much does she
collect altogether?

A taxi company has 9 cars.
If each car holds 16.4 gallons of gasoline,
how many gallons will it take to fill all
of the cars?

Rounding money

Round to the nearest dollar.

$3.95 rounds to $4

$2.25 rounds to $2

Round to the nearest ten dollars.

$15.50 rounds to $20

$14.40 rounds to $10

Round to the nearest dollar.

$2.60 rounds to $8.49 rounds to $3.39 rounds to

$9.55 rounds to $1.75 rounds to $4.30 rounds to

$7.15 rounds to $6.95 rounds to $2.53 rounds to

Round to the nearest ten dollars.

$37.34 rounds to $21.75 rounds to $85.03 rounds to

$71.99 rounds to $66.89 rounds to $52.99 rounds to

$55.31 rounds to $12.79 rounds to $15.00 rounds to

Round to the nearest hundred dollars.

$307.12 rounds to $175.50 rounds to $115.99 rounds to

$860.55 rounds to $417.13 rounds to $650.15 rounds to

$739.10 rounds to $249.66 rounds to $367.50 rounds to

Estimating sums of money

☆

Round to the leading digit. Estimate the sum.

$$\begin{array}{rl} \$3.26 \rightarrow & \$3 \\ + \ \$4.82 \rightarrow & + \ \$5 \\ \hline \text{is about} & \underline{\$8} \end{array} \qquad \begin{array}{rl} \$68.53 \rightarrow & \$70 \\ + \ \$34.60 \rightarrow & + \ \$30 \\ \hline \text{is about} & \underline{\$100} \end{array}$$

Round to the leading digit. Estimate the sum.

$$\begin{array}{rl} \$52.61 \rightarrow \\ + \ \$27.95 \rightarrow \underline{\quad} \\ \hline \text{is about} \end{array} \qquad \begin{array}{rl} \$19.20 \rightarrow \\ + \ \$22.13 \rightarrow \underline{\quad} \\ \hline \text{is about} \end{array} \qquad \begin{array}{rl} \$70.75 \rightarrow \\ + \ \$12.49 \rightarrow \underline{\quad} \\ \hline \text{is about} \end{array}$$

$$\begin{array}{rl} \$701.34 \rightarrow \\ + \ \$100.80 \rightarrow \underline{\quad} \\ \hline \text{is about} \end{array} \qquad \begin{array}{rl} \$339.50 \rightarrow \\ + \ \$422.13 \rightarrow \underline{\quad} \\ \hline \text{is about} \end{array} \qquad \begin{array}{rl} \$160.07 \rightarrow \\ + \ \$230.89 \rightarrow \underline{\quad} \\ \hline \text{is about} \end{array}$$

$$\begin{array}{rl} \$25.61 \rightarrow \\ + \ \$72.51 \rightarrow \underline{\quad} \\ \hline \text{is about} \end{array} \qquad \begin{array}{rl} \$61.39 \rightarrow \\ + \ \$19.50 \rightarrow \underline{\quad} \\ \hline \text{is about} \end{array} \qquad \begin{array}{rl} \$18.32 \rightarrow \\ + \ \$13.90 \rightarrow \underline{\quad} \\ \hline \text{is about} \end{array}$$

$$\begin{array}{rl} \$587.35 \rightarrow \\ + \ 251.89 \rightarrow \underline{\quad} \\ \hline \text{is about} \end{array} \qquad \begin{array}{rl} \$109.98 \rightarrow \\ + \ \$210.09 \rightarrow \underline{\quad} \\ \hline \text{is about} \end{array} \qquad \begin{array}{rl} \$470.02 \rightarrow \\ + \ \$203.17 \rightarrow \underline{\quad} \\ \hline \text{is about} \end{array}$$

Round to the leading digit. Estimate the sum.

$\$75.95 + \$17.95 \rightarrow$ ⬜ $\qquad\qquad$ $\$41.67 + \$20.35 \rightarrow$ ⬜

$\$49.19 + \$38.70 \rightarrow$ ⬜ $\qquad\qquad$ $\$784.65 + \$101.05 \rightarrow$ ⬜

$\$516.50 + \$290.69 \rightarrow$ ⬜ $\qquad\qquad$ $\$58.78 + \$33.25 \rightarrow$ ⬜

$\$82.90 + \$11.79 \rightarrow$ ⬜ $\qquad\qquad$ $\$90.09 + \$14.50 \rightarrow$ ⬜

Estimating differences of money

Round the numbers to the leading digit. Estimate the differences.

$17.90 →
− $12.30 → _____
is about   [   ]

$6.40 →
− $3.75 → _____
is about   [   ]

$87.45 →
− $54.99 → _____
is about   [   ]

$34.90 →
− $12.60 → _____
is about   [   ]

$8.68 →
− $4.39 → _____
is about   [   ]

$363.24 →
− $127.66 → _____
is about   [   ]

$78.75 →
+ $24.99 → _____
is about   [   ]

$64.21 →
− $28.56 → _____
is about   [   ]

$723.34 →
− $487.12 → _____
is about   [   ]

Round the numbers to the leading digit. Estimate the differences.

$8.12 − $1.35
→   =   [   ]

$49.63 − $27.85
→   =   [   ]

$7.50 − $3.15
→   =   [   ]

$85.15 − $42.99
→   =   [   ]

$5.85 − $4.75
→   =   [   ]

$634.60 − $267.25
→   =   [   ]

$37.35 − $16.99
→   =   [   ]

$842.17 − $169.54
→   =   [   ]

$56.95 − $20.58
→   =   [   ]

$628.37 − $252.11
→   =   [   ]

Estimating sums and differences

Round the numbers to the leading digit. Estimate the sum or difference.

$$
\begin{array}{rcl}
3{,}576 & \to & 4{,}000 \\
+\ 1{,}307 & \to & +1{,}000 \\
\hline
\text{is about} & & 5{,}000
\end{array}
\qquad
\begin{array}{rcl}
198{,}248 & \to & 200{,}000 \\
-\ 116{,}431 & \to & -100{,}000 \\
\hline
\text{is about} & & 100{,}000
\end{array}
$$

Round the numbers to the leading digit. Estimate the sum or difference.

$$
\begin{array}{rcl}
685 & \to & \underline{} \\
+\ 489 & \to & \underline{} \\
\hline
\text{is about} & & \underline{}
\end{array}
\qquad
\begin{array}{rcl}
21{,}481 & \to & \underline{} \\
-\ 12{,}500 & \to & \underline{} \\
\hline
\text{is about} & & \underline{}
\end{array}
\qquad
\begin{array}{rcl}
7{,}834 & \to & \underline{} \\
+\ 3{,}106 & \to & \underline{} \\
\hline
\text{is about} & & \underline{}
\end{array}
$$

$$
\begin{array}{rcl}
682{,}778 & \to & \underline{} \\
+\ 130{,}001 & \to & \underline{} \\
\hline
\text{is about} & & \underline{}
\end{array}
\qquad
\begin{array}{rcl}
58{,}499 & \to & \underline{} \\
-\ 22{,}135 & \to & \underline{} \\
\hline
\text{is about} & & \underline{}
\end{array}
\qquad
\begin{array}{rcl}
902{,}276 & \to & \underline{} \\
-\ 615{,}999 & \to & \underline{} \\
\hline
\text{is about} & & \underline{}
\end{array}
$$

$$
\begin{array}{rcl}
46{,}801 & \to & \underline{} \\
+\ 34{,}700 & \to & \underline{} \\
\hline
\text{is about} & & \underline{}
\end{array}
\qquad
\begin{array}{rcl}
9{,}734 & \to & \underline{} \\
-\ 8{,}306 & \to & \underline{} \\
\hline
\text{is about} & & \underline{}
\end{array}
\qquad
\begin{array}{rcl}
65{,}606 & \to & \underline{} \\
+\ 85{,}943 & \to & \underline{} \\
\hline
\text{is about} & & \underline{}
\end{array}
$$

$$
\begin{array}{rcl}
5{,}218 & \to & \underline{} \\
-\ 3{,}673 & \to & \underline{} \\
\hline
\text{is about} & & \underline{}
\end{array}
\qquad
\begin{array}{rcl}
745 & \to & \underline{} \\
+\ 451 & \to & \underline{} \\
\hline
\text{is about} & & \underline{}
\end{array}
\qquad
\begin{array}{rcl}
337{,}297 & \to & \underline{} \\
-\ 168{,}931 & \to & \underline{} \\
\hline
\text{is about} & & \underline{}
\end{array}
$$

Write < or > for each problem.

329 + 495 ____ 800   11,569 – 6,146 ____ 6,000

563 – 317 ____ 300   8,193 – 6,668 ____ 1,000

41,924 – 12,445 ____ 50,000   634,577 + 192,556 ____ 800,000

18,885 + 12,691 ____ 30,000   713,096 – 321,667 ____ 400,000

Estimating products

Round to the leading digit. Estimate the product.

3,456 x 6
3,000 x 6 = 18,000

73 x 46
70 x 50 = 3,500

Round to the leading digit. Estimate the sum.

1,908 x 8
___ x 8 = ___

5 x 6,099
5 x ___ = ___

7 x 1,108
7 x ___ = ___

5,239 x 9
___ x 9 = ___

81 x 32
___ x ___ = ___

19 x 62
___ x ___ = ___

39 x 44
___ x ___ = ___

94 x 12
___ x ___ = ___

Estimate the product.

6 x 7,243	4,785 x 4	3 x 8,924
2,785 x 5	6,298 x 4	7 x 7,105
8 x 2,870	4,176 x 7	5 x 4,803
6,777 x 9	6 x 8,022	3,785 x 4
42 x 51	54 x 28	23 x 75
16 x 32	47 x 54	59 x 52
17 x 74	33 x 22	81 x 18
31 x 91	38 x 87	46 x 77

Estimating quotients

Round to compatible numbers. Estimate the quotient.

$3,156 \div 6$
$3,000 \div 6 = \boxed{500}$

$2,159 \div 5$
$2,500 \div 5 = \boxed{500}$

Round to compatible numbers. Estimate the quotient.

$1,934 \div 8$
$\underline{} \div 8 =$

$4,066 \div 5$
$ \div 5 =$

$1,108 \div 4$
$ \div 4 =$

$5,657 \div 9$
$ \div 9 =$

$3,998 \div 6$
$ \div 6 =$

$5,525 \div 7$
$ \div 7 =$

$1,701 \div 3$
$ \div 3 =$

$1,304 \div 2$
$ \div 2 =$

Estimate the quotient.

$4,798 \div 7$ $8,205 \div 9$ $5,022 \div 5$

$3,785 \div 4$ $5,528 \div 6$ $2,375 \div 8$

$1,632 \div 3$ $4,251 \div 4$ $4,754 \div 9$

$7,352 \div 8$ $1,774 \div 2$ $3,322 \div 7$

$3,591 \div 6$ $2,887 \div 5$ $5,746 \div 2$

$3,703 \div 3$ $2,392 \div 6$ $6,621 \div 8$

Rounding mixed numbers

Circle the fractions that are more than $\frac{1}{2}$.

$\frac{3}{7}$ $\frac{2}{9}$ $\frac{6}{7}$ $\frac{5}{9}$ $\frac{3}{8}$ $\frac{1}{7}$ $\frac{2}{3}$ $\frac{4}{7}$

$\frac{7}{10}$ $\frac{2}{5}$ $\frac{1}{3}$ $\frac{5}{6}$ $\frac{3}{4}$ $\frac{2}{9}$ $\frac{5}{8}$ $\frac{3}{5}$

Circle the fractions that are less than $\frac{1}{2}$.

$\frac{1}{8}$ $\frac{3}{9}$ $\frac{4}{5}$ $\frac{2}{7}$ $\frac{3}{5}$ $\frac{2}{5}$ $\frac{7}{10}$ $\frac{2}{9}$

$\frac{3}{4}$ $\frac{1}{3}$ $\frac{4}{9}$ $\frac{3}{10}$ $\frac{5}{6}$ $\frac{1}{4}$ $\frac{3}{7}$ $\frac{5}{9}$

Round to the closest whole number.

$4\frac{3}{8}$ ▨ $2\frac{6}{7}$ ▨ $5\frac{3}{4}$ ▨ $3\frac{2}{9}$ ▨

$2\frac{5}{6}$ ▨ $1\frac{7}{8}$ ▨ $2\frac{2}{5}$ ▨ $5\frac{1}{7}$ ▨

$3\frac{1}{6}$ ▨ $5\frac{3}{8}$ ▨ $3\frac{3}{5}$ ▨ $7\frac{8}{13}$ ▨

$6\frac{3}{5}$ ▨ $1\frac{1}{4}$ ▨ $4\frac{5}{6}$ ▨ $9\frac{3}{4}$ ▨

$5\frac{2}{3}$ ▨ $3\frac{3}{7}$ ▨ $1\frac{6}{7}$ ▨ $6\frac{3}{4}$ ▨

Calculate the mean

What is the mean of 6 and 10? $(6+10) \div 2 = 8$

David is 9, Asha is 10, and
Daniel is 5. What is their mean age? $(9 + 10 + 5) \div 3 = 8$ years

Calculate the mean of these amounts.

9 and 5

6 and 8

5 and 7

11 and 7

8 and 12

13 and 15

19 and 21

40 and 60

Calculate the mean of these amounts.

5, 7, and 3

11, 9, and 7

14, 10, and 6

12, 8, and 4

7, 3, 5, and 9

$1, $1.50, $2.50, and $3

16¢, 9¢, 12¢, and 3¢

5 g, 7 g, 8 g, and 8 g

Calculate these answers.

The mean of two numbers is 7. If one of the numbers
is 6, what is the other number?

The mean of three numbers is 4. If two of the numbers
are 4 and 5, what is the third number?

The mean of four numbers is 12. If three of the numbers
are 9, 15, and 8, what is the fourth number?

Two children record their
last five spelling-test scores.

| Gayle | 17 | 18 | 16 | 14 | 15 |
| Sally | 19 | 20 | 12 | 13 | 11 |

Which child has the best mean score?

Mean, median, and mode

Sian throws a dice 7 times. Here are her results:
4, 2, 1, 2, 4, 2, 6

What is the mean? $(4 + 2 + 1 + 2 + 4 + 2 + 6) \div 7 = 3$

What is the median? Put the numbers in order of size and find the middle number, example, 1, 2, 2, 2, 4, 4, 6.

The median is 2.

What is the mode?   The most common result, which is 2.

A school soccer team scores the following number of goals in their first 9 matches:
2, 2, 1, 3, 2, 1, 2, 4, 1

What is the mean score?

What is the median score?

Write down the mode for their results.

The ages of the local hockey players are:
17, 15, 16, 19, 17, 19, 22, 17, 18, 21, 17

What is the mean of their ages?

What is their median age?

Write down the mode for their ages.

The results of Susan's last 11 spelling tests were:
15, 12, 15, 17, 11, 16, 19, 11, 3, 11, 13

What is the mean of her scores?

What is her median score?

Write down the mode for her scores.

Line graphs

Look at this graph.

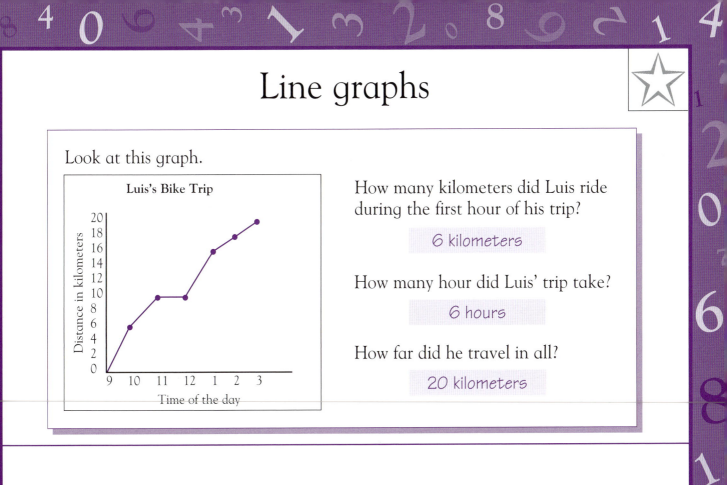

How many kilometers did Luis ride during the first hour of his trip?

6 kilometers

How many hour did Luis' trip take?

6 hours

How far did he travel in all?

20 kilometers

Luis stopped for lunch for one hour. What time did he stop?

Did Luis cover more distance between 12 and 1 or between 1 and 2

Between which two hours did Luis travel 4 kilometers?

During which hours did Luis ride the fastest?

Did Luis travel farther before or after his lunch break?

How much longer did it take Luis to ride 10 kilometers after lunch?

Coordinates

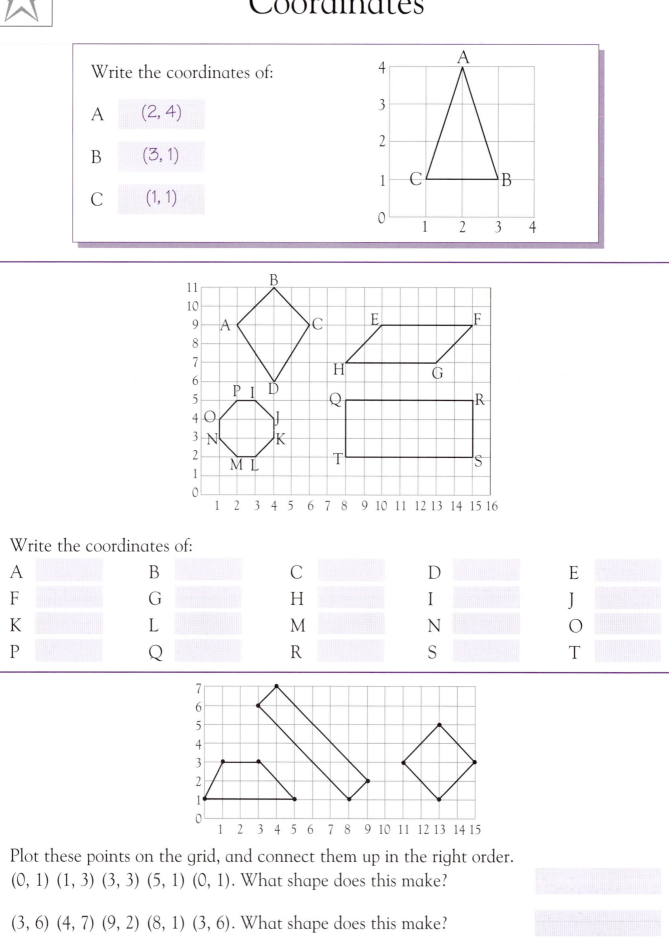

Write the coordinates of:

A   (2, 4)

B   (3, 1)

C   (1, 1)

Write the coordinates of:

A	B	C	D	E
F	G	H	I	J
K	L	M	N	O
P	Q	R	S	T

Plot these points on the grid, and connect them up in the right order.

(0, 1) (1, 3) (3, 3) (5, 1) (0, 1). What shape does this make?

(3, 6) (4, 7) (9, 2) (8, 1) (3, 6). What shape does this make?

(11, 3) (13, 5) (15, 3) (13, 1) (11, 3). What shape does this make?

122

Drawing angles

Acute angles are between 0° and 90°.   Obtuse angles are between 90° and 180°.

When you get to 180° you have a straight line.

Use a protractor to draw these angles. Remember to mark the angle you have drawn.

150°	135°
45°	110°
10°	20°

Reading and writing numbers

264,346 in words is Two hundred sixty-four thousand, three hundred forty-six

One million, three hundred twelve thousand, five hundred two is 1,312,502

Write each of these numbers in words.

326,208

704,543

240,701

278,520

Write each of these in numbers.

Five hundred seventeen thousand, forty-two

Six hundred ninety-four thousand, seven hundred eleven

Eight hundred nine thousand, two hundred three

Nine hundred thousand, four hundred four

Write each of these numbers in words.

9,307,012

5,042,390

9,908,434

8,400,642

Write each of these in numbers.

Eight million, two hundred fifty-one

Two million, forty thousand, four hundred four

Seven million, three hundred two thousand, one hundred one

Two million, five hundred forty-one thousand, five

Multiplying and dividing by 10

Write the answer in the box.

26 x 10 = 260

40 ÷ 10 = 4

Write the answer in the box.

76 x 10 =

43 x 10 =

93 x 10 =

66 x 10 =

13 x 10 =

47 x 10 =

147 x 10 =

936 x 10 =

284 x 10 =

364 x 10 =

821 x 10 =

473 x 10 =

Write the answer in the box.

30 ÷ 10 =

20 ÷ 10 =

70 ÷ 10 =

60 ÷ 10 =

50 ÷ 10 =

580 ÷ 10 =

310 ÷ 10 =

270 ÷ 10 =

100 ÷ 10 =

540 ÷ 10 =

890 ÷ 10 =

710 ÷ 10 =

Write the number that has been multiplied by 10.

x 10 = 370

x 10 = 640

x 10 = 740

x 10 = 810

x 10 = 100

x 10 = 830

x 10 = 7,140

x 10 = 3,070

x 10 = 5,290

x 10 = 2,640

x 10 = 8,290

x 10 = 6,480

Write the number that has been divided by 10.

÷ 10 = 3

÷ 10 = 2

÷ 10 = 9

÷ 10 = 42

÷ 10 = 93

÷ 10 = 74

÷ 10 = 57

÷ 10 = 38

÷ 10 = 86

Continue each pattern.

Steps of 9: 5 14 23 **32** **41** **50**

Steps of 14: 20 34 48 **62** **76** **90**

Continue each pattern.

21	38	55	72	89	106	123	140
13	37	61	85	109	133	157	181
7	25	43	61	79	97	115	133
32	48	64	80	96	112	128	144
12	31	50	69	88	107	126	145
32	54	76	98	120	142	164	186
24	64	104	144	184	224	264	304
4	34	64	94	124	154	184	214
36	126	216	306	396	486	576	666
12	72	132	192	252	312	372	432
25	45	65	85	105	125	145	165
22	72	122	172	222	272	322	372
25	100	175	250	325	400	475	550
60	165	270	375	480	585	690	795
8	107	206	305	404	503	602	701
10	61	112	163	214	265	316	367
26	127	228	329	430	531	632	733
48	100	152	204	256	308	360	412

Recognizing multiples of 6, 7, and 8 ☆

Circle the multiples of 6.

8   (12)   15   (18)   20   (24)

Circle the multiples of 6.

8	22	14	18	36	40
16	38	44	25	30	60
6	21	19	54	56	24
12	48	10	20	35	26
42	39	23	28	36	32

Circle the multiples of 7.

7	17	24	59	42	55
15	20	21	46	12	70
14	27	69	36	47	49
65	19	57	28	38	63
33	34	35	37	60	56

Circle the multiples of 8.

40	26	15	25	38	56
26	8	73	41	64	12
75	58	62	24	31	72
12	80	32	46	38	78
16	42	66	28	48	68

Circle the number that is a multiple of 6 and 7.

18   54   42   21   28   63

Circle the numbers that are multiples of 6 and 8.

16   24   36   48   54   42

Circle the number that is a multiple of 7 and 8.

24   32   40   28   42   56

Factors of numbers from 1 to 30

The factors of 10 are   1   2   5   10

Circle the factors of 4.   (1)   (2)   3   (4)

Write all the factors of each number.

The factors of 26 are

The factors of 30 are

The factors of 9 are

The factors of 12 are

The factors of 15 are

The factors of 22 are

The factors of 20 are

The factors of 21 are

The factors of 24 are

Circle all the factors of each number.

Which numbers are factors of 14?   1   2   3   5   7   9   12   14

Which numbers are factors of 13?   1   2   3   4   5   6   7   8   9   10   11   13

Which numbers are factors of 7?   1   2   3   4   5   6   7

Which numbers are factors of 11?   1   2   3   4   5   6   7   8   9   10   11

Which numbers are factors of 6?   1   2   3   4   5   6

Which numbers are factors of 8?   1   2   3   4   5   6   7   8

Which numbers are factors of 17?   1   2   5   7   12   14   16   17

Which numbers are factors of 18?   1   2   3   4   5   6   8   9   10   12   18

Some numbers only have factors of 1 and themselves. They are called prime numbers. Write down all the prime numbers that are less than 30 in the box.

Recognizing equivalent fractions

Make each pair of fractions equal by writing a number in the box.

$$\frac{1}{2} = \frac{2}{4} \qquad\qquad \frac{1}{3} = \frac{2}{6}$$

Make each pair of fractions equal by writing a number in the box.

$$\frac{1}{2} = \frac{\square}{10} \qquad \frac{3}{4} = \frac{\square}{8} \qquad \frac{1}{3} = \frac{\square}{9}$$

$$\frac{2}{3} = \frac{\square}{12} \qquad \frac{6}{12} = \frac{\square}{6} \qquad \frac{4}{8} = \frac{\square}{2}$$

$$\frac{1}{5} = \frac{\square}{10} \qquad \frac{4}{12} = \frac{\square}{6} \qquad \frac{3}{5} = \frac{\square}{10}$$

$$\frac{1}{4} = \frac{\square}{8} \qquad \frac{6}{18} = \frac{\square}{3} \qquad \frac{3}{12} = \frac{\square}{4}$$

$$\frac{3}{9} = \frac{1}{\square} \qquad \frac{4}{10} = \frac{2}{\square} \qquad \frac{3}{4} = \frac{9}{\square}$$

$$\frac{4}{16} = \frac{1}{\square} \qquad \frac{15}{20} = \frac{3}{\square} \qquad \frac{6}{12} = \frac{1}{\square}$$

$$\frac{3}{5} = \frac{6}{\square} \qquad \frac{3}{6} = \frac{1}{\square} \qquad \frac{9}{12} = \frac{3}{\square}$$

Make each row of fractions equal by writing a number in each box.

$$\frac{1}{2} = \frac{\square}{4} = \frac{3}{\square} = \frac{\square}{8} = \frac{\square}{10} = \frac{6}{\square}$$

$$\frac{1}{4} = \frac{2}{\square} = \frac{\square}{12} = \frac{4}{\square} = \frac{5}{\square} = \frac{\square}{24}$$

$$\frac{3}{4} = \frac{6}{\square} = \frac{\square}{12} = \frac{12}{\square} = \frac{\square}{20} = \frac{18}{\square}$$

$$\frac{1}{3} = \frac{\square}{6} = \frac{3}{\square} = \frac{4}{\square} = \frac{\square}{15} = \frac{12}{\square}$$

$$\frac{1}{5} = \frac{\square}{10} = \frac{\square}{15} = \frac{4}{\square} = \frac{5}{\square} = \frac{\square}{30}$$

$$\frac{2}{3} = \frac{\square}{6} = \frac{\square}{9} = \frac{8}{\square} = \frac{10}{\square} = \frac{14}{\square}$$

Rounding decimals

Round each decimal to the nearest whole number.

3.4   3

5.7   6

4.5   5

If the whole number has 5 after it, round it to the whole number above.

Round each decimal to the nearest whole number.

6.2		2.5		1.5		3.8	
5.5		2.8		3.2		8.5	
5.4		7.9		3.7		2.3	
1.1		8.6		8.3		9.2	
4.7		6.3		7.3		8.7	

Round each decimal to the nearest whole number.

14.4		42.3		74.1		59.7	
29.9		32.6		63.5		96.4	
18.2		37.5		39.6		76.3	
40.1		28.7		26.9		12.5	
29.5		38.5		87.2		41.6	

Round each decimal to the nearest whole number.

137.6		423.5		426.2		111.8	
641.6		333.5		805.2		246.8	
119.5		799.6		562.3		410.2	
682.4		759.6		531.5		829.9	
743.4		831.1		276.7		649.3	

Real-life problems

Write the answer in the box.

Yasmin has $4.60 and she is given another $1.20.
How much money does she have?

$5.80

$$
\begin{array}{r}
\$4.60 \\
+\ \$1.20 \\
\hline
\$5.80
\end{array}
$$

David has 120 marbles.
He divides them equally among his 5 friends.
How many marbles
does each get?   24

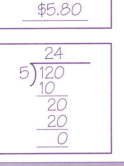

```
      24
   ┌──────
 5 )120
     10
     ──
     20
     20
     ──
      0
```

Write the answer in the box.

Michael buys a ball for $5.50 and a flashlight for $3.65.
How much does he spend?

How much does he have left from $10?

The 32 children of a class bring in $5 each for a school trip.
What is the total of the amount brought in?

A set of 5 shelves can be made from a piece of wood 4 yards long.
What fraction of a yard will each shelf be?

Each of 5 children has $16.
How much do they have altogether?

If the above total were shared among 8 children, how much would
each child have?

Real-life problems

Find the answer to each problem.

A box is 16 in. wide. How wide will 6 boxes side by side be?

96 in.

$$\begin{array}{r} \overset{3}{16 \text{ in.}} \\ \times\ 6 \\ \hline 96 \text{ in.} \end{array}$$

Josh is 1.20 m tall. His sister is 1.55 m tall. How much taller than Josh is his sister?

0.35 m

$$\begin{array}{r} 1.55 \text{ m} \\ -\ 1.20 \text{ m} \\ \hline 0.35 \text{ m} \end{array}$$

Find the answer to each problem.

A can contains 56 g of lemonade mix. If 12 g are used, how much is left?

A large jar of coffee weighs 280 g. A smaller jar weighs 130 g. How much heavier is the larger jar than the smaller jar?

There are 7 shelves of books. 5 shelves are 1.2 m long. 2 shelves are 1.5 m long. What is the total length of the 7 shelves?

A rock star can sign 36 photographs in a minute. How many can he sign in 30 seconds?

Shana has read 5 pages of a 20-page comic book. If it has taken her 9 minutes, how long is it likely to take her to read the whole comic book?

Problems involving time

Find the answer to this problem.

A train leaves the station at 7:30 A.M. and arrives at the end of the line at 10:45 A.M. How long did the journey take?

3 hours 15 minutes

7:30 → 10:30 = 3 h
10:30 → 10:45 = 15 min
Total = 3 h 15 min

Find the answer to each problem.

A film starts at 7:00 P.M. and finishes at 8:45 P.M. How long is the film?

A cake takes 2 hours 25 minutes to bake. If it begins baking at 1:35 P.M., at what time will the cake be done?

Sanjay needs to clean his bedroom and wash the car. It takes him 1 hour 10 minutes to clean his room and 45 minutes to clean the car. If he starts at 10:00 A.M., at what time will he finish?

A car is taken in for repair at 7:00 A.M. It is finished at 1:50 P.M. How long did the repairs take?

Claire has to be at school by 8:50 A.M. If she takes 1 hour 30 minutes to get ready, and the trip takes 35 minutes, at what time does she need to get up?

A bus leaves the bus station at 8:45 A.M. and arrives back at 10:15 A.M. How long has its trip taken?

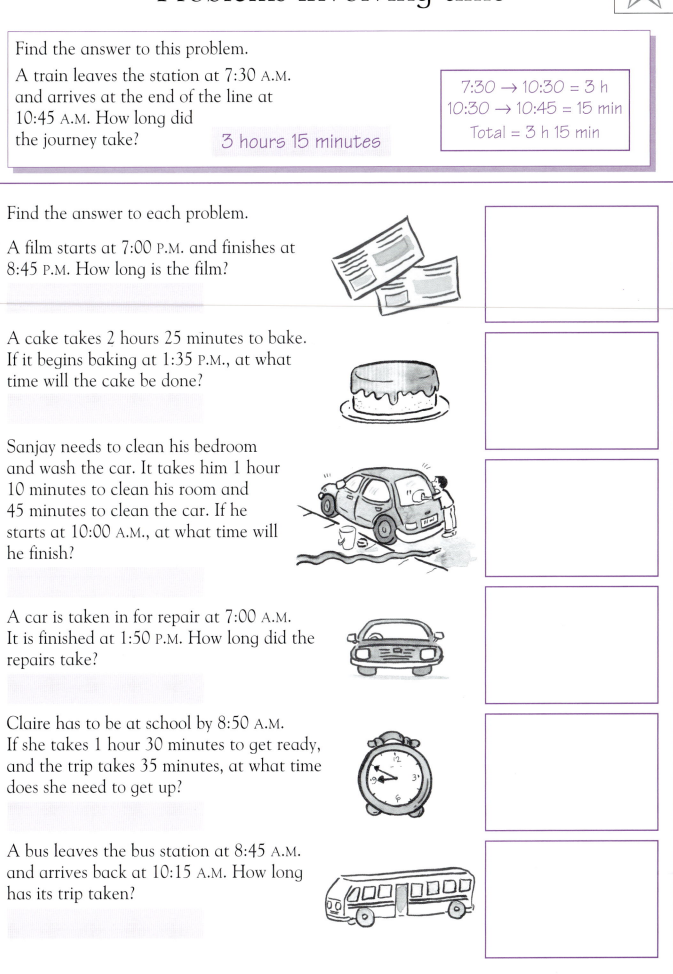

Elapsed time

Write the answer in the box.

10:40   11:40   12:40   1:20

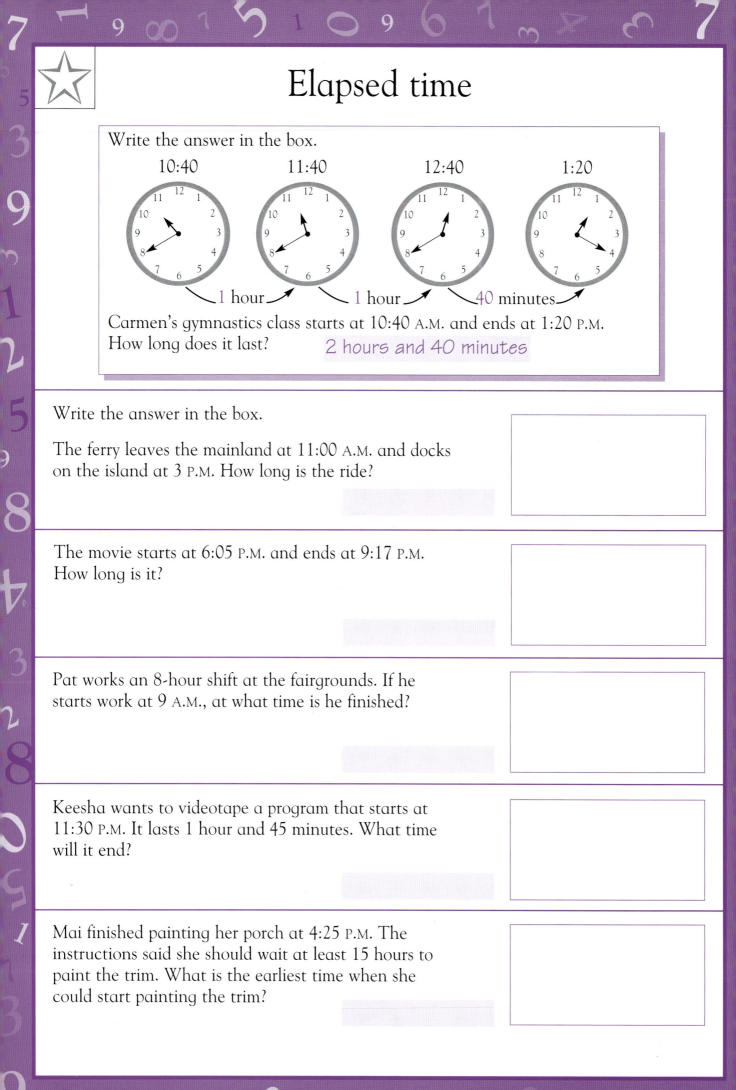

1 hour → 1 hour → 40 minutes →

Carmen's gymnastics class starts at 10:40 A.M. and ends at 1:20 P.M. How long does it last?   2 hours and 40 minutes

---

Write the answer in the box.

The ferry leaves the mainland at 11:00 A.M. and docks on the island at 3 P.M. How long is the ride?

The movie starts at 6:05 P.M. and ends at 9:17 P.M. How long is it?

Pat works an 8-hour shift at the fairgrounds. If he starts work at 9 A.M., at what time is he finished?

Keesha wants to videotape a program that starts at 11:30 P.M. It lasts 1 hour and 45 minutes. What time will it end?

Mai finished painting her porch at 4:25 P.M. The instructions said she should wait at least 15 hours to paint the trim. What is the earliest time when she could start painting the trim?

Recognizing multiples

⭐

Circle the multiples of 10.

| 14 | (20) | 25 | (30) | 47 | (60) |

Circle the multiples of 6.

| 20 | 48 | 56 | 72 | 25 | 35 |
| 1 | 3 | 6 | 16 | 26 | 36 |

Circle the multiples of 7.

| 14 | 24 | 35 | 27 | 47 | 49 |
| 63 | 42 | 52 | 37 | 64 | 71 |

Circle the multiples of 8.

| 25 | 31 | 48 | 84 | 32 | 8 |
| 18 | 54 | 64 | 35 | 72 | 28 |

Circle the multiples of 9.

17	81	27	35	92	106
45	53	108	90	33	95
64	9	28	18	36	98

Circle the multiples of 10.

| 15 | 35 | 20 | 46 | 90 | 100 |
| 44 | 37 | 30 | 29 | 50 | 45 |

Circle the multiples of 11.

24	110	123	54	66	90
45	33	87	98	99	121
43	44	65	55	21	22

Circle the multiples of 12.

136	134	144	109	108	132
24	34	58	68	48	60
35	29	72	74	84	94

Bar graphs

Use this bar graph to answer each question.

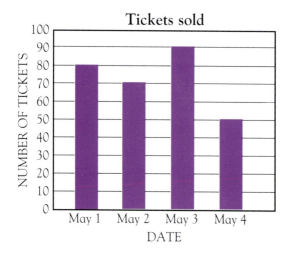

Caps sold

What color cap was sold the most?   red

How many more green
caps were sold than blue caps?   10

Use this bar graph to answer each question.

Tickets sold

How many tickets
were sold on May 1?

How many more
tickets were sold on
May 2 than on May 4?

On which date were 90 tickets sold?

Use this bar graph to answer each question.

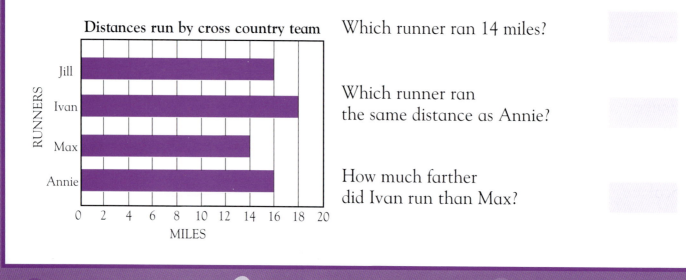

Distances run by cross country team

Which runner ran 14 miles?

Which runner ran
the same distance as Annie?

How much farther
did Ivan run than Max?

Triangles

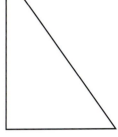

Look at these different triangles.

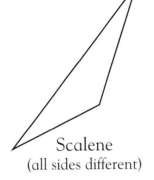

Equilateral
(all sides equal;
is also isosceles)

Isosceles
(two sides equal)

Scalene
(all sides different)

Right angle
(may be isosceles or
scalene, but one angle
must be a right angle)

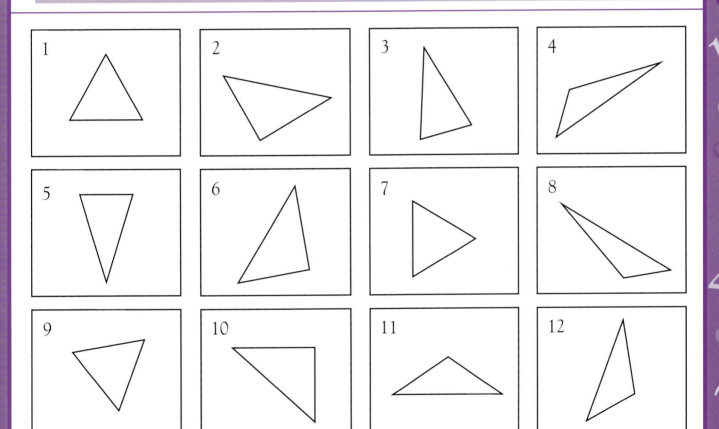

List the triangles that are:

Equilateral _____

Isosceles _____

Scalene _____

Right angle _____

Place value to 10,000,000

★

How many hundreds are there in 7,000?   70   hundreds
(70 x 100 = 7,000)

What is the value of the 9 in 694?   90   (because the 9 is in the tens column)

Write how many tens there are in:

400 _____ tens   600 _____ tens   900 _____ tens

200 _____ tens   1,300 _____ tens   4,700 _____ tens

4,800 _____ tens   1,240 _____ tens   1,320 _____ tens

2,630 _____ tens   5,920 _____ tens   4,350 _____ tens

What is the value of the 7 in these numbers?

76 _____   720 _____   137 _____

7,122 _____   74,301 _____   724 _____

What is the value of the 3 in these numbers?

324,126 _____   3,927,141 _____   214,623 _____

8,254,320 _____   3,711,999 _____   124,372 _____

Write how many hundreds there are in:

6,400 _____ hundreds   8,500 _____ hundreds

19,900 _____ hundreds   36,200 _____ hundreds

524,600 _____ hundreds   712,400 _____ hundreds

What is the value of the 8 in these numbers?

8,214,631 _____   2,398,147 _____   463,846 _____

287,034 _____   8,110,927 _____   105,428 _____

Multiplying and dividing by 10

Write the answer in the box.

37 x 10 = **370**   58 ÷ 10 = **5.8**

Write the product in the box.

94 x 10 =   13 x 10 =   37 x 10 =

36 x 10 =   47 x 10 =   54 x 10 =

236 x 10 =   419 x 10 =   262 x 10 =

531 x 10 =   674 x 10 =   801 x 10 =

Write the quotient in the box.

92 ÷ 10 =   48 ÷ 10 =   37 ÷ 10 =

18 ÷ 10 =   29 ÷ 10 =   54 ÷ 10 =

345 ÷ 10 =   354 ÷ 10 =   723 ÷ 10 =

531 ÷ 10 =   262 ÷ 10 =   419 ÷ 10 =

Find the missing factor.

_____ x 10 = 230   _____ x 10 = 750   _____ x 10 = 990

_____ x 10 = 480   _____ x 10 = 130   _____ x 10 = 250

_____ x 10 = 520   _____ x 10 = 390   _____ x 10 = 270

_____ x 10 = 620   _____ x 10 = 860   _____ x 10 = 170

Find the dividend.

_____ ÷ 10 = 4.7   _____ ÷ 10 = 6.8   _____ ÷ 10 = 12.4

_____ ÷ 10 = 25.7   _____ ÷ 10 = 36.2   _____ ÷ 10 = 31.4

_____ ÷ 10 = 40.8   _____ ÷ 10 = 67.2   _____ ÷ 10 = 80.9

_____ ÷ 10 = 92.4   _____ ÷ 10 = 32.7   _____ ÷ 10 = 56.3

Appropriate units of measure

Choose the best units to measure the length of each item.

inches	feet	yards

notebook	car	swimming pool
inches	feet	yards

Choose the best units to measure the length of each item.

inches	feet	yards

bed	bicycle	toothbrush	football field

shoe	driveway	canoe	fence

The height of a door is about 7 _____ .

The length of a pencil is about 7 _____ .

The height of a flagpole is about 7 _____ .

Choose the best units to measure the weight of each item.

ounces	pounds	tons

train	kitten	watermelon	tennis ball

shoe	bag of potatoes	elephant	washing machine

The weight of a hamburger is about 6 _____ .

The weight of a bag of apples is about 5 _____ .

The weight of a truck is about 4 _____ .

Identifying patterns

Continue each pattern.

Intervals of 6:	1	7	13	19	25	31	37
Intervals of 3:	27	24	21	18	15	12	9

Continue each pattern.

0	10	20				
15	20	25				
5	7	9				
2	9	16				
4	7	10			19	
2	10	18		34		

Continue each pattern.

44	38	32				
33	29	25				
27	23	19				
56	48	40			16	
49	42	35				
28	25	22				10

Continue each pattern.

36	30	24		12		
5	14	23				
3	8	13				
47	40	33			12	
1	4	7				

Factors of numbers from 31 to 65

The factors of 40 are   1   2   4   5   8   10   20   40

Circle the factors of 56.

(1)   (2)   3   (4)   5   6   (7)   (8)   (14)   (28)   32   (56)

Find all the factors of each number.

The factors of 31 are

The factors of 47 are

The factors of 60 are

The factors of 50 are

The factors of 42 are

The factors of 32 are

The factors of 48 are

The factors of 35 are

The factors of 52 are

Circle all the factors of each number.

Which numbers are factors of 39?

1   2   3   4   5   8   9   10   13   14   15   20   25   39

Which numbers are factors of 45?

1   3   4   5   8   9   12   15   16   21   24   36   40   44   45

Which numbers are factors of 61?

1   3   4   5   6   10   15   16   18   20   26   31   40   61

Which numbers are factors of 65?

1   2   4   5   6   8   9   10   12   13   14   15   30   60   65

Some numbers have only factors of 1 and themselves. They are called prime numbers.
Write all the prime numbers between 31 and 65 in the box.

Greatest common factor

Circle the common factors.
Write the greatest common factor (GCF).

24:　①,　②,　③,　4,　⑥,　8,　12,　24
60:　①,　②,　③,　4,　5,　⑥,　8,　10,　12,　60　　　The GCF is 6
42:　①,　②,　③,　⑥,　7,　14

Find the factors. Circle the common factors.

45:

36:

28:

54:

Find the factors. Write the GCF.

35:

80:

The GCF is

32:

64:

The GCF is

12:

44:

15:

12, 24

The GCF is

54:

72:

18:

The GCF is

Writing equivalent fractions

Make these fractions equal by writing the missing number.

$$\frac{20}{100} = \frac{2}{10} = \frac{1}{5}$$

$$\frac{5}{15} = \frac{1}{3}$$

Make these fractions equal by writing a number in the box.

$$\frac{10}{100} = \frac{\square}{10} \qquad \frac{8}{100} = \frac{\square}{25} \qquad \frac{4}{100} = \frac{\square}{25}$$

$$\frac{2}{20} = \frac{\square}{10} \qquad \frac{5}{100} = \frac{\square}{20} \qquad \frac{6}{20} = \frac{\square}{10}$$

$$\frac{3}{5} = \frac{\square}{20} \qquad \frac{5}{6} = \frac{\square}{12} \qquad \frac{2}{8} = \frac{\square}{24}$$

$$\frac{2}{3} = \frac{\square}{24} \qquad \frac{2}{18} = \frac{\square}{9} \qquad \frac{4}{50} = \frac{\square}{25}$$

$$\frac{11}{12} = \frac{\square}{36} \qquad \frac{12}{15} = \frac{\square}{5} \qquad \frac{8}{20} = \frac{\square}{5}$$

$$\frac{2}{12} = \frac{1}{\square} \qquad \frac{5}{20} = \frac{1}{\square} \qquad \frac{5}{8} = \frac{10}{\square}$$

$$\frac{7}{8} = \frac{21}{\square} \qquad \frac{15}{100} = \frac{3}{\square} \qquad \frac{6}{24} = \frac{1}{\square}$$

$$\frac{5}{25} = \frac{1}{\square} \qquad \frac{8}{20} = \frac{2}{\square} \qquad \frac{15}{20} = \frac{3}{\square}$$

$$\frac{5}{30} = \frac{1}{\square} \qquad \frac{12}{14} = \frac{6}{\square} \qquad \frac{1}{5} = \frac{4}{\square}$$

$$\frac{9}{18} = \frac{1}{\square} \qquad \frac{24}{30} = \frac{4}{\square} \qquad \frac{25}{30} = \frac{5}{\square}$$

$$\frac{1}{8} = \frac{\square}{16} = \frac{3}{\square} = \frac{\square}{32} = \frac{\square}{40} = \frac{6}{\square}$$

$$\frac{20}{100} = \frac{\square}{25} = \frac{2}{\square} = \frac{1}{\square} = \frac{\square}{50} = \frac{\square}{200}$$

$$\frac{2}{5} = \frac{6}{\square} = \frac{\square}{20} = \frac{10}{\square} = \frac{\square}{50} = \frac{\square}{40}$$

$$\frac{1}{6} = \frac{\square}{12} = \frac{3}{\square} = \frac{4}{\square} = \frac{5}{\square} = \frac{6}{\square}$$

$$\frac{2}{3} = \frac{\square}{24} = \frac{\square}{36} = \frac{\square}{21} = \frac{6}{\square} = \frac{\square}{300}$$

Fraction models

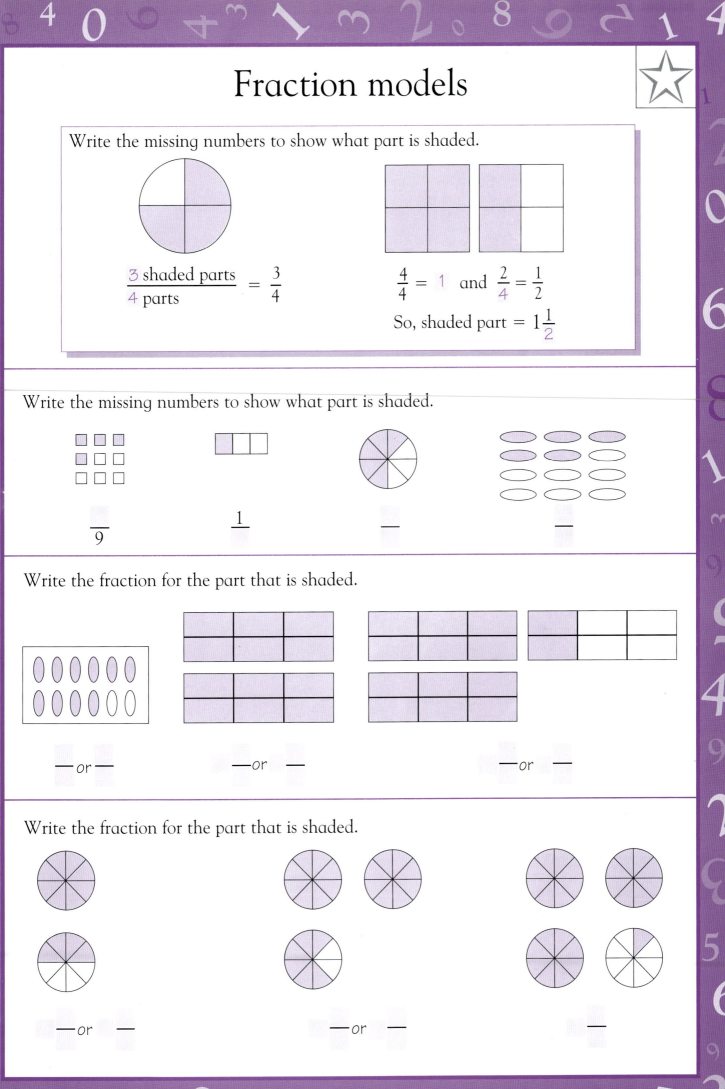

Write the missing numbers to show what part is shaded.

$$\frac{3 \text{ shaded parts}}{4 \text{ parts}} = \frac{3}{4}$$

$$\frac{4}{4} = 1 \quad \text{and} \quad \frac{2}{4} = \frac{1}{2}$$

So, shaded part $= 1\frac{1}{2}$

Write the missing numbers to show what part is shaded.

$$\frac{}{9} \qquad \frac{1}{} \qquad \frac{}{} \qquad \frac{}{}$$

Write the fraction for the part that is shaded.

$$\frac{}{} \text{ or } \frac{}{} \qquad \frac{}{} \text{ or } \frac{}{} \qquad \frac{}{} \text{ or } \frac{}{}$$

Write the fraction for the part that is shaded.

$$\frac{}{} \text{ or } \frac{}{} \qquad \frac{}{} \text{ or } \frac{}{} \qquad \frac{}{}$$

145

Multiplying by one-digit numbers

Find each product. Remember to regroup.

$$
\begin{array}{r}
\scriptstyle 1\;1 \\
465 \\
\times\quad 3 \\
\hline
1{,}395
\end{array}
\qquad
\begin{array}{r}
\scriptstyle 3 \\
391 \\
\times\quad 4 \\
\hline
1{,}564
\end{array}
\qquad
\begin{array}{r}
\scriptstyle 3\;4 \\
278 \\
\times\quad 5 \\
\hline
1{,}390
\end{array}
$$

Find each product.

$$
\begin{array}{r}
563 \\
\times\quad 3 \\
\hline
\end{array}
\qquad
\begin{array}{r}
910 \\
\times\quad 2 \\
\hline
\end{array}
\qquad
\begin{array}{r}
437 \\
\times\quad 3 \\
\hline
\end{array}
\qquad
\begin{array}{r}
812 \\
\times\quad 2 \\
\hline
\end{array}
$$

$$
\begin{array}{r}
572 \\
\times\quad 4 \\
\hline
\end{array}
\qquad
\begin{array}{r}
831 \\
\times\quad 3 \\
\hline
\end{array}
\qquad
\begin{array}{r}
406 \\
\times\quad 5 \\
\hline
\end{array}
\qquad
\begin{array}{r}
394 \\
\times\quad 6 \\
\hline
\end{array}
$$

Find each product.

$$
\begin{array}{r}
318 \\
\times\quad 3 \\
\hline
\end{array}
\qquad
\begin{array}{r}
223 \\
\times\quad 4 \\
\hline
\end{array}
\qquad
\begin{array}{r}
542 \\
\times\quad 4 \\
\hline
\end{array}
\qquad
\begin{array}{r}
217 \\
\times\quad 3 \\
\hline
\end{array}
$$

$$
\begin{array}{r}
127 \\
\times\quad 4 \\
\hline
\end{array}
\qquad
\begin{array}{r}
275 \\
\times\quad 5 \\
\hline
\end{array}
\qquad
\begin{array}{r}
798 \\
\times\quad 6 \\
\hline
\end{array}
\qquad
\begin{array}{r}
365 \\
\times\quad 6 \\
\hline
\end{array}
$$

$$
\begin{array}{r}
100 \\
\times\quad 5 \\
\hline
\end{array}
\qquad
\begin{array}{r}
372 \\
\times\quad 4 \\
\hline
\end{array}
\qquad
\begin{array}{r}
881 \\
\times\quad 4 \\
\hline
\end{array}
\qquad
\begin{array}{r}
953 \\
\times\quad 3 \\
\hline
\end{array}
$$

Solve each problem.

A middle school has 255 students. A high school has 6 times as many students. How many children are there at the high school?

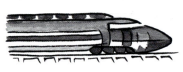

A train can carry 365 passengers. How many could it carry on

four trips?

six trips?

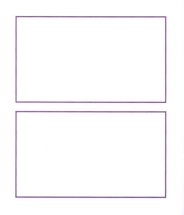

Multiplying by one-digit numbers

Find each product. Remember to regroup.

```
  33              12              44
 456             823             755
x   6           x   8           x   9
-----           -----           -----
2,736           6,584           6,795
```

Find each product.

```
 394             736             827             943
x   7           x   7           x   8           x   9
-----           -----           -----           -----


 643             199             821             547
x   6           x   6           x   7           x   8
-----           -----           -----           -----


 501             377             843             222
x   7           x   8           x   8           x   9
-----           -----           -----           -----


 471             223             606             513
x   9           x   8           x   6           x   7
-----           -----           -----           -----


 500             800             900             200
x   9           x   9           x   8           x   9
-----           -----           -----           -----
```

Solve each problem.

A crate holds 550 apples. How many apples are there in 8 crates?

Keyshawn swims 760 laps each week. How many laps does he swim in 5 weeks?

Real-life problems

Find the answer to each problem.

Jacob spent $4.68 at the store and had $4.77 left.
How much did he have to start with?

$9.45

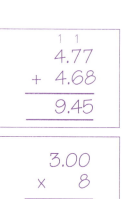
```
   1  1
   4.77
+  4.68
───────
   9.45
```

Tracy receives a weekly allowance of $3.00 a week.
How much will she have if she saves all of it for 8 weeks?

$24.00

```
   3.00
×     8
───────
  24.00
```

Find the answer to each problem.

A theater charges $4 for each matinee
ticket. If it sells 360 tickets for a matinee
performance, how much does it take in?

David has saved $9.59. His sister
has $3.24 less. How much does
she have?

The cost for 9 children to go to a
theme park is $72. How much does
each child pay? If only 6 children
go, what will the cost be?

Paul has $3.69. His sister gives him
another $5.25, and he goes out and
buys a CD single for $3.99. How
much does he have left?

Ian has $20 in savings. He
decides to spend $\frac{1}{4}$ of it. How
much will he have left?

Real-life problems

Find the answer to each problem.

Nina has an hour to do her homework. She plans to spend $\frac{1}{3}$ of her time on math. How many minutes will she spend doing math?

20 minutes

1 hour is 60 minutes

$$3\overline{)60}^{\,20}$$

In gym class, David makes 2 long jumps of 1.78 m and 2.19 m. How far does he jump altogether?

3.97 m

$$\begin{array}{r} {}^{1}\;1.78\,\text{m} \\ +\;2.19\,\text{m} \\ \hline 3.97\,\text{m} \end{array}$$

Find the answer to each problem.

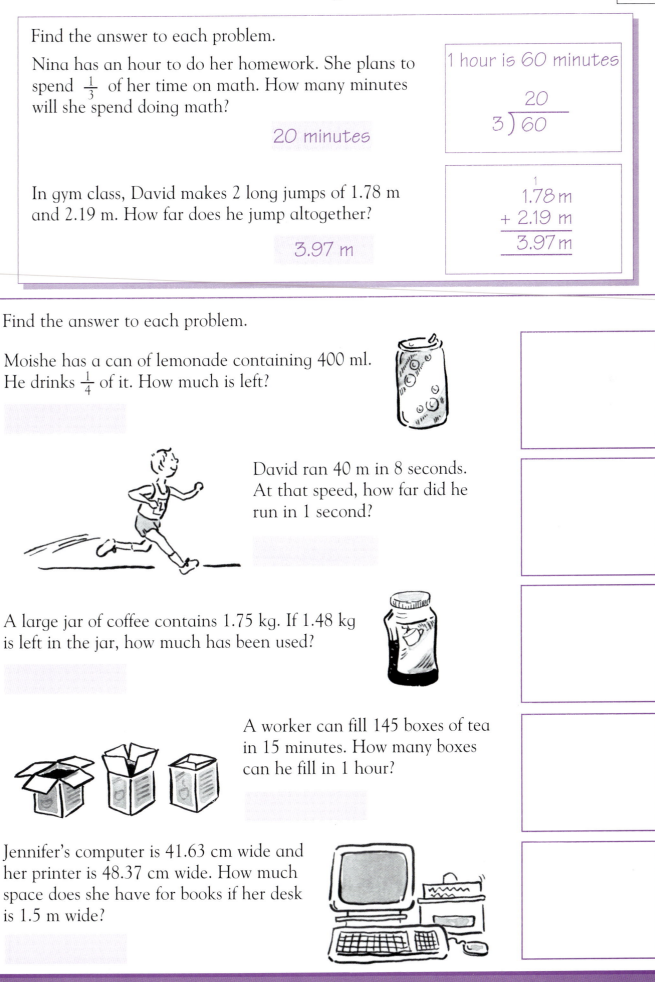

Moishe has a can of lemonade containing 400 ml. He drinks $\frac{1}{4}$ of it. How much is left?

David ran 40 m in 8 seconds. At that speed, how far did he run in 1 second?

A large jar of coffee contains 1.75 kg. If 1.48 kg is left in the jar, how much has been used?

A worker can fill 145 boxes of tea in 15 minutes. How many boxes can he fill in 1 hour?

Jennifer's computer is 41.63 cm wide and her printer is 48.37 cm wide. How much space does she have for books if her desk is 1.5 m wide?

Problems involving time

Find the answer to each problem.

Caitlin spends 35 minutes on her homework each day. How many minutes does she spend on her homework in one week from Monday through Friday?

175 minutes

$$
\begin{array}{r}
{\scriptstyle 2} \\
35 \\
\times \quad 5 \\
\hline
175
\end{array}
$$

Jenny spends 175 minutes on her homework from Monday through Friday. How much time does she spend on homework each day?

35 minutes

$$
\begin{array}{r}
35 \\
5\overline{)175}
\end{array}
$$

Find the answer to each problem.

Amy works from 9 A.M. until 5 P.M. She has a lunch break from noon until 1 P.M. How many hours does she work in a 5-day week?

School children have a 15-minute break in the morning and a 10-minute break in the afternoon. How many minutes of break do they have in a week?

It takes 2 hours for one person to do a job. If John shares the work with 3 of his friends, how long will it take?

Mr. Tambo spent 7 days building a patio. If he worked a total of 56 hours and he divided the work evenly among the seven days, how long did he work each day?

It took Ben 45 hours to build a remote-controlled airplane. If he spent 5 hours a day working on it:

How many days did it take?

How many hours per day would he have needed to finish it in 5 days?

Multiplying and dividing

Write the answer in the box.

26 x 10 = 260   26 x 100 = 2,600

400 ÷ 10 = 40   400 ÷ 100 = 4

Write the product in the box.

33 x 10 =   21 x 10 =   42 x 10 =

94 x 100 =   36 x 100 =   81 x 100 =

416 x 10 =   204 x 10 =   513 x 10 =

767 x 100 =   821 x 100 =   245 x 100 =

Write the quotient in the box.

120 ÷ 10 =   260 ÷ 10 =   470 ÷ 10 =

300 ÷ 100 =   800 ÷ 100 =   400 ÷ 100 =

20 ÷ 10 =   30 ÷ 10 =   70 ÷ 10 =

500 ÷ 100 =   100 ÷ 100 =   900 ÷ 100 =

Write the number that has been multiplied by 100.

x 100 = 5,900   x 100 = 71,400

x 100 = 72,100   x 100 = 23,400

x 100 = 1,100   x 100 = 47,000

x 100 = 8,400   x 100 = 44,100

Write the number that has been divided by 100.

÷ 100 = 2   ÷ 100 = 8

÷ 100 = 21   ÷ 100 = 18

÷ 100 = 86   ÷ 100 = 21

÷ 100 = 10   ÷ 100 = 59

Identifying patterns

Continue each pattern.

Steps of 2:	$\frac{1}{2}$	$2\frac{1}{2}$	$4\frac{1}{2}$	$6\frac{1}{2}$	$8\frac{1}{2}$	$10\frac{1}{2}$
Steps of 5:	3.5	8.5	13.5	18.5	23.5	28.5

Continue each pattern.

$5\frac{1}{2}$	$10\frac{1}{2}$	$15\frac{1}{2}$			
$1\frac{1}{4}$	$3\frac{1}{4}$	$5\frac{1}{4}$			
$8\frac{1}{3}$	$9\frac{1}{3}$	$10\frac{1}{3}$		$12\frac{1}{3}$	
$55\frac{3}{4}$	$45\frac{3}{4}$	$35\frac{3}{4}$			
$42\frac{1}{2}$	$38\frac{1}{2}$	$34\frac{1}{2}$			$22\frac{1}{2}$
7.5	6.5	5.5			
28.4	25.4	22.4		16.4	
81.6	73.6	65.6			
6.3	10.3	14.3			
12.1	13.1	14.1			17.1
14.6	21.6	28.6			
$11\frac{1}{2}$	$10\frac{1}{2}$	$9\frac{1}{2}$			
8.4	11.4	14.4		20.4	
$7\frac{3}{4}$	$13\frac{3}{4}$	$19\frac{3}{4}$			$37\frac{3}{4}$
57.5	48.5	39.5			

Products with odd and even numbers

Find the products of these numbers.

3 and 4   The product of 3 and 4 is 12.   6 and 8   The product of 6 and 8 is 48.

Find the products of these odd and even numbers.

5 and 6 _____   3 and 2 _____

7 and 4 _____   8 and 3 _____

6 and 3 _____   2 and 9 _____

10 and 3 _____   12 and 5 _____

What do you notice about your answers? _____
_____

Find the products of these odd numbers.

5 and 7 _____   3 and 9 _____

5 and 11 _____   7 and 3 _____

9 and 5 _____   11 and 7 _____

13 and 3 _____   1 and 5 _____

What do you notice about your answers? _____
_____

Find the products of these even numbers.

2 and 4 _____   4 and 6 _____

6 and 2 _____   4 and 8 _____

10 and 2 _____   4 and 10 _____

6 and 10 _____   6 and 8 _____

What do you notice about your answers? _____
_____

Can you write a rule for the products with odd and even numbers?
_____

The factors of 66 are   1   2   3   6   11   22   33   66

Circle the factors of 94.   (1)   (2)   28   32   43   (47)   71   86   (94)

Write the factors of each number in the box.

The factors of 70 are

The factors of 85 are

The factors of 69 are

The factors of 83 are

The factors of 75 are

The factors of 96 are

The factors of 63 are

The factors of 99 are

The factors of 72 are

Circle the factors of 68.

    1   2   3   4   5   6   7   8   9   11   12   17   34   35   62   68

Circle the factors of 95.

    1   2   3   4   5   15   16   17   19   24   37   85   90   95   96

Circle the factors of 88.

    1   2   3   4   5   6   8   10   11   15   22   25   27   44   87   88

Circle the factors of 73.

    1   2   4   5   6   8   9   10   12   13   14   15   30   60   73

A prime number only has two factors, 1 and itself.
Write all the prime numbers between 66 and 100 in the box.

Multiplying by two-digit numbers

Write the product for each problem.

$$\begin{array}{r} {}^{1}_{1} \\ 56 \\ \times\ 32 \\ \hline 112 \\ 1,680 \\ \hline 1,792 \end{array}$$

$$\begin{array}{r} {}^{2}_{1} \\ 45 \\ \times\ 43 \\ \hline 135 \\ 1,800 \\ \hline 1,935 \end{array}$$

Write the product for each problem.

56 x 23	23 x 24	47 x 25	84 x 22
73 x 34	52 x 35	64 x 33	51 x 32

Write the product for each problem.

41 x 62	65 x 54	72 x 68	84 x 71
92 x 63	57 x 82	38 x 94	26 x 75

Multiplying by two-digit numbers

Write the product for each problem.

```
    7          7
    6          6
   39         68
 x 87       x 98
  273        544
3,120      6,120
3,393      6,664
```

Write the product for each problem.

87 x 98	76 x 78	99 x 69	85 x 98

88 x 95	67 x 76	94 x 69	89 x 47

Write the product for each problem.

87 x 79	46 x 67	58 x 59	73 x 98

95 x 67	58 x 88	78 x 97	96 x 79

Answer Section with Parents' Notes

Grade 5
ages 10–11
Workbook

This section provides answers to all the activities in the book. These pages will enable you to mark your children's work, or they can be used by your children if they prefer to do their own marking.

The notes for each page help to explain common errors and problems and, where appropriate, indicate the kind of practice needed to ensure that your children understand where and how they have made errors.

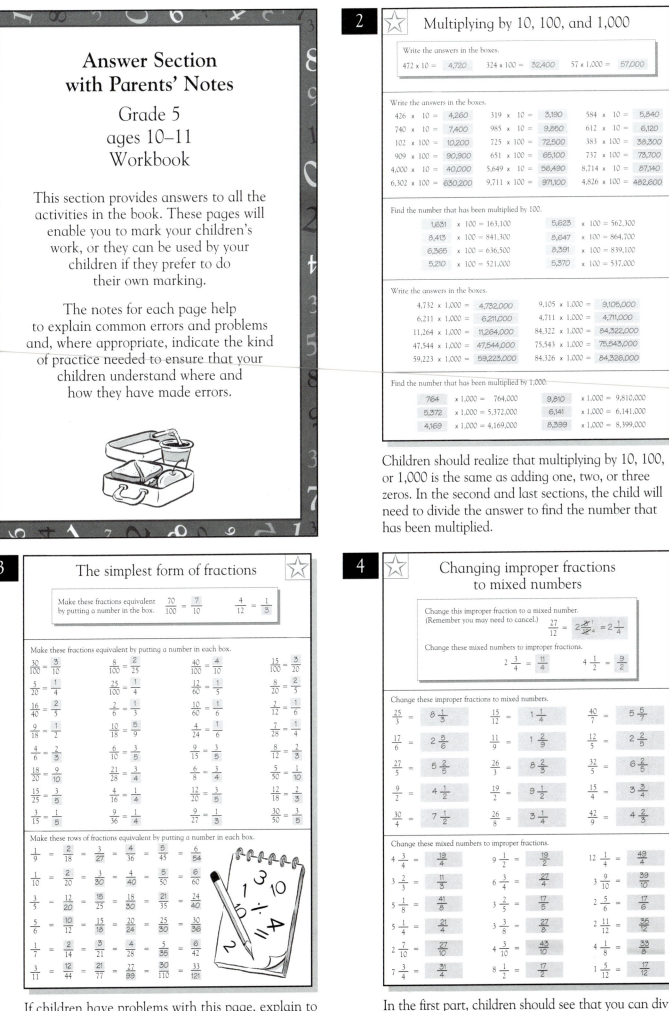

Multiplying by 10, 100, and 1,000

Write the answers in the boxes.

$472 \times 10 = 4{,}720$ $324 \times 100 = 32{,}400$ $57 \times 1{,}000 = 57{,}000$

Write the answers in the boxes.

$426 \times 10 = 4{,}260$	$319 \times 10 = 3{,}190$	$584 \times 10 = 5{,}840$
$740 \times 10 = 7{,}400$	$985 \times 10 = 9{,}850$	$612 \times 10 = 6{,}120$
$102 \times 100 = 10{,}200$	$725 \times 100 = 72{,}500$	$383 \times 100 = 38{,}300$
$909 \times 100 = 90{,}900$	$651 \times 100 = 65{,}100$	$737 \times 100 = 73{,}700$
$4{,}000 \times 10 = 40{,}000$	$5{,}649 \times 10 = 56{,}490$	$8{,}714 \times 10 = 87{,}140$
$6{,}302 \times 100 = 630{,}200$	$9{,}711 \times 100 = 971{,}100$	$4{,}826 \times 100 = 482{,}600$

Find the number that has been multiplied by 100.

$1{,}631 \times 100 = 163{,}100$	$5{,}623 \times 100 = 562{,}300$
$8{,}413 \times 100 = 841{,}300$	$8{,}647 \times 100 = 864{,}700$
$6{,}365 \times 100 = 636{,}500$	$8{,}391 \times 100 = 839{,}100$
$5{,}210 \times 100 = 521{,}000$	$5{,}370 \times 100 = 537{,}000$

Write the answers in the boxes.

$4{,}732 \times 1{,}000 = 4{,}732{,}000$	$9{,}105 \times 1{,}000 = 9{,}105{,}000$
$6{,}211 \times 1{,}000 = 6{,}211{,}000$	$4{,}711 \times 1{,}000 = 4{,}711{,}000$
$11{,}264 \times 1{,}000 = 11{,}264{,}000$	$84{,}322 \times 1{,}000 = 84{,}322{,}000$
$47{,}544 \times 1{,}000 = 47{,}544{,}000$	$75{,}543 \times 1{,}000 = 75{,}543{,}000$
$59{,}223 \times 1{,}000 = 59{,}223{,}000$	$84{,}326 \times 1{,}000 = 84{,}326{,}000$

Find the number that has been multiplied by 1,000.

$764 \times 1{,}000 = 764{,}000$	$9{,}810 \times 1{,}000 = 9{,}810{,}000$
$5{,}372 \times 1{,}000 = 5{,}372{,}000$	$6{,}141 \times 1{,}000 = 6{,}141{,}000$
$4{,}169 \times 1{,}000 = 4{,}169{,}000$	$8{,}399 \times 1{,}000 = 8{,}399{,}000$

Children should realize that multiplying by 10, 100, or 1,000 is the same as adding one, two, or three zeros. In the second and last sections, the child will need to divide the answer to find the number that has been multiplied.

---

3   The simplest form of fractions

Make these fractions equivalent by putting a number in the box. $\frac{70}{100} = \frac{7}{10}$ $\frac{4}{12} = \frac{1}{3}$

Make these fractions equivalent by putting a number in each box.

$\frac{30}{100} = \frac{3}{10}$	$\frac{8}{100} = \frac{2}{25}$	$\frac{40}{100} = \frac{4}{10}$	$\frac{15}{100} = \frac{3}{20}$
$\frac{5}{20} = \frac{1}{4}$	$\frac{25}{100} = \frac{1}{4}$	$\frac{12}{60} = \frac{1}{5}$	$\frac{8}{20} = \frac{2}{5}$
$\frac{16}{40} = \frac{2}{5}$	$\frac{2}{6} = \frac{1}{3}$	$\frac{10}{60} = \frac{1}{6}$	$\frac{2}{12} = \frac{1}{6}$
$\frac{9}{18} = \frac{1}{2}$	$\frac{10}{18} = \frac{5}{9}$	$\frac{4}{24} = \frac{1}{6}$	$\frac{7}{28} = \frac{1}{4}$
$\frac{4}{6} = \frac{2}{3}$	$\frac{6}{10} = \frac{3}{5}$	$\frac{9}{15} = \frac{3}{5}$	$\frac{8}{12} = \frac{2}{3}$
$\frac{18}{20} = \frac{9}{10}$	$\frac{21}{28} = \frac{3}{4}$	$\frac{6}{8} = \frac{3}{4}$	$\frac{5}{50} = \frac{1}{10}$
$\frac{15}{25} = \frac{3}{5}$	$\frac{4}{16} = \frac{1}{4}$	$\frac{12}{20} = \frac{3}{5}$	$\frac{12}{18} = \frac{2}{3}$
$\frac{3}{15} = \frac{1}{5}$	$\frac{9}{36} = \frac{1}{4}$	$\frac{9}{27} = \frac{1}{3}$	$\frac{30}{50} = \frac{3}{5}$

Make these rows of fractions equivalent by putting a number in each box.

$\frac{1}{9}$ =	$\frac{2}{18}$ =	$\frac{3}{27}$ =	$\frac{4}{36}$ =	$\frac{5}{45}$ =	$\frac{6}{54}$
$\frac{1}{10}$ =	$\frac{2}{20}$ =	$\frac{3}{30}$ =	$\frac{4}{40}$ =	$\frac{5}{50}$ =	$\frac{6}{60}$
$\frac{3}{5}$ =	$\frac{12}{20}$ =	$\frac{15}{25}$ =	$\frac{18}{30}$ =	$\frac{21}{35}$ =	$\frac{24}{40}$
$\frac{5}{6}$ =	$\frac{10}{12}$ =	$\frac{15}{18}$ =	$\frac{20}{24}$ =	$\frac{25}{30}$ =	$\frac{30}{36}$
$\frac{1}{7}$ =	$\frac{2}{14}$ =	$\frac{3}{21}$ =	$\frac{4}{28}$ =	$\frac{5}{35}$ =	$\frac{6}{42}$
$\frac{3}{11}$ =	$\frac{12}{44}$ =	$\frac{21}{77}$ =	$\frac{27}{99}$ =	$\frac{30}{110}$ =	$\frac{33}{121}$

If children have problems with this page, explain to them that fractions remain the same as long as you multiply or divide the numerator and denominator by the same number.

---

4   Changing improper fractions to mixed numbers

Change this improper fraction to a mixed number.
(Remember you may need to cancel.) $\frac{27}{12} = 2\frac{3}{12}^{1}_{4} = 2\frac{1}{4}$

Change these mixed numbers to improper fractions.

$2\frac{3}{4} = \frac{11}{4}$ $4\frac{1}{2} = \frac{9}{2}$

Change these improper fractions to mixed numbers.

$\frac{25}{3} = 8\frac{1}{3}$	$\frac{15}{12} = 1\frac{1}{4}$	$\frac{40}{7} = 5\frac{5}{7}$
$\frac{17}{6} = 2\frac{5}{6}$	$\frac{11}{9} = 1\frac{2}{9}$	$\frac{12}{5} = 2\frac{2}{5}$
$\frac{27}{5} = 5\frac{2}{5}$	$\frac{26}{3} = 8\frac{2}{3}$	$\frac{32}{5} = 6\frac{2}{5}$
$\frac{9}{2} = 4\frac{1}{2}$	$\frac{19}{2} = 9\frac{1}{2}$	$\frac{15}{4} = 3\frac{3}{4}$
$\frac{30}{4} = 7\frac{1}{2}$	$\frac{26}{8} = 3\frac{1}{4}$	$\frac{42}{9} = 4\frac{2}{3}$

Change these mixed numbers to improper fractions.

$4\frac{3}{4} = \frac{19}{4}$	$9\frac{1}{2} = \frac{19}{2}$	$12\frac{1}{4} = \frac{49}{4}$
$3\frac{2}{3} = \frac{11}{3}$	$6\frac{3}{4} = \frac{27}{4}$	$3\frac{9}{10} = \frac{39}{10}$
$5\frac{1}{8} = \frac{41}{8}$	$3\frac{2}{5} = \frac{17}{5}$	$2\frac{5}{6} = \frac{17}{6}$
$5\frac{1}{4} = \frac{21}{4}$	$3\frac{3}{8} = \frac{27}{8}$	$2\frac{11}{12} = \frac{35}{12}$
$2\frac{7}{10} = \frac{27}{10}$	$4\frac{3}{10} = \frac{43}{10}$	$4\frac{1}{8} = \frac{33}{8}$
$7\frac{3}{4} = \frac{31}{4}$	$8\frac{1}{2} = \frac{17}{2}$	$1\frac{5}{12} = \frac{17}{12}$

In the first part, children should see that you can divide the denominator by the numerator and place the remainder over the denominator. Use card circles cut into equal parts to reinforce the idea, e.g. how many whole circles can you make from 17 quarter circles?

5

Rounding decimals

Write these decimals to the nearest tenth.

6.23 is 6.2   6.27 is 6.3

If the second decimal place is a 5, we round up the first decimal place to the next larger number.

6.25 is 6.3

Write these decimals to the nearest tenth.

9.21 is 9.2	4.38 is 4.4	2.47 is 2.5
3.48 is 3.5	8.17 is 8.2	6.28 is 6.3
7.14 is 7.1	3.91 is 3.9	2.56 is 2.6
8.41 is 8.4	2.36 is 2.4	1.53 is 1.5

Write these decimals to the nearest tenth.

9.35 is 9.4	8.71 is 8.7	6.05 is 6.1
1.19 is 1.2	3.65 is 3.7	4.21 is 4.2
8.55 is 8.6	7.35 is 7.4	9.14 is 9.1
6.83 is 6.8	2.15 is 2.2	6.34 is 6.3

Write these decimals to the nearest tenth.

25.61 is 25.6	14.35 is 14.4	11.24 is 11.2
16.85 is 16.9	24.34 is 24.3	71.36 is 71.4
26.85 is 26.9	11.54 is 11.5	37.25 is 37.3
92.42 is 92.4	95.65 is 95.7	27.36 is 27.4
45.17 is 45.2	36.75 is 36.8	22.05 is 22.1

If children experience difficulties, point out that the significant digit to look at is in the second decimal place. The use of a number line may be helpful where the child is still unsure. In the second section, the concept of .05 is introduced. This must be rounded up.

6

Adding with different numbers of digits

Find the total for each problem.

```
  432        11
+  43       176
 ----      + 97
  475       ----
            273
```

Remember to regroup if you need to.

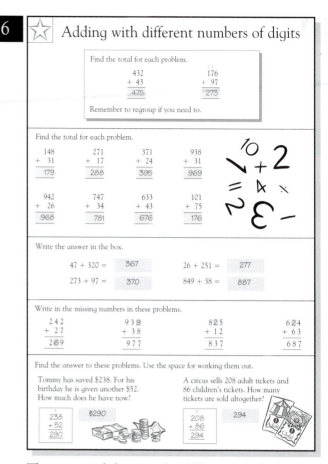

Find the total for each problem.

```
 148      271      371      938
+ 31     + 17     + 24     + 31
 ---      ---      ---      ---
 179      288      395      969

 942      747      633      101
+ 26     + 34     + 43     + 75
 ---      ---      ---      ---
 968      781      676      176
```

Write the answer in the box.

47 + 320 = 367   26 + 251 = 277

273 + 97 = 370   849 + 38 = 887

Write in the missing numbers in these problems.

```
 242      939      825      624
+ 27     + 38     + 12     + 63
 ---      ---      ---      ---
 269      977      837      687
```

Find the answer to these problems. Use the space for working them out.

Tommy has saved $238. For his birthday he is given another $52. How much does he have now?

```
  1
 238     $290
+ 52
 ---
 290
```

A circus sells 208 adult tickets and 86 children's tickets. How many tickets are sold altogether?

```
  1
 208     294
+ 86
 ---
 294
```

This page and the next should be straightforward. Any errors will probably be due to a failure to carry, or particularly in the second section, may occur where children have added digits with different place values.

7

Adding with different numbers of digits

Work out the answer to each problem.

```
 1 11              1 11
   987           2,767
+ 423,123      + 12,844
 --------       -------
 424,110         15,611
```

Remember to regroup if you need to.

Work out the answer to each problem.

```
   3,587       8,537,227           27
+ 17,628      +  86,518      + 9,964
 -------       ---------      ------
  21,215       8,623,745       9,991

     436       387,177          6,770
+ 12,844      +  8,381      + 772,142
 -------       -------       -------
  13,280       395,558        778,912
```

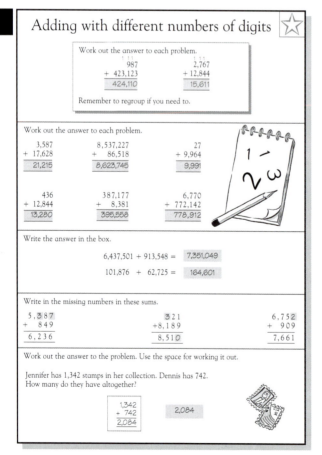

Write the answer in the box.

6,437,501 + 913,548 = 7,351,049

101,876 + 62,725 = 164,601

Write in the missing numbers in these sums.

```
 5,387           321         6,752
+  849        +8,189        +  909
 -----         -----         -----
 6,236         8,510         7,661
```

Work out the answer to the problem. Use the space for working it out.

Jennifer has 1,342 stamps in her collection. Dennis has 742. How many do they have altogether?

```
 1,342       2,084
+  742
 -----
 2,084
```

For problems in which the two numbers are not aligned vertically, ensure that children line up the digits in the ones place on the right side of the numbers. The most common error is not aligning the correct places.

Subtracting one number from another

Find the difference for each problem.

```
   7 13         3 12 11
   834           431
 -  44         -  84
  ----          ----
   790           347
```

Find the difference for each problem.

```
 835      490      175      428
-  23     - 70     - 54     - 67
 ---      ---      ---      ---
 812      420      121      361

 587      674      389      270
-  43     - 62     - 58     - 30
 ---      ---      ---      ---
 544      612      331      240

 483      951      746      234
-  35     - 28     - 17     - 16
 ---      ---      ---      ---
 448      923      729      218
```

Write the answer in the box.

491 – 31 = 460   654 – 22 = 632

874 – 63 = 811   577 – 26 = 551

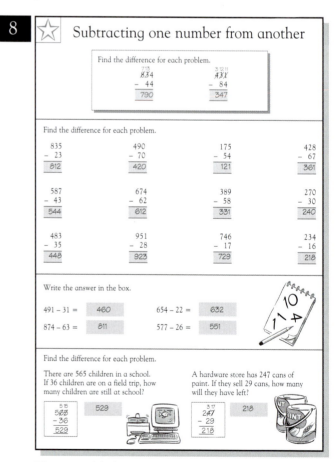

Find the difference for each problem.

There are 565 children in a school. If 36 children are on a field trip, how many children are still at school?

```
  5 5
  565     529
- 36
 ---
 529
```

A hardware store has 247 cans of paint. If they sell 29 cans, how many will they have left?

```
  3 17
  247     218
- 29
 ---
 218
```

The most likely errors to occur in the first section will involve subtractions where a larger digit has to be taken away from a smaller digit. Children often take the smaller digit that is on the top away from the larger digit on the bottom.

Subtracting one number from another

Work out the answer to each problem.

```
  1 16 16 7 15        1 10 14   3 12
   27,685          2,147,423
 −  8,726          − 165,351
   18,959          1,982,072
```

Work out the answer to each problem.

```
   568,231        6,262,411         11,684          337,481
 −   3,846      − 347,566        −  2,845        −  19,804
   564,385        5,914,845          8,839          317,677


 6,157,965          892,112         67,444           82,818
−3,633,976        − 746,489       − 29,545        −  7,465
 2,523,989          145,623         37,899           75,353


   952,812        3,732,522         38,529          116,387
 − 387,341      −     3,176       − 25,892        −   2,798
   565,471        3,729,346         12,637          113,589
```

Write the answer in the box.

4,555,562 − 1,624,871 = **2,930,691**

962,118 − 8,467 = **953,651**

Work out the answer to the problem. Use the space for working it out.

2,826 people went to see a rock concert. 135 had to leave early to catch their train. How many were left at the end?

```
  7 12
  2,826
 −  135        2,691
  2,691
```

See the notes for page 7.

10

Real-life problems

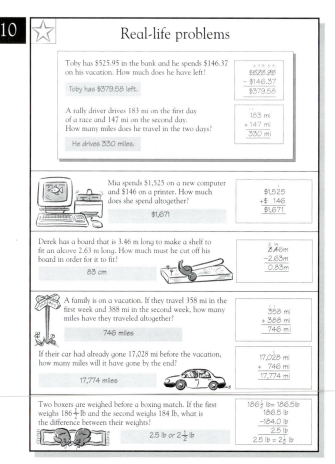

Toby has $525.95 in the bank and he spends $146.37 on his vacation. How much does he have left?

Toby has $379.58 left.

```
  4 11 5  8 15
  $525.95
 −$146.37
  $379.58
```

A rally driver drives 183 mi on the first day of a race and 147 mi on the second day. How many miles does he travel in the two days?

He drives 330 miles.

```
  1 1
  183 mi
 + 147 mi
  330 mi
```

Mia spends $1,525 on a new computer and $146 on a printer. How much does she spend altogether?

$1,671

```
     1
  $1,525
 +$  146
  $1,671
```

Derek has a board that is 3.46 m long to make a shelf to fit an alcove 2.63 m long. How much must he cut off his board in order for it to fit?

83 cm

```
   3 14
  3.46m
 −2.63m
  0.83m
```

A family is on a vacation. If they travel 358 mi in the first week and 388 mi in the second week, how many miles have they traveled altogether?

746 miles

```
    1
  358 mi
 + 388 mi
  746 mi
```

If their car had already gone 17,028 mi before the vacation, how many miles will it have gone by the end?

17,774 miles

```
  17,028 mi
 +   746 mi
  17,774 mi
```

Two boxers are weighed before a boxing match. If the first weighs $186\frac{1}{2}$ lb and the second weighs 184 lb, what is the difference between their weights?

2.5 lb or $2\frac{1}{2}$ lb

```
  186½ lb= 186.5lb
            186.5 lb
          −184.0 lb
             2.5 lb
  2.5 lb = 2½ lb
```

In this page and the following two pages children can apply the skills of addition and subtraction to real-life problems, using various units of measurement. If the child is unsure which operation to use, discuss whether the answer will be larger or smaller.

11

Everyday problems

An electrician buys 415 ft of cable. If he uses 234 ft, how much does he have left?

He has 181 ft of cable left.

```
  3 11
  4̸1̸5 ft
 − 234 ft
   181 ft
```

Simon travels by train for 110 mi, by bus for 56 mi and then walks the final 5 mi. How far does he travel?

Simon travels 171 mi.

```
  110 mi
   56 mi
 +  5 mi
  171 mi
```

Mr. Hindley works 185 hours a month. His wife works 73 hours a month. How many hours do they work altogether in a month?

258 hours

```
    1
  185hrs
 +73hrs
  258hrs
```

A school collects money for the local shelter. If the pupils collect $275 in the first month, $210 in the second month, and $136 in the third month, how much do they collect altogether?

$621

```
    1 1
  $275
  $210
 +$136
  $621
```

Danny's car finishes the race in 12.75 seconds, Rachelle's car finishes in 14.83 seconds. Whose car won the race?

Danny's car won the race.

```
   7 13
  14.8̸3 sec
 −12.75 sec
   2.08 sec
```

How much faster was the winning car?

The winning car was 2.08 seconds faster.

A builder buys 8,755 lb of sand, but uses only 6,916 lb. How much does he have left?

1,839 lb

```
  7 17 4 15
  8,7̸5̸5 lb
 −6,916 lb
  1,839 lb
```

See the notes for page 10. Point out that an answer that will be larger will require addition, while one that will be smaller will require subtraction.

12

Everyday problems

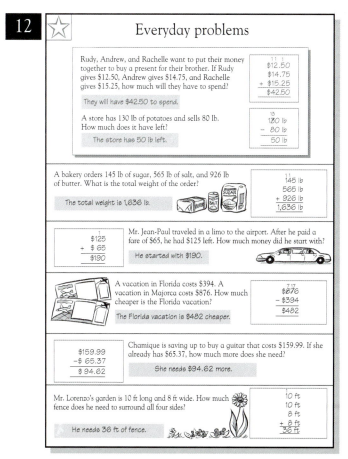

Rudy, Andrew, and Rachelle want to put their money together to buy a present for their brother. If Rudy gives $12.50, Andrew gives $14.75, and Rachelle gives $15.25, how much will they have to spend?

They will have $42.50 to spend.

```
     1 1  1
  $12.50
  $14.75
 +$15.25
  $42.50
```

A store has 130 lb of potatoes and sells 80 lb. How much does it have left?

The store has 50 lb left.

```
    13
  130 lb
 − 80 lb
   50 lb
```

A bakery orders 145 lb of sugar, 565 lb of salt, and 926 lb of butter. What is the total weight of the order?

The total weight is 1,636 lb.

```
     1 1
   145 lb
   565 lb
 + 926 lb
  1,636 lb
```

Mr. Jean-Paul traveled in a limo to the airport. After he paid a fare of $65, he had $125 left. How much money did he start with?

He started with $190.

```
    1
  $125
 +$ 65
  $190
```

A vacation in Florida costs $394. A vacation in Majorca costs $876. How much cheaper is the Florida vacation?

The Florida vacation is $482 cheaper.

```
   7 17
  $8̸7̸6
 −$394
  $482
```

Chamique is saving up to buy a guitar that costs $159.99. If she already has $65.37, how much more does she need?

She needs $94.62 more.

```
  $159.99
 −$ 65.37
  $ 94.62
```

Mr. Lorenzo's garden is 10 ft long and 8 ft wide. How much fence does he need to surround all four sides?

He needs 36 ft of fence.

```
   10 ft
   10 ft
    8 ft
 +  8 ft
   36 ft
```

See the notes for pages 10 and 11.

13 — Decimal addition

Write in the answers to these problems.

$$\begin{array}{r}{\scriptstyle 1\ 1}\\ 47.15 \\ +\ 19.36 \\ \hline 66.51 \end{array} \qquad \begin{array}{r}{\scriptstyle 1\ 1}\\ 43.99 \\ +\ 12.76 \\ \hline 56.75 \end{array}$$

Write the answer to each problem.

53.72 +77.92 **131.64**	84.17 +68.21 **152.38**	29.36 +66.84 **96.20**	23.56 +79.14 **102.70**	62.49 +18.75 **81.24**
35.67 +12.99 **48.66**	29.88 +43.02 **72.90**	67.39 +81.70 **149.09**	49.32 +14.95 **64.27**	27.22 +38.84 **66.06**

Write the answer to each problem.

76.30 +22.97 **99.27**	44.29 +11.04 **55.33**	81.97 +69.14 **151.11**	29.86 +76.33 **106.19**	68.25 +84.36 **152.61**
83.90 +30.24 **114.14**	45.83 +45.71 **91.54**	52.17 +90.21 **142.38**	84.93 +29.37 **114.30**	72.83 +41.16 **113.99**

Write the answer to each problem.

37.89 + 82.15 = **120.04**   32.44 + 21.88 = **54.32**   37.19 + 28.24 = **65.43**

68.67 + 29.82 = **98.49**   21.99 + 79.32 = **101.31**   52.45 + 34.58 = **87.03**

84.77 + 39.12 = **123.89**   63.84 + 29.81 = **93.65**   34.43 + 25.64 = **60.07**

33.97 + 24.62 = **58.59**   76.39 + 43.78 = **120.17**   52.38 + 38.43 = **90.81**

This page and the next page should follow on from earlier addition work. On these two pages, children are dealing with two decimal places. The most likely mistakes will be errors involving carrying, or in the third section, where they are working horizontally.

14 — Decimal addition

Write the sum for each problem.

$$\begin{array}{r}{\scriptstyle 1\ 1}\\ 296.48 \\ +\ 131.70 \\ \hline 428.18 \end{array} \qquad \begin{array}{r}{\scriptstyle 1\ 1}\\ 73.00 \\ +\ 269.23 \\ \hline 342.23 \end{array}$$

Write the sum for each problem.

491.83 + 37.84 **529.67**	964.71 + 321.2 **1,285.91**	32.045 + 204.99 **237.035**	306 + 844.24 **1,150.24**
471.932 + 755.26 **1,227.192**	842.01 + 11.842 **853.852**	675.82 + 105 **780.82**	37.82 + 399.71 **437.53**
65.24 + 605.27 **670.51**	178.935 + 599.41 **778.345**	184.70 + 372.81 **557.51**	443.27 + 75 **518.27**
563 + 413.98 **976.98**	703.95 + 85.11 **789.06**	825.36 + 249.857 **1,075.217**	529.3 + 482.56 **1,011.86**

Write the sum for each problem.

421 + 136.25 = **557.25**   92.31 + 241.73 = **334.04**

501.8 + 361.93 = **863.73**   558.32 + 137.945 = **696.265**

27 + 142.07 = **169.07**   75.31 + 293.33 = **368.64**

153.3 + 182.02 = **335.32**   491.445 + 105.37 = **596.815**

253.71 + 62 = **315.71**   829.2 + 63.74 = **892.94**

Watch out for misalignment when children work on horizontal subtractions.

15 — Decimal subtraction

Write the difference for each problem.

$$\begin{array}{r}{\scriptstyle 8\ 16}\\ 59.\cancel{76} \\ -\ 21.47 \\ \hline 38.29 \end{array} \qquad \begin{array}{r}{\scriptstyle 0\ 16}\\ 57.\cancel{18} \\ -\ 22.09 \\ \hline 35.09 \end{array}$$

Write the difference for each problem.

64.92 – 26.35 **38.57**	64.21 – 16.02 **48.19**	73.71 –19.24 **54.47**	92.63 – 67.14 **25.49**
45.76 – 16.18 **29.58**	73.52 – 39.27 **34.25**	98.98 –39.19 **59.79**	53.58 – 14.39 **39.19**
94.87 – 65.28 **29.59**	21.74 – 12.1 **9.64**	62.35 – 13.16 **49.19**	81.94 – 28.15 **53.79**
62.95 – 33.37 **29.58**	81.42 –25.04 **56.38**	48.52 – 14.49 **34.03**	61.55 – 13.26 **48.29**

Write the difference for each problem.

51.52 – 12.13 = **39.39**   72.41 – 23.18 = **49.23**

91.91 – 22.22 = **69.69**   53.84 – 19.65 = **34.19**

41.82 – 18.13 = **23.69**   51.61 – 23.14 = **28.47**

83.91 – 14.73 = **69.18**   64.65 – 37.26 = **27.39**

53.21 – 35.12 = **18.09**   77.31 – 28.15 = **49.16**

On this page and the next two pages, the most likely errors will result from a failure to use decomposition where necessary (see notes for pages 8 and 9). Watch out for misalignment when children work on horizontal subtractions.

16 — Decimal subtraction

Write the difference for each problem.

$$\begin{array}{r}{\scriptstyle 7\ 11}\\ 68.\cancel{17} \\ -\ 11.40 \\ \hline 56.77 \end{array} \qquad \begin{array}{r}{\scriptstyle 1\ 10}\\ 39.2\cancel{0} \\ -\ 13.15 \\ \hline 26.05 \end{array}$$

Work out the difference for each problem.

87.23 – 24.4 **62.83**	95.15 – 31.356 **63.794**	66.37 – 21.9 **44.47**	85 – 26.32 **58.68**
72.28 – 1.3 **70.98**	63.14 – 32 **31.14**	99.235 – 33.70 **65.535**	62.1 – 29.34 **32.76**
77.3 – 24.42 **52.88**	55.492 – 27.66 **27.832**	68 – 31.5 **36.5**	35.612 – 13.207 **22.405**
82.35 – 23.40 **58.95**	63.20 – 15.36 **47.84**	53.64 – 23 **30.64**	35.612 – 26.19 **9.422**

Write the difference for each problem.

63.4 – 24.51 = **38.89**   92.197 – 63.28 = **28.917**

91.3 – 33 = **58.3**   41.24 – 14.306 = **26.934**

52.251 – 22.42 = **29.831**   72.6 – 53.71 = **18.89**

92.84 – 23 = **69.84**   61.16 – 24.4 = **36.76**

81.815 – 55.90 = **25.915**   94.31 – 27.406 = **66.904**

On this page, the most common error will result from not writing the numbers to the same number of decimal places before subtracting.

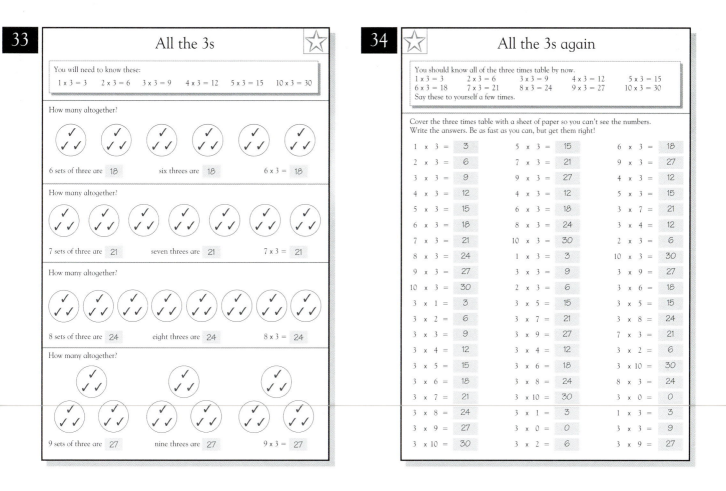

33 — All the 3s ⭐

You will need to know these:

1 x 3 = 3   2 x 3 = 6   3 x 3 = 9   4 x 3 = 12   5 x 3 = 15   10 x 3 = 30

How many altogether?

6 sets of three are 18   six threes are 18   6 x 3 = 18

How many altogether?

7 sets of three are 21   seven threes are 21   7 x 3 = 21

How many altogether?

8 sets of three are 24   eight threes are 24   8 x 3 = 24

How many altogether?

9 sets of three are 27   nine threes are 27   9 x 3 = 27

---

34 ⭐ — All the 3s again

You should know all of the three times table by now.

1 x 3 = 3   2 x 3 = 6   3 x 3 = 9   4 x 3 = 12   5 x 3 = 15
6 x 3 = 18   7 x 3 = 21   8 x 3 = 24   9 x 3 = 27   10 x 3 = 30

Say these to yourself a few times.

Cover the three times table with a sheet of paper so you can't see the numbers.
Write the answers. Be as fast as you can, but get them right!

1 x 3 = 3	5 x 3 = 15	6 x 3 = 18
2 x 3 = 6	7 x 3 = 21	9 x 3 = 27
3 x 3 = 9	9 x 3 = 27	4 x 3 = 12
4 x 3 = 12	4 x 3 = 12	5 x 3 = 15
5 x 3 = 15	6 x 3 = 18	3 x 7 = 21
6 x 3 = 18	8 x 3 = 24	3 x 4 = 12
7 x 3 = 21	10 x 3 = 30	2 x 3 = 6
8 x 3 = 24	1 x 3 = 3	10 x 3 = 30
9 x 3 = 27	3 x 3 = 9	3 x 9 = 27
10 x 3 = 30	2 x 3 = 6	3 x 6 = 18
3 x 1 = 3	3 x 5 = 15	3 x 5 = 15
3 x 2 = 6	3 x 7 = 21	3 x 8 = 24
3 x 3 = 9	3 x 9 = 27	7 x 3 = 21
3 x 4 = 12	3 x 4 = 12	3 x 2 = 6
3 x 5 = 15	3 x 6 = 18	3 x 10 = 30
3 x 6 = 18	3 x 8 = 24	8 x 3 = 24
3 x 7 = 21	3 x 10 = 30	3 x 0 = 0
3 x 8 = 24	3 x 1 = 3	1 x 3 = 3
3 x 9 = 27	3 x 0 = 0	3 x 3 = 9
3 x 10 = 30	3 x 2 = 6	3 x 9 = 27

---

35 — All the 4s ⭐

You should know these:

1 x 4 = 4   2 x 4 = 8   3 x 4 = 12   4 x 4 = 16   5 x 4 = 20   10 x 4 = 40

How many altogether?

6 sets of four are 24   six fours are 24   6 x 4 = 24

How many altogether?

7 sets of four are 28   seven fours are 28   7 x 4 = 28

How many altogether?

8 sets of four are 32   eight fours are 32   8 x 4 = 32

How many altogether?

9 sets of four are 36   nine fours are 36   9 x 4 = 36

---

36 ⭐ — All the 4s again

You should know all of the four times table by now.

1 x 4 = 4   2 x 4 = 8   3 x 4 = 12   4 x 4 = 16   5 x 4 = 20
6 x 4 = 24   7 x 4 = 28   8 x 4 = 32   9 x 4 = 36   10 x 4 = 40

Say these to yourself the a few times.

Cover the four times table with a sheet of paper so you can't see the numbers.
Write the answers. Be as fast as you can, but get them right!

1 x 4 = 4	5 x 4 = 20	6 x 4 = 24
2 x 4 = 8	7 x 4 = 28	9 x 4 = 36
3 x 4 = 12	9 x 4 = 36	4 x 1 = 4
4 x 4 = 16	3 x 4 = 12	5 x 4 = 20
5 x 4 = 20	6 x 4 = 24	4 x 7 = 28
6 x 4 = 24	8 x 4 = 32	3 x 4 = 12
7 x 4 = 28	10 x 4 = 40	2 x 4 = 8
8 x 4 = 32	1 x 4 = 4	10 x 4 = 40
9 x 4 = 36	4 x 4 = 16	4 x 3 = 12
10 x 4 = 40	2 x 4 = 8	4 x 6 = 24
4 x 1 = 4	4 x 5 = 20	4 x 5 = 20
4 x 2 = 8	4 x 7 = 28	4 x 8 = 32
4 x 3 = 12	4 x 9 = 36	7 x 4 = 28
4 x 4 = 16	4 x 4 = 16	4 x 2 = 8
4 x 5 = 20	4 x 6 = 24	4 x 10 = 40
4 x 6 = 24	4 x 8 = 32	8 x 4 = 32
4 x 7 = 28	4 x 10 = 40	4 x 0 = 0
4 x 8 = 32	4 x 1 = 4	1 x 4 = 4
4 x 9 = 36	4 x 0 = 0	4 x 4 = 16
4 x 10 = 40	4 x 2 = 8	4 x 9 = 36

37

Speed trials

You should know all of the 1, 2, 3, 4, 5, and 10 times tables by now, but how quickly can you do them?
Ask someone to time you as you do this page.
Remember, you must be fast but also correct.

4 x 2 = 8	6 x 3 = 18	9 x 5 = 45
8 x 3 = 24	3 x 4 = 12	8 x 10 = 80
7 x 4 = 28	7 x 5 = 35	7 x 2 = 14
6 x 5 = 30	3 x 10 = 30	6 x 3 = 18
8 x 10 = 80	1 x 2 = 2	5 x 4 = 20
8 x 2 = 16	7 x 3 = 21	4 x 5 = 20
5 x 3 = 15	4 x 4 = 16	3 x 10 = 30
9 x 4 = 36	6 x 5 = 30	2 x 2 = 4
5 x 5 = 25	4 x 10 = 40	1 x 3 = 3
7 x 10 = 70	6 x 2 = 12	0 x 4 = 0
0 x 2 = 0	5 x 3 = 15	10 x 5 = 50
4 x 3 = 12	8 x 4 = 32	9 x 2 = 18
6 x 4 = 24	0 x 5 = 0	8 x 3 = 24
3 x 5 = 15	2 x 10 = 20	7 x 4 = 28
4 x 10 = 40	7 x 2 = 14	6 x 5 = 30
7 x 2 = 14	8 x 3 = 24	5 x 10 = 50
3 x 3 = 9	9 x 4 = 36	4 x 0 = 0
2 x 4 = 8	5 x 5 = 25	3 x 2 = 6
7 x 5 = 35	7 x 10 = 70	2 x 8 = 16
9 x 10 = 90	5 x 2 = 10	1 x 9 = 9

38

Some of the 6s

You should already know parts of the 6 times table because they are parts of the 1, 2, 3, 4, 5, and 10 times tables.
  1 x 6 = 6   2 x 6 = 12   3 x 6 = 18
  4 x 6 = 24   5 x 6 = 30   10 x 6 = 60
Find out if you can remember them quickly and correctly.

Cover the six times table with paper so you can't see the numbers.
Write the answers as quickly as you can.

What is three sixes?	18	What is ten sixes?	60
What is two sixes?	12	What is four sixes?	24
What is one six?	6	What is five sixes?	30

Write the answers as quickly as you can.

How many sixes make 12?	2	How many sixes make 6?	1
How many sixes make 30?	5	How many sixes make 18?	3
How many sixes make 24?	4	How many sixes make 60?	10

Write the answers as quickly as you can.

Multiply six by three.	18	Multiply six by ten.	60
Multiply six by two.	12	Multiply six by five.	30
Multiply six by one.	6	Multiply six by four.	24

Write the answers as quickly as you can.

4 x 6 = 24	2 x 6 = 12	10 x 6 = 60
5 x 6 = 30	1 x 6 = 6	3 x 6 = 18

Write the answers as quickly as you can.
A box contains six eggs. A man buys five boxes. How many eggs does he have? 30

A pack contains six sticks of gum.
How many sticks will there be in 10 packs? 60

39

The rest of the 6s

You need to learn these:
  6 x 6 = 36   7 x 6 = 42   8 x 6 = 48   9 x 6 = 54

This work will help you remember the 6 times table.

Complete these sequences.

6   12   18   24   30   36   42   48   54   60

  5 x 6 = 30   so   6 x 6 = 30 plus another 6 = 36

18   24   30   36   42   48   54   60

  6 x 6 = 36   so   7 x 6 = 36 plus another 6 = 42

6   12   18   24   30   36   42   48   54   60

  7 x 6 = 42   so   8 x 6 = 42 plus another 6 = 48

6   12   18   24   30   36   42   48   54   60

  8 x 6 = 48   so   9 x 6 = 48 plus another 6 = 54

6   12   18   24   30   36   42   48   54   60

Test yourself on the rest of the 6 times table.
Cover the above part of the page with a sheet of paper.

What is six sixes?	36	What is seven sixes?	42
What is eight sixes?	48	What is nine sixes?	54

8 x 6 = 48   7 x 6 = 42   6 x 6 = 36   9 x 6 = 54

40

Practice the 6s

You should know all of the 6 times table now, but how quickly can you remember it?
Ask someone to time you as you do this page.
Remember, you must be fast but also correct.

1 x 6 = 6	2 x 6 = 12	7 x 6 = 42
2 x 6 = 12	4 x 6 = 24	3 x 6 = 18
3 x 6 = 18	6 x 6 = 36	9 x 6 = 54
4 x 6 = 24	8 x 6 = 48	6 x 4 = 24
5 x 6 = 30	10 x 6 = 60	1 x 6 = 6
6 x 6 = 36	1 x 6 = 6	6 x 2 = 12
7 x 6 = 42	3 x 6 = 18	6 x 8 = 48
8 x 6 = 48	5 x 6 = 30	0 x 6 = 0
9 x 6 = 54	7 x 6 = 42	6 x 3 = 18
10 x 6 = 60	9 x 6 = 54	5 x 6 = 30
6 x 1 = 6	6 x 3 = 18	6 x 7 = 42
6 x 2 = 12	6 x 5 = 30	2 x 6 = 12
6 x 3 = 18	6 x 7 = 42	6 x 9 = 54
6 x 4 = 24	6 x 9 = 54	4 x 6 = 24
6 x 5 = 30	6 x 2 = 12	8 x 6 = 48
6 x 6 = 36	6 x 4 = 24	10 x 6 = 60
6 x 7 = 42	6 x 6 = 36	6 x 5 = 30
6 x 8 = 48	6 x 8 = 48	6 x 0 = 0
6 x 9 = 54	6 x 10 = 60	6 x 1 = 6
6 x 10 = 60	6 x 0 = 0	6 x 6 = 36

41 — Speed trials

41

You should know all of the 1, 2, 3, 4, 5, 6, and 10 times tables by now, but how quickly can you remember them?
Ask someone to time you as you do this page.
Remember, you must be fast but also correct.

4 x 6 = 24	6 x 3 = 18	9 x 6 = 54
5 x 3 = 15	8 x 6 = 48	8 x 6 = 48
7 x 3 = 21	6 x 6 = 36	7 x 3 = 21
6 x 5 = 30	3 x 10 = 30	6 x 6 = 36
6 x 10 = 60	6 x 2 = 12	5 x 4 = 20
8 x 2 = 16	7 x 3 = 21	4 x 6 = 24
5 x 3 = 15	4 x 6 = 24	3 x 6 = 18
9 x 6 = 54	6 x 5 = 30	2 x 6 = 12
5 x 5 = 25	6 x 10 = 60	6 x 3 = 18
7 x 6 = 42	6 x 2 = 12	0 x 6 = 0
0 x 2 = 0	5 x 3 = 15	10 x 5 = 50
6 x 3 = 18	8 x 4 = 32	6 x 2 = 12
6 x 6 = 36	0 x 6 = 0	8 x 3 = 24
3 x 5 = 15	5 x 10 = 50	7 x 6 = 42
4 x 10 = 40	7 x 6 = 42	6 x 5 = 30
7 x 10 = 70	8 x 3 = 24	5 x 10 = 50
3 x 6 = 18	9 x 6 = 54	6 x 0 = 0
2 x 4 = 8	5 x 5 = 25	3 x 10 = 30
6 x 9 = 54	7 x 10 = 70	2 x 8 = 16
9 x 10 = 90	5 x 6 = 30	1 x 8 = 8

42 — Some of the 7s

42

You should already know parts of the 7 times table because they are parts of the 1, 2, 3, 4, 5, 6 and 10 times tables.
1 x 7 = 7   2 x 7 = 14   3 x 7 = 21   4 x 7 = 28
5 x 7 = 35   6 x 7 = 42   10 x 7 = 70
Find out if you can remember them quickly and correctly.

Cover the seven times table with paper and write the answers to these questions as quickly as you can.

What is three sevens?	21	What is ten sevens?	70
What is two sevens?	14	What is four sevens?	28
What is six sevens?	42	What is five sevens?	35

Write the answers as quickly as you can.

How many sevens make 14?	2	How many sevens make 42?	6
How many sevens make 35?	5	How many sevens make 21?	3
How many sevens make 28?	4	How many sevens make 70?	10

Write the answers as quickly as you can.

Multiply seven by three.	21	Multiply seven by ten.	70
Multiply seven by two.	14	Multiply seven by five.	35
Multiply seven by six.	42	Multiply seven by four.	28

Write the answers as quickly as you can.

4 x 7 = 28	2 x 7 = 14	10 x 7 = 70
5 x 7 = 35	1 x 7 = 7	3 x 7 = 21

Write the answers as quickly as you can.
A bag has seven candies. Ann buys five bags. How many candies does she have? 35

How many days are there in six weeks? 42

43 — The rest of the 7s

43

You should now know all of the 1, 2, 3, 4, 5, 6, and 10 times tables.
You need to learn only these parts of the seven times table.
7 x 7 = 49   8 x 7 = 56   9 x 7 = 63

This work will help you remember the 7 times table.

Complete these sequences.

7   14   21   28   35   42   49   56   63   70

6 x 7 = 42   so   7 x 7 = 42 plus another 7 = 49

21   28   35   42   49   56   63   70

7 x 7 = 49   so   8 x 7 = 49 plus another 7 = 56

7   14   21   28   35   42   49   56   63   70

8 x 7 = 56   so   9 x 7 = 56 plus another 7 = 63

7   14   21   28   35   42   49   56   63   70

Test yourself on the rest of the 7 times table.
Cover the section above with a sheet of paper.

What is seven sevens? 49   What is eight sevens? 56

What is nine sevens? 63   What is ten sevens? 70

8 x 7 = 56   7 x 7 = 49   9 x 7 = 63   10 x 7 = 70

How many days are there in eight weeks? 56

A package contains seven pens.
How many pens will there be in nine packets? 63

How many sevens make 56? 8

44 — Practice the 7s

44

You should know all of the 7 times table now, but how quickly can you remember it?
Ask someone to time you as you do this page.
Remember, you must be fast but also correct.

1 x 7 = 7	2 x 7 = 14	7 x 6 = 42
2 x 7 = 14	4 x 7 = 28	3 x 7 = 21
3 x 7 = 21	6 x 7 = 42	9 x 7 = 63
4 x 7 = 28	8 x 7 = 56	7 x 4 = 28
5 x 7 = 35	10 x 7 = 70	1 x 7 = 7
6 x 7 = 42	1 x 7 = 7	7 x 2 = 14
7 x 7 = 49	3 x 7 = 21	7 x 8 = 56
8 x 7 = 56	5 x 7 = 35	0 x 7 = 0
9 x 7 = 63	7 x 7 = 49	7 x 3 = 21
10 x 7 = 70	9 x 7 = 63	5 x 7 = 35
7 x 1 = 7	7 x 3 = 21	7 x 7 = 49
7 x 2 = 14	7 x 5 = 35	2 x 7 = 14
7 x 3 = 21	7 x 7 = 49	7 x 9 = 63
7 x 4 = 28	7 x 9 = 63	4 x 7 = 28
7 x 5 = 35	7 x 2 = 14	8 x 7 = 56
7 x 6 = 42	7 x 4 = 28	10 x 7 = 70
7 x 7 = 49	7 x 6 = 42	7 x 5 = 35
7 x 8 = 56	7 x 8 = 56	7 x 0 = 0
7 x 9 = 63	7 x 10 = 70	7 x 1 = 7
7 x 10 = 70	7 x 0 = 0	6 x 7 = 42

45

Speed trials

You should know all of the 1, 2, 3, 4, 5, 6, 7, and 10 times tables by now, but how quickly can you remember them?
Ask someone to time you as you do this page.
Remember, you must be fast but also correct.

4 x 7 = 28	7 x 3 = 21	9 x 7 = 63
5 x 10 = 50	8 x 7 = 56	7 x 6 = 42
7 x 5 = 35	6 x 6 = 36	8 x 3 = 24
6 x 5 = 30	5 x 10 = 50	6 x 6 = 36
6 x 10 = 60	6 x 3 = 18	7 x 4 = 28
8 x 7 = 56	7 x 5 = 35	4 x 6 = 24
5 x 8 = 40	4 x 6 = 24	3 x 7 = 21
9 x 6 = 54	6 x 5 = 30	2 x 8 = 16
5 x 7 = 35	7 x 10 = 70	7 x 3 = 21
7 x 6 = 42	6 x 7 = 42	0 x 6 = 0
0 x 5 = 0	5 x 7 = 35	10 x 7 = 70
6 x 3 = 18	8 x 4 = 32	6 x 2 = 12
6 x 7 = 42	0 x 7 = 0	8 x 7 = 56
3 x 5 = 15	5 x 8 = 40	7 x 7 = 49
4 x 7 = 28	7 x 6 = 42	6 x 5 = 30
7 x 10 = 70	8 x 3 = 24	5 x 10 = 50
7 x 8 = 56	9 x 6 = 54	7 x 0 = 0
2 x 7 = 14	7 x 7 = 49	3 x 10 = 30
4 x 9 = 36	9 x 10 = 90	2 x 7 = 14
9 x 10 = 90	5 x 6 = 30	7 x 8 = 56

46

Some of the 8s

You should already know some of the 8 times table because it is part of the 1, 2, 3, 4, 5, 6, 7, and 10 times tables.
1 x 8 = 8   2 x 8 = 16   3 x 8 = 24   4 x 8 = 32
5 x 8 = 40   6 x 8 = 48   7 x 8 = 56   10 x 8 = 80
Find out if you can remember them quickly and correctly.

Cover the 8 times table with paper so you can't see the numbers.
Write the answers as quickly as you can.

What is three eights? 24		What is ten eights? 80
What is two eights? 16		What is four eights? 32
What is six eights? 48		What is five eights? 40

Write the answers as quickly as you can.

How many eights equal 16? 2	How many eights equal 40? 5
How many eights equal 32? 4	How many eights equal 24? 3
How many eights equal 56? 7	How many eights equal 48? 6

Write the answers as quickly as you can.

Multiply eight by three. 24	Multiply eight by ten. 80
Multiply eight by two. 16	Multiply eight by five. 40
Multiply eight by six. 48	Multiply eight by four. 32

Write the answers as quickly as you can.

6 x 8 = 48	2 x 8 = 16	10 x 8 = 80
5 x 8 = 40	7 x 8 = 56	3 x 8 = 24

Write the answers as quickly as you can.
A pizza has eight slices. John buys six pizzas.
How many slices does he have? 48
Which number multiplied by 8 gives the answer 56? 7

The rest of the 8s

You need to learn only these parts of the eight times table.
8 x 8 = 64   9 x 8 = 72

This work will help you remember the 8 times table.

Complete these sequences.

8   16   24   32   40   48   56   64   72   80

7 x 8 = 56   so   8 x 8 = 56 plus another 8 = 64

24   32   40   48   56   64   72   80

8 x 8 = 64   so   9 x 8 = 64 plus another 8 = 72

8   16   24   32   40   48   56   64   72   80

8   16   24   32   40   48   56   64   72   80

Test yourself on the rest of the 8 times table.
Cover the section above with a sheet of paper.

What is seven eights? 56	What is eight eights? 64
What is nine eights? 72	What is eight nines? 72

8 x 8 = 64   9 x 8 = 72   8 x 9 = 72   10 x 8 = 80

What number multiplied by 8 gives the answer 72? 9

A number multiplied by 8 gives the answer 80. What is the number? 10

David puts out building bricks in piles of 8.
How many bricks will there be in 10 piles? 80

What number multiplied by 5 gives the answer 40? 8

How many 8s make 72? 9

Practice the 8s

You should know all of the 8 times table now, but how quickly can you remember it?
Ask someone to time you as you do this page.
Be fast but also correct.

1 x 8 = 8	2 x 8 = 16	8 x 6 = 48
2 x 8 = 16	4 x 8 = 32	3 x 8 = 24
3 x 8 = 24	6 x 8 = 48	9 x 8 = 72
4 x 8 = 32	8 x 8 = 64	8 x 4 = 32
5 x 8 = 40	10 x 8 = 80	1 x 8 = 8
6 x 8 = 48	1 x 8 = 8	8 x 2 = 16
7 x 8 = 56	3 x 8 = 24	7 x 8 = 56
8 x 8 = 64	5 x 8 = 40	0 x 8 = 0
9 x 8 = 72	7 x 8 = 56	8 x 3 = 24
10 x 8 = 80	9 x 8 = 72	5 x 8 = 40
8 x 1 = 8	8 x 3 = 24	8 x 8 = 64
8 x 2 = 16	8 x 5 = 40	2 x 8 = 16
8 x 3 = 24	8 x 8 = 64	8 x 9 = 72
8 x 4 = 32	8 x 9 = 72	4 x 8 = 32
8 x 5 = 40	8 x 2 = 16	8 x 6 = 48
8 x 6 = 48	8 x 4 = 32	10 x 8 = 80
8 x 7 = 56	8 x 6 = 48	8 x 5 = 40
8 x 8 = 64	8 x 8 = 64	8 x 0 = 0
8 x 9 = 72	8 x 10 = 80	8 x 1 = 8
8 x 10 = 80	8 x 0 = 0	6 x 8 = 48

Speed trials ☆

You should know all of the 1, 2, 3, 4, 5, 6, 7, 8, and 10 times tables now,
but how quickly can you remember them?
Ask someone to time you as you do this page.
Be fast but also correct.

4 x 8 = 32	7 x 8 = 56	9 x 8 = 72
5 x 10 = 50	8 x 7 = 56	7 x 6 = 42
7 x 8 = 56	6 x 8 = 48	8 x 3 = 24
8 x 5 = 40	8 x 10 = 80	8 x 8 = 64
6 x 10 = 60	6 x 3 = 18	7 x 4 = 28
8 x 7 = 56	7 x 7 = 49	4 x 8 = 32
5 x 8 = 40	5 x 6 = 30	3 x 7 = 21
9 x 8 = 72	6 x 7 = 42	2 x 8 = 16
8 x 8 = 64	7 x 10 = 70	7 x 3 = 21
7 x 6 = 42	6 x 9 = 54	0 x 8 = 0
7 x 5 = 35	5 x 8 = 40	10 x 8 = 80
6 x 8 = 48	8 x 4 = 32	6 x 2 = 12
6 x 7 = 42	0 x 8 = 0	8 x 6 = 48
5 x 7 = 35	5 x 9 = 45	7 x 8 = 56
8 x 4 = 32	7 x 6 = 42	6 x 5 = 30
7 x 10 = 70	8 x 3 = 24	8 x 10 = 80
2 x 8 = 16	9 x 6 = 54	8 x 7 = 56
4 x 7 = 28	8 x 6 = 48	5 x 10 = 50
6 x 9 = 54	9 x 10 = 90	8 x 2 = 16
9 x 10 = 90	6 x 6 = 36	8 x 9 = 72

50

☆ Some of the 9s

You should already know nearly all of the 9 times table because it is part of the
1, 2, 3, 4, 5, 6, 7, 8, and 10 times tables.
1 x 9 = 9   2 x 9 = 18   3 x 9 = 27   4 x 9 = 36   5 x 9 = 45
6 x 9 = 54   7 x 9 = 63   8 x 9 = 72   10 x 9 = 90
Find out if you can remember them quickly and correctly.

Cover the nine times table so you can't see the numbers.
Write the answers as quickly as you can.

What is three nines? 27	What is ten nines? 90
What is two nines? 18	What is four nines? 36
What is six nines? 54	What is five nines? 45
What is seven nines? 63	What is eight nines? 72

Write the answers as quickly as you can.

How many nines equal 18? 2	How many nines equal 54? 6
How many nines equal 90? 10	How many nines equal 27? 3
How many nines equal 72? 8	How many nines equal 36? 4
How many nines equal 45? 5	How many nines equal 63? 7

Write the answers as quickly as you can.

Multiply nine by seven. 63	Multiply nine by ten. 90
Multiply nine by two. 18	Multiply nine by five. 45
Multiply nine by six. 54	Multiply nine by four. 36
Multiply nine by three. 27	Multiply nine by eight. 72

Write the answers as quickly as you can.

6 x 9 = 54	2 x 9 = 18	10 x 9 = 90
5 x 9 = 45	3 x 9 = 27	8 x 9 = 72
0 x 9 = 0	7 x 9 = 63	4 x 9 = 36

51

The rest of the 9s ☆

You need to learn only this part of the nine times table.
9 x 9 = 81

This work will help you remember the 9 times table.
Complete these sequences.

9   18   27   36   45   54   63   72   81   90

8 x 9 = 72   so   9 x 9 = 72 plus another 9 = 81

27   36   45   54   63   72   81   90

9   18   27   36   45   54   63   72   81   90

9   18   27   36   45   54   63   72   81   90

Look for a pattern in the nine times table.

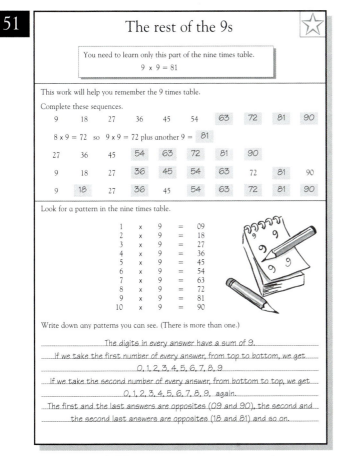

1	x	9	=	09
2	x	9	=	18
3	x	9	=	27
4	x	9	=	36
5	x	9	=	45
6	x	9	=	54
7	x	9	=	63
8	x	9	=	72
9	x	9	=	81
10	x	9	=	90

Write down any patterns you can see. (There is more than one.)

The digits in every answer have a sum of 9.
If we take the first number of every answer, from top to bottom, we get
0, 1, 2, 3, 4, 5, 6, 7, 8, 9.
If we take the second number of every answer, from bottom to top, we get
0, 1, 2, 3, 4, 5, 6, 7, 8, 9, again.
The first and the last answers are opposites (09 and 90), the second and
the second last answers are opposites (18 and 81) and so on.

☆ Practice the 9s

You should know all of the 9 times table now, but how quickly can you remember it?
Ask someone to time you as you do this page.
Be fast and correct.

1 x 9 = 9	2 x 9 = 18	9 x 6 = 54
2 x 9 = 18	4 x 9 = 36	3 x 9 = 27
3 x 9 = 27	6 x 9 = 54	9 x 9 = 81
4 x 9 = 36	9 x 7 = 63	9 x 4 = 36
5 x 9 = 45	10 x 9 = 90	1 x 9 = 9
6 x 9 = 54	1 x 9 = 9	9 x 2 = 18
7 x 9 = 63	3 x 9 = 27	7 x 9 = 63
8 x 9 = 72	5 x 9 = 45	0 x 9 = 0
9 x 9 = 81	7 x 9 = 63	9 x 3 = 27
10 x 9 = 90	9 x 9 = 81	5 x 9 = 45
9 x 1 = 9	9 x 3 = 27	9 x 9 = 81
9 x 2 = 18	9 x 5 = 45	2 x 9 = 18
9 x 3 = 27	0 x 9 = 0	8 x 9 = 72
9 x 4 = 36	9 x 1 = 9	4 x 9 = 36
9 x 5 = 45	9 x 2 = 18	9 x 7 = 63
9 x 6 = 54	9 x 4 = 36	10 x 9 = 90
9 x 7 = 63	9 x 6 = 54	9 x 5 = 45
9 x 8 = 72	9 x 8 = 72	9 x 0 = 0
9 x 9 = 81	9 x 10 = 90	9 x 1 = 9
9 x 10 = 90	9 x 0 = 0	6 x 9 = 54

Encourage children to notice patterns. It does not
matter how they express these. One pattern is to
deduct 1 from the number being multiplied. This
gives the first digit of the answer. Then deduct this
first digit from 9 to get the second digit of the answer.

Speed trials

You should know all of the times tables by now, but how quickly can you remember them?
Ask someone to time you as you do this page.
Be fast and correct.

6 x 8 = 48	4 x 8 = 32	8 x 10 = 80
9 x 10 = 90	9 x 8 = 72	7 x 9 = 63
5 x 8 = 40	6 x 6 = 36	8 x 5 = 40
7 x 5 = 35	8 x 9 = 72	8 x 7 = 56
6 x 4 = 24	6 x 4 = 24	7 x 4 = 28
8 x 8 = 64	7 x 3 = 21	4 x 9 = 36
5 x 10 = 50	5 x 9 = 45	6 x 7 = 42
9 x 8 = 72	6 x 8 = 48	4 x 6 = 24
8 x 3 = 24	7 x 7 = 49	7 x 8 = 56
7 x 7 = 49	6 x 9 = 54	6 x 9 = 54
9 x 5 = 45	7 x 8 = 56	10 x 8 = 80
4 x 8 = 32	8 x 4 = 32	6 x 5 = 30
6 x 7 = 42	0 x 9 = 0	8 x 8 = 64
2 x 9 = 18	10 x 10 = 100	7 x 6 = 42
8 x 4 = 32	7 x 6 = 42	6 x 8 = 48
7 x 10 = 70	8 x 7 = 56	9 x 10 = 90
2 x 8 = 16	9 x 6 = 54	8 x 4 = 32
4 x 7 = 28	8 x 6 = 48	7 x 10 = 70
6 x 9 = 54	9 x 9 = 81	5 x 8 = 40
9 x 9 = 81	6 x 7 = 42	8 x 9 = 72

54

Times tables for division

Knowing the times tables can also help with division problems.
Look at these examples.
3 x 6 = 18 which means that 18 ÷ 3 = 6 and that 18 ÷ 6 = 3
4 x 5 = 20 which means that 20 ÷ 4 = 5 and that 20 ÷ 5 = 4
9 x 3 = 27 which means that 27 ÷ 3 = 9 and that 27 ÷ 9 = 3

Use your knowledge of the times tables to work these division problems.

3 x 8 = 24 which means that 24 ÷ 3 = 8 and that 24 ÷ 8 = 3
4 x 7 = 28 which means that 28 ÷ 4 = 7 and that 28 ÷ 7 = 4
3 x 5 = 15 which means that 15 ÷ 3 = 5 and that 15 ÷ 5 = 3
4 x 3 = 12 which means that 12 ÷ 3 = 4 and that 12 ÷ 4 = 3
3 x 10 = 30 which means that 30 ÷ 3 = 10 and that 30 ÷ 10 = 3
4 x 8 = 32 which means that 32 ÷ 4 = 8 and that 32 ÷ 8 = 4
3 x 9 = 27 which means that 27 ÷ 3 = 9 and that 27 ÷ 9 = 3
4 x 10 = 40 which means that 40 ÷ 4 = 10 and that 40 ÷ 10 = 4

These division problems help practice the 3 and 4 times tables.

20 ÷ 4 = 5	15 ÷ 3 = 5	16 ÷ 4 = 4
24 ÷ 4 = 6	27 ÷ 3 = 9	30 ÷ 3 = 10
12 ÷ 3 = 4	18 ÷ 3 = 6	28 ÷ 4 = 7
24 ÷ 3 = 8	32 ÷ 4 = 8	21 ÷ 3 = 7

How many fours in 36? 9	Divide 27 by three. 9
Divide 28 by 4. 7	How many threes in 21? 7
How many fives in 35? 7	Divide 40 by 5. 8
Divide 15 by 3. 5	How many eights in 48? 6

55

Times tables for division

This page will help you remember times tables by dividing by 2, 3, 4, 5, and 10.

20 ÷ 5 = 4   18 ÷ 3 = 6   60 ÷ 10 = 6

Complete the problems.

40 ÷ 10 = 4	14 ÷ 2 = 7	32 ÷ 4 = 8
25 ÷ 5 = 5	21 ÷ 3 = 7	16 ÷ 4 = 4
24 ÷ 4 = 6	28 ÷ 4 = 7	12 ÷ 2 = 6
45 ÷ 5 = 9	35 ÷ 5 = 7	12 ÷ 3 = 4
10 ÷ 2 = 5	40 ÷ 10 = 4	12 ÷ 4 = 3
20 ÷ 10 = 2	20 ÷ 2 = 10	20 ÷ 2 = 10
6 ÷ 2 = 3	18 ÷ 3 = 6	20 ÷ 4 = 5
24 ÷ 3 = 8	32 ÷ 4 = 8	20 ÷ 5 = 4
30 ÷ 5 = 6	40 ÷ 5 = 8	20 ÷ 10 = 2
30 ÷ 10 = 3	80 ÷ 10 = 8	18 ÷ 2 = 9
40 ÷ 5 = 8	6 ÷ 2 = 3	18 ÷ 3 = 6
21 ÷ 3 = 7	15 ÷ 3 = 5	15 ÷ 3 = 5
14 ÷ 2 = 7	24 ÷ 4 = 6	15 ÷ 5 = 3
27 ÷ 3 = 9	15 ÷ 5 = 3	24 ÷ 3 = 8
90 ÷ 10 = 9	10 ÷ 10 = 1	24 ÷ 4 = 6
15 ÷ 5 = 3	4 ÷ 2 = 2	50 ÷ 5 = 10
15 ÷ 3 = 5	9 ÷ 3 = 3	50 ÷ 10 = 5
20 ÷ 5 = 4	4 ÷ 4 = 1	30 ÷ 3 = 10
20 ÷ 4 = 5	10 ÷ 5 = 2	30 ÷ 5 = 6
16 ÷ 2 = 8	100 ÷ 10 = 10	30 ÷ 10 = 3

Times tables for division

This page will help you remember times tables by dividing by 2, 3, 4, 5, 6, and 10.

30 ÷ 6 = 5   12 ÷ 6 = 2   60 ÷ 10 = 6

Complete the problems.

18 ÷ 6 = 3	27 ÷ 3 = 9	48 ÷ 6 = 8
30 ÷ 10 = 3	18 ÷ 6 = 3	35 ÷ 5 = 7
14 ÷ 2 = 7	20 ÷ 2 = 10	36 ÷ 4 = 9
18 ÷ 3 = 6	24 ÷ 6 = 4	24 ÷ 3 = 8
20 ÷ 4 = 5	24 ÷ 3 = 8	20 ÷ 2 = 10
15 ÷ 5 = 3	24 ÷ 4 = 6	30 ÷ 6 = 5
36 ÷ 6 = 6	30 ÷ 10 = 3	25 ÷ 5 = 5
50 ÷ 10 = 5	18 ÷ 2 = 9	32 ÷ 4 = 8
8 ÷ 2 = 4	18 ÷ 3 = 6	27 ÷ 3 = 9
15 ÷ 3 = 5	36 ÷ 4 = 9	16 ÷ 2 = 8
16 ÷ 4 = 4	36 ÷ 6 = 6	42 ÷ 6 = 7
25 ÷ 5 = 5	40 ÷ 5 = 8	5 ÷ 5 = 1
6 ÷ 6 = 1	100 ÷ 10 = 10	4 ÷ 4 = 1
10 ÷ 10 = 1	16 ÷ 4 = 4	28 ÷ 4 = 7
42 ÷ 6 = 7	42 ÷ 6 = 7	14 ÷ 2 = 7
24 ÷ 4 = 6	48 ÷ 6 = 8	24 ÷ 6 = 4
54 ÷ 6 = 9	54 ÷ 6 = 9	18 ÷ 6 = 3
90 ÷ 10 = 9	60 ÷ 6 = 10	54 ÷ 6 = 9
30 ÷ 6 = 5	60 ÷ 10 = 6	60 ÷ 6 = 10
30 ÷ 5 = 6	30 ÷ 6 = 5	40 ÷ 5 = 8

Times tables for division

This page will help you remember times tables by dividing by 2, 3, 4, 5, 6, and 7.

14 ÷ 7 = 2   28 ÷ 7 = 4   70 ÷ 7 = 10

Complete the problems.

21 ÷ 7 = 3	18 ÷ 6 = 3	49 ÷ 7 = 7
35 ÷ 5 = 7	28 ÷ 7 = 4	35 ÷ 5 = 7
14 ÷ 2 = 7	24 ÷ 6 = 4	35 ÷ 7 = 5
18 ÷ 6 = 3	24 ÷ 4 = 6	24 ÷ 6 = 4
20 ÷ 5 = 4	24 ÷ 2 = 12	21 ÷ 3 = 7
15 ÷ 3 = 5	21 ÷ 7 = 3	70 ÷ 7 = 10
36 ÷ 4 = 9	42 ÷ 7 = 6	42 ÷ 7 = 6
56 ÷ 7 = 8	18 ÷ 3 = 6	32 ÷ 4 = 8
18 ÷ 2 = 9	49 ÷ 7 = 7	27 ÷ 3 = 9
15 ÷ 5 = 3	36 ÷ 4 = 9	16 ÷ 4 = 4
49 ÷ 7 = 7	36 ÷ 6 = 6	42 ÷ 6 = 7
25 ÷ 5 = 5	40 ÷ 5 = 8	45 ÷ 5 = 9
7 ÷ 7 = 1	70 ÷ 7 = 10	40 ÷ 4 = 10
63 ÷ 7 = 9	24 ÷ 3 = 8	24 ÷ 3 = 8
42 ÷ 7 = 6	42 ÷ 6 = 7	14 ÷ 7 = 2
24 ÷ 6 = 4	48 ÷ 6 = 8	24 ÷ 4 = 6
54 ÷ 6 = 9	54 ÷ 6 = 9	18 ÷ 3 = 6
28 ÷ 7 = 4	60 ÷ 6 = 10	56 ÷ 7 = 8
30 ÷ 6 = 5	63 ÷ 7 = 9	63 ÷ 7 = 9
35 ÷ 7 = 5	25 ÷ 5 = 5	48 ÷ 6 = 8

Times tables for division

This page will help you remember times tables by dividing by 2, 3, 4, 5, 6, 7, 8, and 9.

16 ÷ 8 = 2   35 ÷ 7 = 5   27 ÷ 9 = 3

Complete the problems.

42 ÷ 6 = 7	81 ÷ 9 = 9	56 ÷ 7 = 8
32 ÷ 8 = 4	56 ÷ 7 = 8	45 ÷ 5 = 9
14 ÷ 7 = 2	72 ÷ 9 = 8	35 ÷ 7 = 5
18 ÷ 9 = 2	24 ÷ 8 = 3	18 ÷ 9 = 2
63 ÷ 7 = 9	27 ÷ 9 = 3	21 ÷ 3 = 7
72 ÷ 9 = 8	72 ÷ 9 = 8	28 ÷ 7 = 4
72 ÷ 8 = 9	42 ÷ 6 = 7	64 ÷ 8 = 8
56 ÷ 7 = 8	27 ÷ 3 = 9	32 ÷ 8 = 4
18 ÷ 6 = 3	14 ÷ 7 = 2	27 ÷ 9 = 3
81 ÷ 9 = 9	36 ÷ 4 = 9	16 ÷ 8 = 2
63 ÷ 9 = 7	36 ÷ 6 = 6	42 ÷ 6 = 7
45 ÷ 5 = 9	48 ÷ 8 = 6	45 ÷ 9 = 5
54 ÷ 9 = 6	21 ÷ 7 = 3	40 ÷ 4 = 10
70 ÷ 7 = 10	24 ÷ 3 = 8	24 ÷ 8 = 3
42 ÷ 7 = 6	40 ÷ 8 = 5	63 ÷ 7 = 9
30 ÷ 5 = 6	45 ÷ 9 = 5	24 ÷ 6 = 4
54 ÷ 6 = 9	54 ÷ 6 = 9	18 ÷ 6 = 3
56 ÷ 8 = 7	42 ÷ 7 = 6	56 ÷ 8 = 7
30 ÷ 5 = 6	63 ÷ 9 = 7	63 ÷ 9 = 7
35 ÷ 7 = 5	50 ÷ 5 = 10	48 ÷ 8 = 6

Times tables practice grids

This is a times tables grid.

X	3	4	5
7	21	28	35
8	24	32	40

Complete each times tables grid.

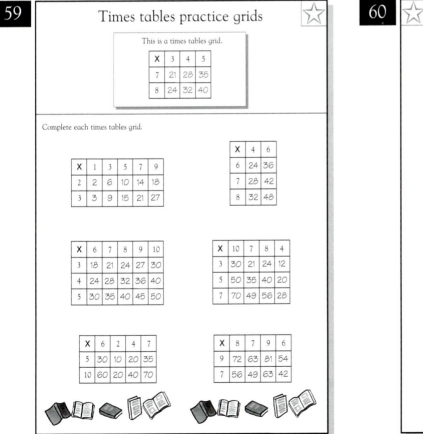

X	1	3	5	7	9
2	2	6	10	14	18
3	3	9	15	21	27

X	4	6
6	24	36
7	28	42
8	32	48

X	6	7	8	9	10
3	18	21	24	27	30
4	24	28	32	36	40
5	30	35	40	45	50

X	10	7	8	4
3	30	21	24	12
5	50	35	40	20
7	70	49	56	28

X	6	2	4	7
5	30	10	20	35
10	60	20	40	70

X	8	7	9	6
9	72	63	81	54
7	56	49	63	42

Times tables practice grids

Here are more times tables grids.

X	2	4	6
5	10	20	30
7	14	28	42

X	8	3	9	2
5	40	15	45	10
6	48	18	54	12
7	56	21	63	14

X	2	3	4	5
8	16	24	32	40
9	18	27	36	45

X	10	9	8	7
6	60	54	48	42
5	50	45	40	35
4	40	36	32	28

X	3	8
2	6	16
3	9	24
4	12	32
5	15	40
6	18	48
7	21	56

X	2	4	6	8
1	2	4	6	8
3	6	12	18	24
5	10	20	30	40
7	14	28	42	56
9	18	36	54	72
0	0	0	0	0

Times tables practice grids

Here are some other times tables grids.

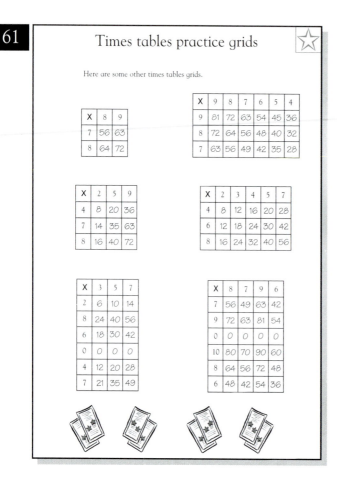

X	8	9
7	56	63
8	64	72

X	9	8	7	6	5	4
9	81	72	63	54	45	36
8	72	64	56	48	40	32
7	63	56	49	42	35	28

X	2	5	9
4	8	20	36
7	14	35	63
8	16	40	72

X	2	3	4	5	7
4	8	12	16	20	28
6	12	18	24	30	42
8	16	24	32	40	56

X	3	5	7
2	6	10	14
8	24	40	56
6	18	30	42
0	0	0	0
4	12	20	28
7	21	35	49

X	8	7	9	6
7	56	49	63	42
9	72	63	81	54
0	0	0	0	0
10	80	70	90	60
8	64	56	72	48
6	48	42	54	36

Speed trials

Try this final test.

27 ÷ 3 = 9	4 x 9 = 36	14 ÷ 2 = 7
7 x 9 = 63	18 ÷ 2 = 9	9 x 9 = 81
64 ÷ 8 = 8	6 x 8 = 48	15 ÷ 3 = 5
90 ÷ 10 = 9	21 ÷ 3 = 7	8 x 8 = 64
6 x 8 = 48	9 x 7 = 63	24 ÷ 4 = 6
45 ÷ 9 = 5	36 ÷ 4 = 9	7 x 8 = 56
3 x 7 = 21	4 x 6 = 24	30 ÷ 5 = 6
9 x 5 = 45	45 ÷ 5 = 9	6 x 6 = 36
48 ÷ 6 = 8	8 x 5 = 40	42 ÷ 6 = 7
7 x 7 = 49	42 ÷ 6 = 7	9 x 5 = 45
3 x 9 = 27	7 x 4 = 28	49 ÷ 7 = 7
56 ÷ 8 = 7	35 ÷ 7 = 5	8 x 6 = 48
36 ÷ 4 = 9	9 x 3 = 27	72 ÷ 8 = 9
24 ÷ 3 = 8	24 ÷ 8 = 3	9 x 7 = 63
36 ÷ 9 = 4	8 x 2 = 16	54 ÷ 9 = 6
6 x 7 = 42	36 ÷ 9 = 4	7 x 6 = 42
4 x 4 = 16	6 x 10 = 60	10 ÷ 10 = 1
32 ÷ 8 = 4	80 ÷ 10 = 8	7 x 7 = 49
49 ÷ 7 = 7	6 x 9 = 54	16 ÷ 8 = 2
25 ÷ 5 = 5	16 ÷ 2 = 8	7 x 9 = 63
56 ÷ 7 = 8	54 ÷ 9 = 6	63 ÷ 7 = 9

Line of symmetry

If a plane figure is cut into two equal parts, the line of the cut is called a line of symmetry.
Draw as many lines of symmetry as you can find on each of these shapes.

Draw a line of symmetry on each of these shapes.

Draw as many lines of symmetry on as you can find on these shapes.

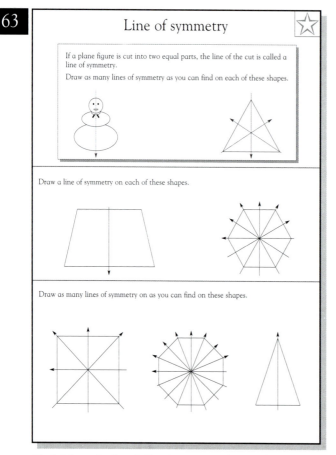

If children find it difficult to see where a line of symmetry falls, talk about where the shape could be folded so that both parts overlap exactly.

Ordering large numbers

Write these numbers in order, starting with the least.

256	9,654,327	39,214	147,243	9,631
256	9,631	39,214	147,243	9,654,327

Write these numbers in order, starting with the least.

72,463	8,730,241	261	5,247	643,292
261	5,247	72,463	643,292	8,730,241
9,641,471	260,453	59,372	657,473	4,290
4,290	59,372	260,453	657,473	9,641,471
327,914	3,647,212	47,900	3,825	416
416	3,825	47,900	327,914	3,647,212
593,103	761	374,239	91,761	1,425
761	1,425	91,761	374,239	593,103
5,600,200	500,200	5,200	50,200	52,000
5,200	50,200	52,000	500,200	5,600,200
6,437	643	64,370	6,430	643,000
643	6,430	6,437	64,370	643,000
9,900	999	900,200	920,200	9,200,000
999	9,900	900,200	920,200	9,200,000

In a country's election O'Neil got 900,550 votes, Schneider got 840,690 votes, Rojas got 8,406,900 votes, Marsalis got 7,964,201 votes and Samperi got 859,999 votes.

Place the candidates in order.

1st ___Rojas___

2nd ___Marsalis___

3rd ___O'Neil___

4th ___Samperi___

5th ___Schneider___

If children are weak on place value, help them identify the significant digits when sorting a group of numbers. Take care when the same digits are used but with different place values.

Rounding whole numbers ☆

Write these numbers to the nearest hundred.

529   500   1687   1,700

If the place to the right of the place we are rounding is 5, round to the number above.

652   700

Round to the nearest hundred.

873	900	295	300	7,348	7,300	3,561	3,600
16,537	16,500	4,855	4,900	569	600	1,200	1,200
22,851	22,900	227	200	782	800	452	500

Round to the nearest ten-thousand.

23,478	20,000	418,700	420,000	58,397	60,000	351,899	350,000
109,544	110,000	31,059	30,000	67,414	70,000	33,500	30,000
89,388	90,000	801,821	800,000	134,800	130,000	45,010	50,000

Round to the nearest ten.

87	90	397	400	52	50	65	70
1,392	1,390	15	20	12,489	12,490	2,861	2,860
75	80	715	720	34	30	18,149	18,150

Round to the nearest thousand.

3,284	3,000	112,810	113,000	10,518	11,000	83,477	83,000
8,499	8,000	225,500	226,000	4,500	5,000	6,112	6,000
1,059	1,000	93,606	94,000	6,752	7,000	2,550	3,000

If children are confused about where to round, help them underline the rounding place and circle the digit to its right– that is the digit to compare to 5.

66

☆ Choosing units of measure

Circle the units that are the closest estimate.

The amount of orange juice in a full glass.

(6 fluid ounces)   4 pints   2 gallons

Circle the units that are the closest estimate.

The weight of a box of cereal	(15 ounces)	3 pounds	2 tons
The length of a football field	20 feet	(100 yards)	1 mile
The area of a rug	90 sq inches	(108 sq feet)	1 sq mile
The amount of cough medicine in a bottle	(3 fluid ounces)	2 cups	1 quart
The distance from home plate to first base	120 inches	(90 feet)	6 yards
The weight of a package of sugar	4 ounces	(5 pounds)	1/2 ton
The length of an airport runway	(2 miles)	50 yards	500 feet
The amount of water in a full pail	8 fluid ounces	2 pints	(3 gallons)
The area of a place mat	(144 sq inches)	6 sq feet	1 sq mile

Children need mental benchmarks for each of the units in order to choose the best unit of measure. Suggest examples, such as the weight of a few raisins for an ounce and the weight of a shoe for a pound.

67

Comparing fractions ☆

Which is greater, $\frac{2}{3}$ or $\frac{3}{4}$? $\frac{3}{4}$

The common denominator of 3 and 4 is 12.

So $\frac{2}{3} = \frac{8}{12}$ and $\frac{3}{4} = \frac{9}{12}$

$\frac{3}{4}$ is greater.

Which is greater?

$\frac{1}{4}$ or $\frac{1}{3}$ $\frac{1}{3}$	$\frac{5}{6}$ or $\frac{7}{9}$ $\frac{5}{6}$	$\frac{1}{2}$ or $\frac{5}{8}$ $\frac{5}{8}$	$\frac{4}{9}$ or $\frac{1}{3}$ $\frac{4}{9}$
$\frac{2}{5}$ or $\frac{3}{8}$ $\frac{2}{5}$	$\frac{7}{10}$ or $\frac{8}{9}$ $\frac{8}{9}$	$\frac{8}{10}$ or $\frac{7}{8}$ $\frac{7}{8}$	$\frac{7}{12}$ or $\frac{2}{3}$ $\frac{2}{3}$
$\frac{2}{3}$ or $\frac{5}{8}$ $\frac{2}{3}$	$\frac{4}{15}$ or $\frac{1}{3}$ $\frac{1}{3}$	$\frac{3}{5}$ or $\frac{2}{3}$ $\frac{2}{3}$	$\frac{3}{8}$ or $\frac{1}{4}$ $\frac{3}{8}$

Which two fractions in each row are equal?

$\frac{1}{4}$	$\frac{4}{8}$	$\frac{3}{12}$	$\frac{7}{8}$	$\frac{5}{8}$	$\frac{1}{4}$ and $\frac{3}{12}$
$\frac{5}{8}$	$\frac{6}{9}$	$\frac{7}{10}$	$\frac{8}{12}$	$\frac{1}{2}$ $\frac{3}{4}$	$\frac{6}{9}$ and $\frac{8}{12}$
$\frac{7}{12}$	$\frac{6}{14}$	$\frac{7}{14}$	$\frac{3}{8}$	$\frac{4}{8}$ $\frac{9}{12}$	$\frac{7}{14}$ and $\frac{4}{8}$
$\frac{3}{8}$	$\frac{3}{9}$	$\frac{2}{6}$	$\frac{4}{7}$	$\frac{9}{10}$ $\frac{6}{7}$	$\frac{3}{9}$ and $\frac{2}{6}$
$\frac{3}{10}$	$\frac{5}{15}$	$\frac{2}{10}$	$\frac{3}{15}$	$\frac{4}{10}$ $\frac{7}{15}$	$\frac{2}{10}$ and $\frac{3}{15}$

Put these fractions in order starting with the least.

$\frac{1}{2}$	$\frac{5}{6}$	$\frac{2}{3}$	$\frac{1}{2}$	$\frac{2}{3}$	$\frac{5}{6}$
$\frac{5}{8}$	$\frac{3}{4}$	$\frac{11}{12}$	$\frac{5}{8}$	$\frac{3}{4}$	$\frac{11}{12}$
$\frac{2}{3}$	$\frac{8}{15}$	$\frac{3}{5}$	$\frac{8}{15}$	$\frac{3}{5}$	$\frac{2}{3}$

Difficulty in finding a common denominator indicates a weakness in times tables knowledge. Children need to convert all the fractions in the later questions into a common form before answering the question. Be careful that they do not try to guess the answer.

☆ Converting fractions to decimals

Convert these fractions to decimals.

$\frac{3}{10} = 0.3$

(because the three goes in the tenths column)

$\frac{7}{100} = 0.07$

(because the seven goes in the hundredths column)

Convert these fractions to decimals.

$\frac{6}{10} = 0.6$	$\frac{9}{100} = 0.09$	$\frac{4}{100} = 0.04$	$\frac{6}{100} = 0.06$
$\frac{4}{10} = 0.4$	$\frac{2}{10} = 0.2$	$\frac{1}{10} = 0.1$	$\frac{7}{100} = 0.07$
$\frac{8}{100} = 0.08$	$\frac{5}{10} = 0.5$	$\frac{7}{10} = 0.7$	$\frac{8}{10} = 0.8$
$\frac{2}{100} = 0.02$	$\frac{5}{100} = 0.05$	$\frac{1}{100} = 0.01$	$\frac{3}{10} = 0.3$

Convert $\frac{1}{4}$ to a decimal.

To do this we have to divide the bottom number into the top.

When we run out of numbers we put in the decimal point and enough zeros to finish the sum. Be careful to keep the decimal point in your answer above the decimal point in the sum.

```
    0.25
4)1.00
    8
    20
    20
     0
```

Convert these fractions to decimals.

$\frac{1}{2} = 0.5$	$\frac{3}{4} = 0.75$	$\frac{2}{5} = 0.4$	$\frac{1}{5} = 0.2$
$\frac{4}{5} = 0.8$	$\frac{3}{8} = 0.375$	$\frac{3}{5} = 0.6$	$\frac{1}{4} = 0.25$

Difficulty in the first section highlights weakness in understanding place value to the first two decimal places. It may be necessary to reinforce understanding of 10ths and 100ths in decimals.

Adding fractions

Work out the answer to the problem.

$\frac{1}{5} + \frac{3}{5} = \frac{4}{5}$ $\frac{4}{9} + \frac{2}{9} = \frac{\cancel{6}}{\cancel{9}_3} = \frac{2}{3}$

Remember to reduce to simplest form if you need to.

Work out the answer to each sum. Reduce to simplest form if you need to.

$\frac{2}{7} + \frac{3}{7} = \frac{5}{7}$ $\frac{2}{9} + \frac{5}{9} = \frac{7}{9}$ $\frac{1}{3} + \frac{1}{3} = \frac{2}{3}$

$\frac{3}{10} + \frac{4}{10} = \frac{7}{10}$ $\frac{1}{8} + \frac{2}{8} = \frac{3}{8}$ $\frac{2}{9} + \frac{3}{9} = \frac{5}{9}$

$\frac{2}{5} + \frac{1}{5} = \frac{3}{5}$ $\frac{1}{7} + \frac{5}{7} = \frac{6}{7}$ $\frac{4}{9} + \frac{1}{9} = \frac{5}{9}$

$\frac{3}{20} + \frac{4}{20} = \frac{7}{20}$ $\frac{3}{100} + \frac{8}{100} = \frac{11}{100}$ $\frac{7}{10} + \frac{2}{10} = \frac{9}{10}$

$\frac{1}{6} + \frac{2}{6} = \frac{3}{6} = \frac{1}{2}$ $\frac{31}{100} + \frac{19}{100} = \frac{50}{100} = \frac{1}{2}$ $\frac{11}{20} + \frac{4}{20} = \frac{15}{20} = \frac{3}{4}$

$\frac{3}{10} + \frac{3}{10} = \frac{6}{10} = \frac{3}{5}$ $\frac{1}{12} + \frac{5}{12} = \frac{6}{12} = \frac{1}{2}$ $\frac{2}{6} + \frac{2}{6} = \frac{4}{6} = \frac{2}{3}$

$\frac{3}{8} + \frac{3}{8} = \frac{6}{8} = \frac{3}{4}$ $\frac{3}{8} + \frac{1}{8} = \frac{4}{8} = \frac{1}{2}$ $\frac{5}{12} + \frac{3}{12} = \frac{8}{12} = \frac{2}{3}$

$\frac{1}{4} + \frac{1}{4} = \frac{2}{4} = \frac{1}{2}$ $\frac{3}{20} + \frac{2}{20} = \frac{5}{20} = \frac{1}{4}$ $\frac{2}{6} + \frac{2}{6} = \frac{4}{6} = \frac{2}{3}$

$\frac{2}{7} + \frac{4}{7} = \frac{6}{7}$ $\frac{2}{9} + \frac{2}{9} = \frac{4}{9}$ $\frac{13}{20} + \frac{5}{20} = \frac{18}{20} = \frac{9}{10}$

$\frac{81}{100} + \frac{9}{100} = \frac{90}{100} = \frac{9}{10}$ $\frac{7}{20} + \frac{6}{20} = \frac{13}{20}$ $\frac{3}{8} + \frac{2}{8} = \frac{5}{8}$

$\frac{6}{10} + \frac{2}{10} = \frac{8}{10} = \frac{4}{5}$ $\frac{29}{100} + \frac{46}{100} = \frac{75}{100} = \frac{3}{4}$ $\frac{73}{100} + \frac{17}{100} = \frac{90}{100} = \frac{9}{10}$

Difficulty in reducing a sum to a simpler form points to a weakness in finding the greatest common factor of the numerator and denominator. Children can reduce the answer in stages, first looking at whether 2 is a common factor, then 3, and so on.

70

Subtracting fractions

Write the answer to each problem.

$\frac{4}{5} - \frac{2}{5} = \frac{2}{5}$ $\frac{8}{9} - \frac{5}{9} = \frac{\cancel{3}}{\cancel{9}_3} = \frac{1}{3}$

Reduce to simplest form if you need to.

Write the answer to each problem. Reduce to simplest form if you need to.

$\frac{3}{5} - \frac{1}{5} = \frac{2}{5}$ $\frac{6}{7} - \frac{3}{7} = \frac{3}{7}$ $\frac{9}{10} - \frac{6}{10} = \frac{3}{10}$

$\frac{7}{10} - \frac{4}{10} = \frac{3}{10}$ $\frac{5}{9} - \frac{4}{9} = \frac{1}{9}$ $\frac{2}{3} - \frac{1}{3} = \frac{1}{3}$

$\frac{7}{8} - \frac{3}{8} = \frac{4}{8} = \frac{1}{2}$ $\frac{14}{20} - \frac{10}{20} = \frac{4}{20} = \frac{1}{5}$ $\frac{5}{6} - \frac{1}{6} = \frac{4}{6} = \frac{2}{3}$

$\frac{11}{12} - \frac{5}{12} = \frac{6}{12} = \frac{1}{2}$ $\frac{17}{20} - \frac{12}{20} = \frac{5}{20} = \frac{1}{4}$ $\frac{9}{12} - \frac{3}{12} = \frac{6}{12} = \frac{1}{2}$

$\frac{8}{10} - \frac{6}{10} = \frac{2}{10} = \frac{1}{5}$ $\frac{12}{12} - \frac{2}{12} = \frac{10}{12} = \frac{5}{6}$ $\frac{9}{10} - \frac{3}{10} = \frac{6}{10} = \frac{3}{5}$

$\frac{8}{9} - \frac{2}{9} = \frac{6}{9} = \frac{2}{3}$ $\frac{7}{8} - \frac{1}{8} = \frac{6}{8} = \frac{3}{4}$ $\frac{9}{12} - \frac{5}{12} = \frac{4}{12} = \frac{1}{3}$

$\frac{3}{4} - \frac{2}{4} = \frac{1}{4}$ $\frac{6}{8} - \frac{3}{8} = \frac{3}{8}$ $\frac{18}{20} - \frac{8}{20} = \frac{10}{20} = \frac{1}{2}$

$\frac{4}{6} - \frac{2}{6} = \frac{2}{6} = \frac{1}{3}$ $\frac{5}{12} - \frac{4}{12} = \frac{1}{12}$ $\frac{3}{8} - \frac{2}{8} = \frac{1}{8}$

$\frac{5}{7} - \frac{1}{7} = \frac{4}{7}$ $\frac{5}{16} - \frac{1}{16} = \frac{4}{16} = \frac{1}{4}$ $\frac{90}{100} - \frac{80}{100} = \frac{10}{100} = \frac{1}{10}$

See the notes on page 69.

71

Adding fractions

Write the answer to each problem.

$\frac{3}{8} + \frac{5}{8} = \frac{8}{8} = 1$ $\frac{3}{4} + \frac{3}{4} = \frac{\cancel{6}}{\cancel{4}_2} = \frac{3}{2} = 1\frac{1}{2}$

Write the answer to each problem.

$\frac{7}{10} + \frac{6}{10} = \frac{13}{10} = 1\frac{3}{10}$ $\frac{6}{7} + \frac{5}{7} = \frac{11}{7} = 1\frac{4}{7}$ $\frac{2}{3} + \frac{2}{3} = \frac{4}{3} = 1\frac{1}{3}$

$\frac{5}{10} + \frac{6}{10} = \frac{11}{10} = 1\frac{1}{10}$ $\frac{8}{13} + \frac{5}{13} = \frac{13}{13} = 1$ $\frac{7}{8} + \frac{4}{8} = \frac{11}{8} = 1\frac{3}{8}$

$\frac{7}{8} + \frac{5}{8} = \frac{12}{8} = \frac{3}{2} = 1\frac{1}{2}$ $\frac{2}{5} + \frac{3}{5} = \frac{5}{5} = 1$ $\frac{5}{8} + \frac{5}{8} = \frac{10}{8} = \frac{5}{4} = 1\frac{1}{4}$

$\frac{10}{20} + \frac{15}{20} = \frac{25}{20} = \frac{5}{4} = 1\frac{1}{4}$ $\frac{2}{3} + \frac{1}{3} = \frac{3}{3} = 1$ $\frac{5}{6} + \frac{5}{6} = \frac{10}{6} = \frac{5}{3} = 1\frac{2}{3}$

$\frac{5}{6} + \frac{3}{6} = \frac{8}{6} = \frac{4}{3} = 1\frac{1}{3}$ $\frac{6}{12} + \frac{7}{12} = \frac{13}{12} = 1\frac{1}{12}$ $\frac{8}{10} + \frac{6}{10} = \frac{14}{10} = \frac{7}{5} = 1\frac{2}{5}$

$\frac{12}{20} + \frac{10}{20} = \frac{22}{20} = \frac{11}{10} = 1\frac{1}{10}$ $\frac{3}{10} + \frac{7}{10} = \frac{10}{10} = 1$ $\frac{75}{100} + \frac{75}{100} = \frac{150}{100} = \frac{3}{2} = 1\frac{1}{2}$

$\frac{10}{20} + \frac{16}{20} = \frac{26}{20} = \frac{13}{10} = 1\frac{3}{10}$ $\frac{4}{5} + \frac{4}{5} = \frac{8}{5} = 1\frac{3}{5}$ $\frac{11}{21} + \frac{17}{21} = \frac{28}{21} = \frac{4}{3} = 1\frac{1}{3}$

If children leave the answer as a fraction or do not reduce it, they are completing only one of the two steps to finding the simplest form. Have them write the answer as a mixed number first, and then reduce the fraction part.

Adding fractions

Write the answer to each problem.

$\frac{2}{3} + \frac{1}{6} = \frac{4}{6} + \frac{1}{6} = \frac{5}{6}$ $\frac{3}{4} + \frac{5}{6} = \frac{9}{12} + \frac{10}{12} = \frac{19}{12} = 1\frac{7}{12}$

Work out the answer to each problem. Rename as a mixed number if you need to.

$\frac{2}{5} + \frac{7}{10} = \frac{4}{10} + \frac{7}{10} = \frac{11}{10} = 1\frac{1}{10}$ $\frac{3}{4} + \frac{7}{10} = \frac{15}{20} + \frac{14}{20} = \frac{29}{20} = 1\frac{9}{20}$

$\frac{1}{4} + \frac{5}{6} = \frac{3}{12} + \frac{10}{12} = \frac{13}{12} = 1\frac{1}{12}$ $\frac{3}{4} + \frac{7}{8} = \frac{6}{8} + \frac{7}{8} = \frac{13}{8} = 1\frac{5}{8}$

$\frac{2}{3} + \frac{1}{4} = \frac{8}{12} + \frac{3}{12} = \frac{11}{12}$ $\frac{5}{6} + \frac{11}{12} = \frac{10}{12} + \frac{11}{12} = \frac{21}{12} = 1\frac{3}{4}$

$\frac{5}{7} + \frac{3}{14} = \frac{10}{14} + \frac{3}{14} = \frac{13}{14}$ $\frac{5}{8} + \frac{7}{10} = \frac{25}{40} + \frac{28}{40} = \frac{53}{40} = 1\frac{13}{40}$

$\frac{3}{4} + \frac{3}{5} = \frac{15}{20} + \frac{12}{20} = \frac{27}{20} = 1\frac{7}{20}$ $\frac{1}{2} + \frac{5}{9} = \frac{9}{18} + \frac{10}{18} = \frac{19}{18} = 1\frac{1}{18}$

$\frac{2}{3} + \frac{7}{9} = \frac{6}{9} + \frac{7}{9} = \frac{13}{9} = 1\frac{4}{9}$ $\frac{1}{3} + \frac{7}{8} = \frac{8}{24} + \frac{21}{24} = \frac{29}{24} = 1\frac{5}{24}$

$\frac{3}{8} + \frac{1}{6} = \frac{9}{24} + \frac{4}{24} = \frac{13}{24}$ $\frac{2}{3} + \frac{4}{5} = \frac{10}{15} + \frac{12}{15} = \frac{22}{15} = 1\frac{7}{15}$

$\frac{4}{5} + \frac{5}{6} = \frac{24}{30} + \frac{25}{30} = \frac{49}{30} = 1\frac{19}{30}$ $\frac{2}{3} + \frac{3}{10} = \frac{20}{30} + \frac{9}{30} = \frac{29}{30}$

Difficulty in finding a common denominator indicates a weakness in finding the least common multiple of two numbers. Children can always find a common denominator by multiplying the given denominators.

73

Subtracting fractions

Work out the answer to the problems.

$$\frac{7}{9} - \frac{1}{3} = \frac{7}{9} - \frac{3}{9} = \frac{4}{9} \qquad \frac{7}{10} - \frac{3}{8} = \frac{28}{40} - \frac{15}{40} = \frac{13}{40}$$

Work out the answer to each problem. Reduce to the simplest form if you need to.

$\frac{5}{8} - \frac{1}{2} = \frac{5}{8} - \frac{4}{8} = \frac{1}{8}$ $\qquad$ $\frac{5}{6} - \frac{1}{4} = \frac{10}{12} - \frac{3}{12} = \frac{7}{12}$

$\frac{9}{10} - \frac{3}{8} = \frac{36}{40} - \frac{15}{40} = \frac{21}{40}$ $\qquad$ $\frac{9}{10} - \frac{5}{8} = \frac{36}{40} - \frac{25}{40} = \frac{11}{40}$

$\frac{6}{7} - \frac{2}{5} = \frac{30}{35} - \frac{14}{35} = \frac{16}{35}$ $\qquad$ $\frac{11}{12} - \frac{1}{6} = \frac{11}{12} - \frac{2}{12} = \frac{9}{12} = \frac{3}{4}$

$\frac{7}{12} - \frac{1}{6} = \frac{7}{12} - \frac{2}{12} = \frac{5}{12}$ $\qquad$ $\frac{7}{10} - \frac{1}{4} = \frac{28}{40} - \frac{10}{40} = \frac{18}{40} = \frac{9}{20}$

$\frac{5}{9} - \frac{1}{3} = \frac{5}{9} - \frac{3}{9} = \frac{2}{9}$ $\qquad$ $\frac{7}{9} - \frac{1}{4} = \frac{28}{36} - \frac{9}{36} = \frac{19}{36}$

$\frac{7}{16} - \frac{1}{8} = \frac{7}{16} - \frac{2}{16} = \frac{5}{16}$ $\qquad$ $\frac{3}{7} - \frac{1}{5} = \frac{15}{35} - \frac{7}{35} = \frac{8}{35}$

$\frac{3}{8} - \frac{1}{6} = \frac{9}{24} - \frac{4}{24} = \frac{5}{24}$ $\qquad$ $\frac{3}{5} - \frac{1}{4} = \frac{12}{20} - \frac{5}{20} = \frac{7}{20}$

$\frac{2}{3} - \frac{1}{2} = \frac{4}{6} - \frac{3}{6} = \frac{1}{6}$ $\qquad$ $\frac{4}{5} - \frac{1}{4} = \frac{16}{20} - \frac{5}{20} = \frac{11}{20}$

See the notes on page 72.

74

Adding mixed numbers

Work out the answer to each problem.

$$8\frac{10}{30} + 1\frac{3}{30} = 9\frac{13}{30} = 9\frac{13}{30} \qquad 3\frac{1}{4} + 1\frac{1}{6} = 3\frac{3}{12} + 1\frac{2}{12} = 4\frac{5}{12}$$

Work out the answer to each problem.

$2\frac{1}{8} + 3\frac{3}{8} = 5\frac{4}{8} = 5\frac{1}{2}$ $\qquad$ $3\frac{5}{6} + 1\frac{1}{8} = 3\frac{20}{24} + 1\frac{3}{24} = 4\frac{23}{24}$

$3\frac{3}{4} + 2\frac{1}{16} = 3\frac{12}{16} + 2\frac{1}{16} = 5\frac{13}{16}$ $\qquad$ $1\frac{2}{3} + 3\frac{2}{7} = 1\frac{14}{21} + 3\frac{6}{21} = 4\frac{20}{21}$

$4\frac{1}{4} + 2\frac{1}{6} = 4\frac{3}{12} + 2\frac{2}{12} = 6\frac{5}{12}$ $\qquad$ $6\frac{1}{6} + 3\frac{2}{9} = 6\frac{3}{18} + 3\frac{4}{18} = 9\frac{7}{18}$

$7\frac{5}{6} + 2\frac{1}{10} = 7\frac{25}{30} + 2\frac{3}{30} = 9\frac{28}{30} = 9\frac{14}{15}$ $\qquad$ $1\frac{7}{12} + 4\frac{1}{12} = 5\frac{8}{12} = 5\frac{2}{3}$

$5\frac{1}{4} + 3\frac{2}{5} = 5\frac{4}{20} + 3\frac{8}{20} = 8\frac{12}{20} = 8\frac{3}{5}$ $\qquad$ $3\frac{3}{8} + 1\frac{1}{4} = 3\frac{3}{8} + 1\frac{2}{8} = 4\frac{5}{8}$

$6\frac{1}{4} + 2\frac{1}{4} = 8\frac{2}{4} = 8\frac{1}{2}$ $\qquad$ $6\frac{2}{3} + 3\frac{1}{10} = 6\frac{20}{30} + 3\frac{3}{30} = 9\frac{23}{30}$

$7\frac{1}{3} + 1\frac{2}{9} = 7\frac{3}{9} + 1\frac{2}{9} = 8\frac{5}{9}$ $\qquad$ $2\frac{2}{5} + 1\frac{3}{10} = 2\frac{4}{10} + 1\frac{3}{10} = 3\frac{7}{10}$

A common error is forgetting to recopy the whole number when renaming the mixed numbers. Children can recopy both whole numbers first, then rename the two fractions.

75

Subtracting mixed numbers

Work out the answer to the problems.

$$2\frac{7}{8} - 1\frac{5}{8} = 1\frac{2}{8} = 1\frac{1}{4} \qquad 9\frac{9}{10} - 6\frac{5}{8} = 9\frac{36}{40} - 6\frac{25}{40} = 3\frac{11}{40}$$

Work out the answer to each problem.

$7\frac{3}{8} - 3\frac{1}{8} = 4\frac{2}{8} = 4\frac{1}{4}$ $\qquad$ $2\frac{14}{15} - 1\frac{4}{9} = 2\frac{42}{45} - 1\frac{20}{45} = 1\frac{22}{45}$

$2\frac{2}{3} - 1\frac{1}{6} = 2\frac{4}{6} - 1\frac{1}{6} = 1\frac{3}{6} = 1\frac{1}{2}$ $\qquad$ $6\frac{4}{5} - 2\frac{1}{2} = 6\frac{8}{10} - 2\frac{5}{10} = 4\frac{3}{10}$

$5\frac{11}{20} - 2\frac{1}{8} = 5\frac{22}{40} - 2\frac{5}{40} = 3\frac{17}{40}$ $\qquad$ $8\frac{11}{12} - 5\frac{5}{12} = 3\frac{6}{12} = 3\frac{1}{2}$

$9\frac{7}{9} - 3\frac{4}{6} = 9\frac{14}{18} - 3\frac{12}{18} = 6\frac{2}{18} = 6\frac{1}{9}$ $\qquad$ $4\frac{7}{8} - 2\frac{1}{4} = 4\frac{7}{8} - 2\frac{2}{8} = 2\frac{5}{8}$

$8\frac{2}{5} - 4\frac{1}{4} = 8\frac{8}{20} - 4\frac{5}{20} = 4\frac{3}{20}$ $\qquad$ $4\frac{5}{6} - 3\frac{1}{4} = 4\frac{10}{12} - 3\frac{3}{12} = 1\frac{7}{12}$

$4\frac{2}{3} - 1\frac{2}{3} = 3\frac{0}{3} = 3$ $\qquad$ $9\frac{8}{9} - 3\frac{3}{4} = 9\frac{32}{36} - 3\frac{27}{36} = 6\frac{5}{36}$

$3\frac{8}{15} - 2\frac{2}{5} = 3\frac{8}{15} - 2\frac{6}{15} = 1\frac{2}{15}$ $\qquad$ $2\frac{7}{9} - 1\frac{1}{5} = 2\frac{35}{45} - 1\frac{9}{45} = 1\frac{26}{45}$

See the notes on page 74.

Adding mixed numbers and fractions

Work out the answer to the problems.

$$4\frac{3}{4} + \frac{3}{4} = 4\frac{6}{4} = 5\frac{2}{4} = 5\frac{1}{2} \qquad 3\frac{1}{2} + \frac{2}{3} = 3\frac{3}{6} + \frac{4}{6} = 3\frac{7}{6} = 4\frac{1}{6}$$

Work out the answer to each problem.

$6\frac{2}{3} + \frac{2}{3} = 6\frac{4}{3} = 7\frac{1}{3}$ $\qquad$ $4\frac{1}{4} + \frac{7}{8} = 4\frac{2}{8} + \frac{7}{8} = 4\frac{9}{8} = 5\frac{1}{8}$

$4\frac{5}{8} + \frac{7}{8} = 4\frac{12}{8} = 5\frac{1}{2}$ $\qquad$ $3\frac{7}{10} + \frac{1}{2} = 3\frac{7}{10} + \frac{5}{10} = 3\frac{12}{10} = 4\frac{1}{5}$

$2\frac{3}{7} + \frac{8}{7} = 2\frac{11}{7} = 3\frac{4}{7}$ $\qquad$ $1\frac{1}{2} + \frac{3}{4} = 1\frac{2}{4} + \frac{3}{4} = 1\frac{5}{4} = 2\frac{1}{4}$

$3\frac{5}{6} + \frac{2}{3} = 3\frac{5}{6} + \frac{4}{6} = 3\frac{9}{6} = 4\frac{1}{2}$ $\qquad$ $5\frac{3}{4} + \frac{4}{5} = 5\frac{15}{20} + \frac{16}{20} = 5\frac{31}{20} = 6\frac{11}{20}$

$3\frac{7}{8} + \frac{1}{4} = 3\frac{7}{8} + \frac{2}{8} = 3\frac{9}{8} = 4\frac{1}{8}$ $\qquad$ $3\frac{6}{7} + \frac{3}{4} = 3\frac{24}{28} + \frac{21}{28} = 3\frac{45}{28} = 4\frac{17}{28}$

$7\frac{7}{8} + \frac{1}{4} = 7\frac{7}{8} + \frac{2}{8} = 7\frac{9}{8} = 8\frac{1}{8}$ $\qquad$ $4\frac{2}{3} + \frac{5}{8} = 4\frac{16}{24} + \frac{15}{24} = 4\frac{31}{24} = 5\frac{7}{24}$

$1\frac{9}{10} + \frac{2}{5} = 1\frac{9}{10} + \frac{4}{10} = 1\frac{13}{10} = 2\frac{3}{10}$ $\qquad$ $8\frac{5}{6} + \frac{3}{5} = 8\frac{25}{30} + \frac{18}{30} = 8\frac{43}{30} = 9\frac{13}{30}$

The most difficult step is renaming the answer as a proper mixed number. If children have trouble, get them to first rename the fractional part as a mixed number, and then add the 1 from this mixed number to the other whole-number part.

Simple use of parentheses ☆

Work out these problems.
$(4 + 6) - (2 + 1) =$ | $10 - 3 = 7$
$(2 \times 5) + (10 - 4) =$ | $10 + 6 = 16$
Remember to work out the parentheses first.

Work out these problems.
$(5 + 3) + (6 - 2) =$ | 12 $(3 - 1) + (12 - 1) =$ | 13
$(6 - 1) - (1 + 2) =$ | 2 $(9 + 5) - (3 + 6) =$ | 5
$(8 + 3) + (12 - 2) =$ | 21 $(14 + 12) - (9 + 4) =$ | 13
$(7 - 2) + (4 + 5) =$ | 14 $(9 - 3) - (4 + 2) =$ | 0

Now try these longer problems.
$(5 + 9) + (12 - 2) - (4 + 3) =$ | 17
$(10 + 5) - (2 + 4) + (9 + 6) =$ | 24
$(19 + 4) - (3 + 2) - (2 + 1) =$ | 15
$(24 - 5) - (3 + 7) - (5 - 2) =$ | 6
$(15 + 3) + (7 - 2) - (5 + 7) =$ | 11

Now try these. Be careful, the parentheses now have multiplication problems.
$(2 \times 3) + (5 \times 2) =$ | 16 $(3 \times 4) - (2 \times 2) =$ | 8
$(7 \times 2) + (3 \times 3) =$ | 23 $(5 \times 4) - (3 \times 2) =$ | 14
$(6 \times 4) - (4 \times 3) =$ | 12 $(9 \times 5) - (4 \times 6) =$ | 21
$(12 \times 4) - (8 \times 3) =$ | 24 $(7 \times 4) - (8 \times 2) =$ | 12

If the answer is 24, which of these problems gives the correct answer? Write the correct letter.
a $(3 + 5) + (3 \times 1)$ c $(3 \times 5) + (3 \times 3)$ e $(5 \times 7) - (2 \times 5)$
b $(3 \times 5) + (3 \times 2)$ d $(2 \times 5) + (2 \times 6)$ f $(6 + 7) + (12 - 2)$
(c)

Errors on this page will most likely be the result of choosing the wrong order of operation. Remind children that they must work out the brackets first, before they add or subtract the results. Concentration and careful reading should prevent any problems.

78

☆ Simple use of parentheses

Work out these problems.
$(3 + 2) \times (4 + 1) =$ | $5 \times 5 = 25$
$(10 \times 5) \div (10 - 5) =$ | $50 \div 5 = 10$
Remember to work out the parentheses first.

Work out these problems.
$(7 + 3) \times (8 - 4) =$ | 40 $(5 - 2) \times (8 - 1) =$ | 21
$(9 + 5) \div (1 + 6) =$ | 2 $(14 - 6) \times (4 + 3) =$ | 56
$(14 + 4) \div (12 - 6) =$ | 3 $(9 + 21) \div (8 - 5) =$ | 10
$(11 - 5) \times (7 + 5) =$ | 72 $(8 + 20) \div (12 - 10) =$ | 14
$(6 + 9) \div (8 - 3) =$ | 3 $(14 - 3) \times (6 + 1) =$ | 77
$(10 + 10) \div (2 + 3) =$ | 4 $(9 + 3) \times (2 + 4) =$ | 72

Now try these.
$(4 \times 3) \div (1 \times 2) =$ | 6 $(5 \times 4) \div (2 \times 2) =$ | 5
$(8 \times 5) \div (4 \times 1) =$ | 10 $(6 \times 4) \div (3 \times 4) =$ | 2
$(2 \times 4) \times (2 \times 3) =$ | 48 $(3 \times 5) \times (1 \times 2) =$ | 30
$(8 \times 4) \div (2 \times 2) =$ | 8 $(6 \times 4) \div (4 \times 2) =$ | 3

If the answer is 30, which of these problems gives the correct answer?
a $(3 \times 5) \times (2 \times 2)$ d $(20 \div 2) \times (12 \div 3)$
b $(4 \times 5) \times (5 \times 2)$ e $(5 \times 12) \div (2 \times 5)$
c $(12 \times 5) \div (8 \div 4)$ f $(9 \times 5) \div (10 \div 2)$ c

If the answer is 8, which of these problems gives the correct answer?
a $(16 \div 2) \div (2 \times 1)$ d $(24 \div 6) \times (8 \div 4)$
b $(9 \div 3) \times (3 \times 2)$ e $(8 \div 4) \times (8 \div 1)$
c $(12 \times 4) \div (6 \times 2)$ f $(16 \div 4) \times (20 \div 4)$ d

This page continues the work of the previous page, but the brackets are multiplied or divided. It may be necessary to remind children to read carefully, as several operations take place in each equation.

Simple use of parentheses ☆

Work out these problems.
$(5 + 3) + (9 - 2) =$ | $8 + 7 = 15$
$(5 + 2) - (4 - 1) =$ | $7 - 3 = 4$
$(4 + 2) \times (3 + 1) =$ | $6 \times 4 = 24$
$(3 \times 5) \div (9 - 6) =$ | $15 \div 3 = 5$
Remember to work out the parentheses first.

Work out these problems.
$(5 + 4) + (7 - 3) =$ | 13 $(9 - 2) + (6 + 4) =$ | 17
$(7 + 3) - (9 - 7) =$ | 8 $(15 - 5) + (2 + 3) =$ | 15
$(11 \times 2) - (3 \times 2) =$ | 16 $(15 \div 3) + (9 \times 2) =$ | 23
$(12 \times 2) - (3 \times 3) =$ | 15 $(6 \div 2) + (8 \times 2) =$ | 19
$(9 \times 3) - (7 \times 3) =$ | 6 $(15 \div 5) + (3 \times 4) =$ | 15
$(20 \div 5) - (8 \div 2) =$ | 0 $(5 \times 10) - (12 \times 4) =$ | 2

Now try these.
$(4 + 8) \div (3 \times 2) =$ | 2 $(6 \times 4) \div (3 \times 2) =$ | 4
$(9 + 5) \div (2 \times 1) =$ | 7 $(7 \times 4) \div (3 + 4) =$ | 4
$(3 + 6) \times (3 \times 3) =$ | 81 $(5 \times 5) \div (10 \div 2) =$ | 5
$(24 \div 2) \times (3 \times 2) =$ | 72 $(8 \times 6) \div (2 \times 12) =$ | 2

Write down the letters of all the problems that make 25.
a $(2 \times 5) \times (3 \times 2)$ d $(40 \div 2) + (10 \div 2)$
b $(5 \times 5) + (7 - 2)$ e $(10 \times 5) - (5 \times 5)$
c $(6 \times 5) - (10 \div 2)$ f $(10 \times 10) \div (10 - 6)$ c, d, e, f

Write down the letters of all the problems that make 20.
a $(10 \div 2) \times (4 \div 4)$ d $(20 \div 4) \times (8 \div 2)$
b $(7 \times 3) - (3 \div 3)$ e $(10 \div 2) + (20 \div 2)$
c $(8 \times 4) - (6 \times 2)$ f $(14 \div 2) + (2 \times 7)$ b, c

This page reinforces all the elements of the previous two pages. Again, the most likely cause of error will be lack of concentration.

☆ Multiplying decimals

Work out these problems.

¹4.6	⁴3.9	³8.4
$\times$ 3	$\times$ 5	$\times$ 8
13.8	19.5	67.2

Work out these problems.

4.7	9.1	5.8	1.7	5.1
$\times$ 3	$\times$ 3	$\times$ 3	$\times$ 2	$\times$ 2
14.1	27.3	17.4	3.4	10.2

7.4	3.6	6.5	4.2	3.8
$\times$ 2	$\times$ 4	$\times$ 4	$\times$ 2	$\times$ 2
14.8	14.4	26.0	8.4	7.6

4.2	4.7	1.8	3.4	3.7
$\times$ 4	$\times$ 4	$\times$ 5	$\times$ 5	$\times$ 5
16.8	18.8	9.0	17.0	18.5

2.5	2.4	5.3	7.2	5.1
$\times$ 5	$\times$ 6	$\times$ 7	$\times$ 8	$\times$ 9
12.5	14.4	37.1	57.6	45.9

7.9	8.6	8.8	7.5	9.9
$\times$ 9	$\times$ 9	$\times$ 8	$\times$ 8	$\times$ 6
71.1	77.4	70.4	60.0	59.4

6.8	5.7	6.9	7.5	8.4
$\times$ 7	$\times$ 6	$\times$ 7	$\times$ 9	$\times$ 9
47.6	34.2	48.3	67.5	75.6

7.3	2.8	3.8	7.7	9.4
$\times$ 8	$\times$ 7	$\times$ 8	$\times$ 7	$\times$ 9
58.4	19.6	30.4	53.9	84.6

Ensure that children work from right to left. Problems will highlight gaps in their knowledge of times tables. Remind them that the number they are multiplying has one decimal place, so their answer must have one decimal place also, and this can be put in at the end.

Multiplying decimals

Work out these problems.

$$\begin{array}{r} \overset{1\,1}{37.5} \\ \times\ \ 2 \\ \hline 75.0 \end{array} \quad \begin{array}{r} \overset{3\,1}{26.2} \\ \times\ \ 5 \\ \hline 131.0 \end{array} \quad \begin{array}{r} \overset{4\,2}{65.3} \\ \times\ \ 9 \\ \hline 587.7 \end{array}$$

Work out these problems.

53.3 × 2 = 106.6	93.2 × 2 = 186.4	51.4 × 2 = 102.8	34.6 × 3 = 103.8	35.2 × 3 = 105.6
46.5 × 4 = 186.0	25.8 × 4 = 103.2	16.4 × 3 = 49.2	47.1 × 5 = 235.5	37.4 × 5 = 187.0
12.4 × 5 = 62.0	46.3 × 5 = 231.5	17.5 × 6 = 105.0	36.5 × 6 = 219.0	72.4 × 7 = 506.8
37.5 × 7 = 262.5	20.3 × 7 = 142.1	73.4 × 7 = 513.8	92.6 × 6 = 555.6	47.9 × 6 = 287.4
53.9 × 8 = 431.2	75.6 × 8 = 604.8	28.8 × 8 = 230.4	79.4 × 8 = 635.2	99.9 × 9 = 899.1
37.9 × 9 = 341.1	14.8 × 9 = 133.2	35.4 × 9 = 318.6	46.8 × 8 = 374.4	27.2 × 7 = 190.4
39.5 × 6 = 237.0	84.2 × 9 = 757.8	68.5 × 8 = 548.0	73.2 × 9 = 658.8	47.6 × 6 = 285.6

This page further revises decimal multiplication, using larger numbers.

82

Real-life problems

Carlos earns $3.50 a day on his paper route. How much does he earn per week?

$24.50

$$\begin{array}{r} \overset{3}{\$3.50} \\ \times\ \ 7 \\ \hline \$24.50 \end{array}$$

When Chanté subtracts the width of her closet from the length of her bedroom wall she finds she has 3.65 m of wall space left. If the closet is 0.87 m wide, what is the length of her bedroom wall?

4.52 m

$$\begin{array}{r} \overset{1\,1}{3.65} \\ +\ 0.87 \\ \hline 4.52 \end{array}$$

Sophie buys her mother a bunch of flowers for $12.95 and her brothers some candy for $2.76. If she has $7.83 left, how much did she start with?

$23.54

$$\begin{array}{r} \overset{1\ 1}{12.95} \\ +\ 2.76 \\ \hline 15.71 \end{array} \quad \begin{array}{r} \overset{1\,1}{15.71} \\ +\ 7.83 \\ \hline 23.54 \end{array}$$

If Pedro were 7.5 cm taller, he would be twice as tall as Ian. Ian is 74.25 cm tall, so how tall is Pedro?

141 cm (1.41 m)

$$\begin{array}{r} \overset{1}{74.25} \\ \times\ \ 2 \\ \hline 148.50 \end{array} \quad \begin{array}{r} 148.5 \\ -\ \ 7.5 \\ \hline 141.0 \end{array}$$

Sasha is making some shelves which are 75.5 cm long. If the wood she is using is 180 cm long, how many pieces will she need to make six shelves?

3 pieces

75.5 × 2 = 151
Sasha can make 2 shelves per piece of wood with some wastage.
6 ÷ 2 = 3

A café uses 27.5 quarts of milk a day. If they have a weekly delivery of 180 quarts, how much will they have left after six days?

15 quarts

$$\begin{array}{r} \overset{4\ 3}{27.5} \\ \times\ \ 6 \\ \hline 165.0 \end{array} \quad \begin{array}{r} \overset{7\,10}{18\cancel{0}} \\ -165 \\ \hline 15 \end{array}$$

Charles has 12.5 m of railway track. Gavin has 8.6 m and Kristy has 4.8 m. If they put their track together how long will their layout be?

25.9 m

$$\begin{array}{r} \overset{1\,1}{12.5} \\ 8.6 \\ +\ \ 4.8 \\ \hline 25.9 \end{array}$$

This page provides an opportunity to apply math skills to real-life problems. Children will need to choose the operation carefully. Some questions require more than one operation.

83

Real-life problems

A novelist writes 9.5 pages of his book a day. How many pages will he write in nine days?

85.5 pages

$$\begin{array}{r} \overset{4}{9.5} \\ \times\ \ 9 \\ \hline 85.5 \end{array}$$

After driving 147.7 mi a driver stops at a service station. If he has another 115.4 mi to go, how long will his trip be?

263.1 mi

$$\begin{array}{r} \overset{1\,1}{147.7} \\ +\ 115.4 \\ \hline 263.1 \end{array}$$

Mr. Mayfield divides his money equally among four separate banks. If he has $98.65 in each bank, what is the total of his savings?

$394.60

$$\begin{array}{r} \overset{3\ 2\ 2}{98.65} \\ \times\ \ 4 \\ \hline 394.60 \end{array}$$

Mrs. Eldon buys two bottles of perfume; one contains 48.5 ml and the other contains 150.5 ml. How much more perfume is in the larger of the two bottles?

102 ml

$$\begin{array}{r} \overset{4\ 10}{15\cancel{0}.5} \\ -\ 48.5 \\ \hline 102.0 \end{array}$$

A teacher spends 5.75 minutes grading each story. How long would it take to grade eight stories?

46 minutes

$$\begin{array}{r} \overset{6\ 4}{5.75} \\ \times\ \ 8 \\ \hline 46.00 \end{array}$$

Eight tiles, each 15.75 cm wide, fit exactly across the width of the bathroom wall. How wide is the bathroom wall?

126 cm (1.26 m)

$$\begin{array}{r} \overset{4\ 6\ 4}{15.75} \\ \times\ \ 8 \\ \hline 126.00 \end{array}$$

Terry has $8.50. If he spends $1.05 a day over the next seven days, how much will he have left at the end of the seven days?

$1.15

$$\begin{array}{r} \overset{3}{1.05} \\ \times\ \ 7 \\ \hline 7.35 \end{array} \quad \begin{array}{r} \overset{4\ 10}{8.\cancel{5}\cancel{0}} \\ -\ 7.35 \\ \hline 1.15 \end{array}$$

A shop sells 427.56 kg of loose peanuts the first week and 246.94 kg the second week. How much did they sell over the two weeks?

674.5 kg

$$\begin{array}{r} \overset{1\ 1\ 1}{427.56} \\ +\ 246.94 \\ \hline 674.50 \end{array}$$

This page also revises various operations applied to real-life situations.

Real-life problems

In a class of 30 children, 6 children are painting. What percent of children are painting?

$\frac{6}{30}$ of the children are painting and to change a fraction to a percent we multiply by 100.

20%

$$\frac{\cancel{6}}{\cancel{30}} \times 100 = 20$$

40% of a class is made up of girls. If there are 12 girls, how many children are in the class?

If 12 girls are 40% of the class, we divide 12 by 40 to find 1%. Then we multiply by 100 to find 100%.

30 children

$$\frac{\cancel{12}}{\cancel{40}} \times 100 = 30$$

A shop has 60 books by a new author. If the shop sells 45 books, what percent does it sell?

75%

$$\frac{\cancel{45}}{\cancel{60}} \times 100 = 75$$

A school disco sells 65% of its tickets. If it had 120 tickets to start with, how many has it sold?

78 tickets

$$\frac{\cancel{120}}{\cancel{100}} \times 65 = 78$$

200 people go on a school trip. If 14% are adults, how many children go on the trip?

172 children

$$100 - 14 = 86\%$$
$$\frac{\cancel{200}}{\cancel{100}} \times 86 = 172$$

A shop sells 150 T-shirts but 12 are returned because they are faulty. What percent of the T-shirts was faulty?

8%

$$\frac{\cancel{12}}{\cancel{150}} \times 100 = 8$$

A group of 120 children are asked their favorite colors.

15% like red. How many children like red? **18**

$$\frac{\cancel{120}}{\cancel{100}} \times 15 = 18$$

20% like green. How many children like green? **24**

$$\frac{\cancel{120}}{\cancel{100}} \times 20 = 24$$

30% like yellow. How many children like yellow? **36**

$$\frac{\cancel{120}}{\cancel{100}} \times 30 = 36$$

35% like blue. How many children like blue? **42**

$$\frac{\cancel{120}}{\cancel{100}} \times 35 = 42$$

In questions 1 and 4, children should see that the answer can be expressed as a fraction, which can then be converted to a percentage by multiplying by 100.

85

Conversions: length ☆

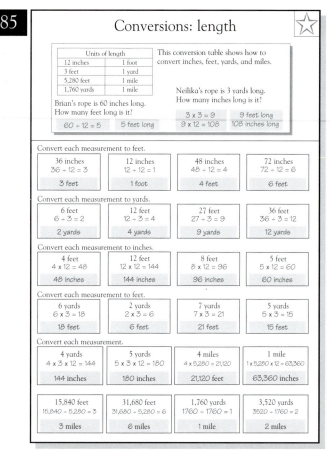

Units of length	
12 inches	1 foot
3 feet	1 yard
5,280 feet	1 mile
1,760 yards	1 mile

This conversion table shows how to convert inches, feet, yards, and miles.

Brian's rope is 60 inches long. How many feet long is it?
60 ÷ 12 = 5 → 5 feet long

Neilika's rope is 3 yards long. How many inches long is it?
3 x 3 = 9 → 9 feet long
9 x 12 = 108 → 108 inches long

Convert each measurement to feet.

36 inches
36 ÷ 12 = 3 → **3 feet**

12 inches
12 ÷ 12 = 1 → **1 foot**

48 inches
48 ÷ 12 = 4 → **4 feet**

72 inches
72 ÷ 12 = 6 → **6 feet**

Convert each measurement to yards.

6 feet
6 ÷ 3 = 2 → **2 yards**

12 feet
12 ÷ 3 = 4 → **4 yards**

27 feet
27 ÷ 3 = 9 → **9 yards**

36 feet
36 ÷ 3 = 12 → **12 yards**

Convert each measurement to inches.

4 feet
4 x 12 = 48 → **48 inches**

12 feet
12 x 12 = 144 → **144 inches**

8 feet
8 x 12 = 96 → **96 inches**

5 feet
5 x 12 = 60 → **60 inches**

Convert each measurement to feet.

6 yards
6 x 3 = 18 → **18 feet**

2 yards
2 x 3 = 6 → **6 feet**

7 yards
7 x 3 = 21 → **21 feet**

5 yards
5 x 3 = 15 → **15 feet**

Convert each measurement.

4 yards
4 x 3 x 12 = 144 → **144 inches**

5 yards
5 x 3 x 12 = 180 → **180 inches**

4 miles
4 x 5,280 = 21,120 → **21,120 feet**

1 mile
1 x 5,280 x 12 = 63,360 → **63,360 inches**

15,840 feet
15,840 ÷ 5,280 = 3 → **3 miles**

31,680 feet
31,680 ÷ 5,280 = 6 → **6 miles**

1,760 yards
1760 ÷ 1760 = 1 → **1 mile**

3,520 yards
3520 ÷ 1760 = 2 → **2 miles**

If children are confused whether to multiply or divide, have them think about whether the new unit is a longer or a shorter unit. If the unit is longer, there will be fewer of them, so division will be the appropriate operation to use.

86

☆ Conversions: capacity

Units of capacity	
8 fluid ounces	1 cup
2 cups	1 pint
2 pints	1 quart
4 quarts	1 gallon

This conversion table shows how to convert ounces, cups pints, quarts, and gallons.

Katya's thermos holds 8 pints. How many cups does it hold?
8 x 2 = 16 → 16 cups

Hannah's thermos holds 6 cups. How many pints does it hold?
6 ÷ 2 = 3 → 3 pints

Convert each measurement to cups.

32 fluid ounces
32 ÷ 8 = 4 → **4 cups**

16 fluid ounces
16 ÷ 8 = 2 → **2 cups**

96 fluid ounces
96 ÷ 8 = 12 → **12 cups**

80 fluid ounces
80 ÷ 8 = 10 → **10 cups**

Convert each measurement to pints.

6 cups
6 ÷ 2 = 3 → **3 pints**

12 cups
12 ÷ 2 = 6 → **6 pints**

36 cups
36 ÷ 2 = 18 → **18 pints**

50 cups
50 ÷ 2 = 25 → **25 pints**

4 quarts
4 x 2 = 8 → **8 pints**

12 quarts
12 x 2 = 24 → **24 pints**

30 quarts
30 x 2 = 60 → **60 pints**

6 quarts
6 x 2 = 12 → **12 pints**

Convert each measurement to gallons.

16 quarts
16 ÷ 4 = 4 → **4 gallons**

32 quarts
32 ÷ 4 = 8 → **8 gallons**

100 quarts
100 ÷ 4 = 25 → **25 gallons**

20 quarts
20 ÷ 4 = 5 → **5 gallons**

Convert each measurement.

3 gallons
3 x 4 x 2 = 24 → **24 pints**

5 quarts
5 x 2 x 2 = 20 → **20 cups**

36 cups
36 ÷ 2 ÷ 2 = 9 → **9 quarts**

72 pints
72 ÷ 2 ÷ 4 = 9 → **9 gallons**

1 quart
1 x 2 x 2 x 8 = 32 → **32 fluid ounces**

240 fluid ounces
240 ÷ 8 ÷ 2 = 15 → **15 pints**

7 quarts
7 x 4 = 28 → **28 cups**

11 gallons
11 x 4 x 2 = 88 → **88 pints**

See the notes for page 85.

87

Fraction of a number ☆

Work out to find the fraction of the number. Write the answer in the box.

$\frac{1}{6}$ of 42
$\frac{1}{6}$ x 42 = $\frac{42}{6}$ = 7
1 x 7 = 7
So, $\frac{1}{6}$ of 42 = 7

$\frac{3}{5}$ of 35
$\frac{1}{5}$ x 35 = $\frac{35}{5}$ = 7
3 x 7 = 21
So, $\frac{3}{5}$ of 35 = 21

$\frac{1}{4}$ of 100 = $\frac{100}{4}$ = 25

$\frac{1}{3}$ of 69 = $\frac{69}{3}$ = 23

Work out to find the fraction of the number. Write the answer in the box.

$\frac{1}{8}$ of 72	9	$\frac{1}{5}$ of 250	50	$\frac{1}{2}$ of 38	19
$\frac{1}{9}$ of 54	6	$\frac{1}{2}$ of 84	42	$\frac{1}{6}$ of 72	12
$\frac{1}{4}$ of 52	13	$\frac{1}{7}$ of 140	20	$\frac{1}{3}$ of 36	12
$\frac{1}{5}$ of 175	35	$\frac{1}{8}$ of 64	8	$\frac{1}{4}$ of 100	25
$\frac{1}{6}$ of 300	50	$\frac{1}{9}$ of 81	9	$\frac{1}{2}$ of 114	57
$\frac{1}{10}$ of 100	10	$\frac{1}{5}$ of 55	11	$\frac{1}{7}$ of 140	20
$\frac{3}{4}$ of 100	75	$\frac{2}{3}$ of 75	50	$\frac{4}{7}$ of 42	24
$\frac{2}{5}$ of 25	10	$\frac{5}{8}$ of 40	25	$\frac{2}{3}$ of 27	18
$\frac{5}{9}$ of 36	20	$\frac{2}{3}$ of 225	150	$\frac{5}{6}$ of 120	100
$\frac{3}{4}$ of 56	42	$\frac{5}{7}$ of 133	95	$\frac{2}{3}$ of 180	120
$\frac{4}{5}$ of 100	80	$\frac{2}{10}$ of 100	20	$\frac{3}{8}$ of 64	24
$\frac{2}{3}$ of 210	140	$\frac{4}{9}$ of 90	40	$\frac{7}{8}$ of 72	63

If children have difficulty with the first step, have them use long division to find the quotient.

☆ Showing decimals

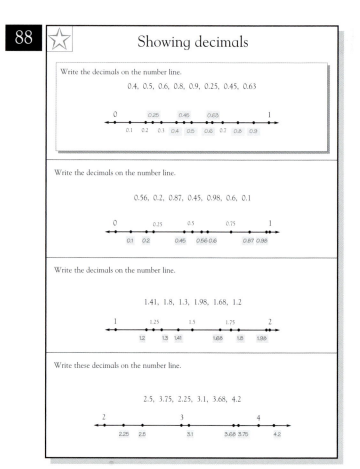

Write the decimals on the number line.

0.4, 0.5, 0.6, 0.8, 0.9, 0.25, 0.45, 0.63

Write the decimals on the number line.

0.56, 0.2, 0.87, 0.45, 0.98, 0.6, 0.1

Write the decimals on the number line.

1.41, 1.8, 1.3, 1.98, 1.68, 1.2

Write these decimals on the number line.

2.5, 3.75, 2.25, 3.1, 3.68, 4.2

If children are confused about where to place the decimals to hundredths, have them first fill in all of the tenths on the number line. Then ask which of those tenths the decimals to hundredths fall between.

89

Area of right-angled triangles

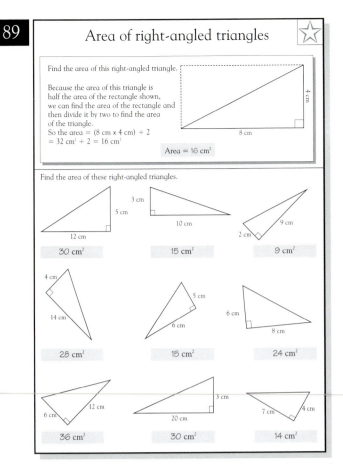

Find the area of this right-angled triangle.

Because the area of this triangle is half the area of the rectangle shown, we can find the area of the rectangle and then divide it by two to find the area of the triangle.
So the area = (8 cm x 4 cm) ÷ 2
= 32 cm² ÷ 2 = 16 cm²

Area = 16 cm²

Find the area of these right-angled triangles.

30 cm² 15 cm² 9 cm²

28 cm² 15 cm² 24 cm²

36 cm² 30 cm² 14 cm²

The operation of multiplying the sides together and dividing by two should offer no serious difficulty to children, but make sure they are really clear about why they are doing this.

Speed problems

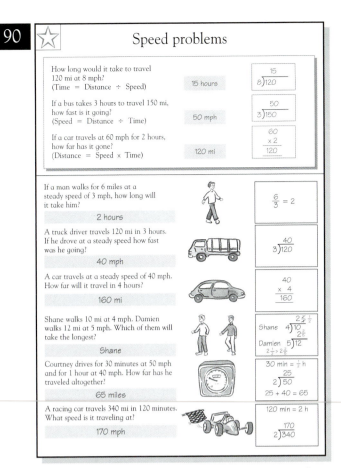

How long would it take to travel 120 mi at 8 mph?
(Time = Distance ÷ Speed)

15 hours

$8)\overline{120}$ → 15

If a bus takes 3 hours to travel 150 mi, how fast is it going?
(Speed = Distance ÷ Time)

50 mph

$3)\overline{150}$ → 50

If a car travels at 60 mph for 2 hours, how far has it gone?
(Distance = Speed × Time)

120 mi

60 × 2 = 120

If a man walks for 6 miles at a steady speed of 3 mph, how long will it take him?

2 hours

$\frac{6}{3} = 2$

A truck driver travels 120 mi in 3 hours. If he drove at a steady speed how fast was he going?

40 mph

$3)\overline{120}$ → 40

A car travels at a steady speed of 40 mph. How far will it travel in 4 hours?

160 mi

40 × 4 = 160

Shane walks 10 mi at 4 mph. Damien walks 12 mi at 5 mph. Which of them will take the longest?

Shane

Shane $4)\overline{10}$ = 2½
Damien $5)\overline{12}$ = 2⅖
2½ > 2⅖

Courtney drives for 30 minutes at 50 mph and for 1 hour at 40 mph. How far has he traveled altogether?

65 miles

30 min = ½ h
$2)\overline{50}$ = 25
25 + 40 = 65

A racing car travels 340 mi in 120 minutes. What speed is it traveling at?

170 mph

120 min = 2 h
$2)\overline{340}$ = 170

If children experience difficulty on this page, ask them what they need to find – speed, distance or time – and refer them to the necessary formula. Encourage them to develop simple examples that will help them to remember the formulas.

Conversion tables

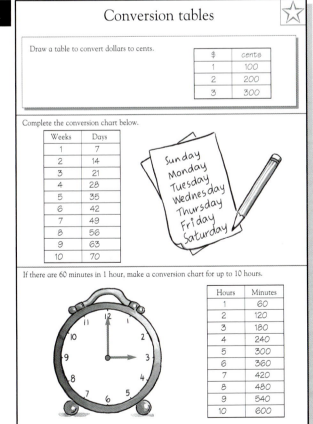

Draw a table to convert dollars to cents.

$	cents
1	100
2	200
3	300

Complete the conversion chart below.

Weeks	Days
1	7
2	14
3	21
4	28
5	35
6	42
7	49
8	56
9	63
10	70

Sunday
Monday
Tuesday
Wednesday
Thursday
Friday
Saturday

If there are 60 minutes in 1 hour, make a conversion chart for up to 10 hours.

Hours	Minutes
1	60
2	120
3	180
4	240
5	300
6	360
7	420
8	480
9	540
10	600

Children will grasp that they are dealing with multiples of 7 and later, 60. Any problems will be due to weaknesses in tables or from missing out numbers as they work down the chart. Encourage care and concentration.

Reading bar graphs

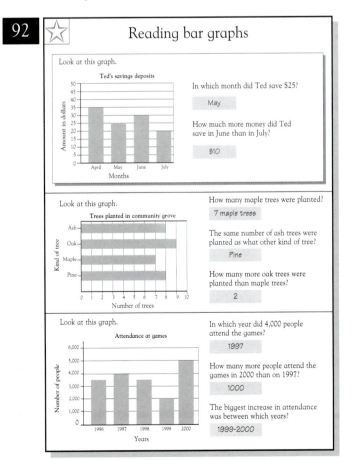

Look at this graph.

Ted's savings deposits

In which month did Ted save $25?

May

How much more money did Ted save in June than in July?

$10

Look at this graph.

Trees planted in community grove

How many maple trees were planted?

7 maple trees

The same number of ash trees were planted as what other kind of tree?

Pine

How many more oak trees were planted than maple trees?

2

Look at this graph.

Attendance at games

In which year did 4,000 people attend the games?

1997

How many more people attend the games in 2000 than on 1997?

1000

The biggest increase in attendance was between which years?

1999-2000

If children have difficulties with computation problems, have them write down each of the numbers they read off the graph before computing with them.

Expanded form ★

What is the value of 3 in 2,308? 300

Write 32,084 in expanded form. 30,000 + 2,000 + 80 + 4

What is the value of 6 in these numbers?

26	6	162	60	36,904	6,000
12,612	600	6,130	6,000	567,902	60,000
13,036	6	9,764	60	17,632	600

What is the value of 4 in these numbers?

14,300	4,000	942	40	8,764	4
10,408	400	1,043	40	45,987	40,000
6,045	40	804,001	4,000	694	4

Circle the numbers that have a 7 with the value of seventy thousand.

457,682   67,924   ⟨870,234⟩   ⟨372,987⟩

⟨171,345⟩   767,707   ⟨79,835⟩   16,757

Write the numbers in expanded form.

34,897	30,000 + 4,000 + 800 + 90 + 7
508,061	500,000 + 8,000 + 60 + 1
50,810	50,000 + 800 + 10
8,945	8,000 + 900 + 40 + 5
60,098	60,000 + 90 + 8

Some children are confused about how to represent the zeros in a number. Be sure they know to skip those terms when they write the expanded form.

★ Cubes of small numbers

What is 2^3? $2 \times 2 \times 2 = 8$

What is the volume of this cube? 2 in. x 2 in. x 2 in. = 8 in.³
You find the volume of a cube in the same way you work out the cube of a number.

Use extra paper here if you need to. What is...

3^3	$3 \times 3 \times 3 = 27$		4^3	$4 \times 4 \times 4 = 64$
6^3	$6 \times 6 \times 6 = 216$		5^3	$5 \times 5 \times 5 = 125$
1^3	$1 \times 1 \times 1 = 1$		2^3	$2 \times 2 \times 2 = 8$

What are the volumes of these cubes?

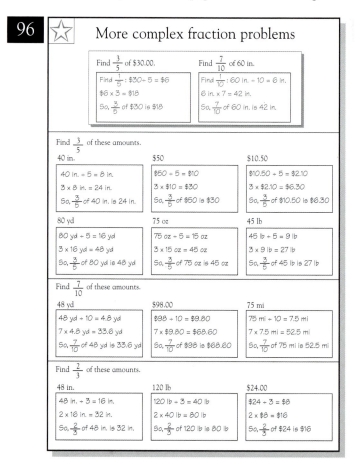

7 in. — 343 in.³
8 in. — 512 in.³
9 in. — 729 in.³
10 in. — 1,000 in.³

The most common mistake children make is confusing three cubed with three times three, especially when they are working quickly through the examples. It is necessary to reinforce the concept of cubing a number. Children may need some paper for their working out.

Multiplying fractions ★

Write the product.

$$\frac{3}{8} \times \frac{4}{7} = \frac{3}{14}$$

$$\frac{1}{5} \times \frac{3}{10} = \frac{3}{2} = 1\frac{1}{2}$$

Write the product.

$$\frac{1}{4} \times \frac{1}{4} = \frac{1}{16} \qquad \frac{3}{10} \times \frac{2}{6} = \frac{1}{10} \qquad 6 \times \frac{3}{4} = \frac{9}{2} = 4\frac{1}{2}$$

$$8 \times \frac{1}{4} = 2 \qquad \frac{2}{5} \times \frac{5}{7} = \frac{2}{7} \qquad \frac{2}{5} \times \frac{5}{6} = \frac{1}{3}$$

$$\frac{2}{5} \times \frac{2}{3} = \frac{4}{15} \qquad 4 \times \frac{3}{16} = \frac{3}{4} \qquad \frac{3}{8} \times 10 = \frac{15}{4} = 3\frac{3}{4}$$

$$\frac{1}{3} \times 15 = 5 \qquad \frac{5}{9} \times \frac{1}{5} = \frac{1}{9} \qquad \frac{3}{4} \times \frac{4}{9} = \frac{1}{3}$$

$$\frac{1}{4} \times \frac{2}{7} = \frac{1}{14} \qquad \frac{2}{9} \times \frac{3}{4} = \frac{1}{6} \qquad 12 \times \frac{3}{10} = \frac{18}{5} = 3\frac{3}{5}$$

$$\frac{2}{3} \times \frac{1}{3} = \frac{2}{9} \qquad \frac{1}{12} \times 2 = \frac{1}{6} \qquad \frac{3}{4} \times \frac{1}{4} = \frac{3}{16}$$

$$\frac{5}{6} \times 8 = \frac{20}{3} = 6\frac{2}{3} \qquad 7 \times \frac{1}{8} = \frac{7}{8} \qquad \frac{1}{6} \times \frac{5}{6} = \frac{5}{36}$$

$$\frac{1}{2} \times 25 = \frac{25}{2} = 12\frac{1}{2} \qquad \frac{7}{10} \times \frac{5}{7} = \frac{1}{2} \qquad 4 \times \frac{3}{4} = 3$$

Some children are confused about how to multiply a fraction by a whole number. Remind them that any whole number is also a fraction with 1 as the denominator.

★ More complex fraction problems

Find $\frac{3}{5}$ of $30.00.
Find $\frac{1}{5}$: $30 ÷ 5 = $6
$6 × 3 = $18
So, $\frac{3}{5}$ of $30 is $18

Find $\frac{7}{10}$ of 60 in.
Find $\frac{1}{10}$: 60 in. ÷ 10 = 6 in.
6 in. × 7 = 42 in.
So, $\frac{7}{10}$ of 60 in. is 42 in.

Find $\frac{3}{5}$ of these amounts.

40 in.	$50	$10.50
40 in. ÷ 5 = 8 in.	$50 ÷ 5 = $10	$10.50 ÷ 5 = $2.10
3 × 8 in. = 24 in.	3 × $10 = $30	3 × $2.10 = $6.30
So, $\frac{3}{5}$ of 40 in. is 24 in.	So, $\frac{3}{5}$ of $50 is $30	So, $\frac{3}{5}$ of $10.50 is $6.30

80 yd	75 oz	45 lb
80 yd ÷ 5 = 16 yd	75 oz ÷ 5 = 15 oz	45 lb ÷ 5 = 9 lb
3 × 16 yd = 48 yd	3 × 15 oz = 45 oz	3 × 9 lb = 27 lb
So, $\frac{3}{5}$ of 80 yd is 48 yd	So, $\frac{3}{5}$ of 75 oz is 45 oz	So, $\frac{3}{5}$ of 45 lb is 27 lb

Find $\frac{7}{10}$ of these amounts.

48 yd	$98.00	75 mi
48 yd ÷ 10 = 4.8 yd	$98 ÷ 10 = $9.80	75 mi ÷ 10 = 7.5 mi
7 × 4.8 yd = 33.6 yd	7 × $9.80 = $68.60	7 × 7.5 mi = 52.5 mi
So, $\frac{7}{10}$ of 48 yd is 33.6 yd	So, $\frac{7}{10}$ of $98 is $68.60	So, $\frac{7}{10}$ of 75 mi is 52.5 mi

Find $\frac{2}{3}$ of these amounts.

48 in.	120 lb	$24.00
48 in. ÷ 3 = 16 in.	120 lb ÷ 3 = 40 lb	$24 ÷ 3 = $8
2 × 16 in. = 32 in.	2 × 40 lb = 80 lb	2 × $8 = $16
So, $\frac{2}{3}$ of 48 in. is 32 in.	So, $\frac{2}{3}$ of 120 lb is 80 lb	So, $\frac{2}{3}$ of $24 is $16

Ensure that children are dividing the amount by the denominator and multiplying the result by the numerator. You could explain that we divide by the bottom to find one part and multiply by the top to find the number of parts we want.

Finding percentages ⭐

Find 30% of 140. $\frac{14\cancel{0}}{10\cancel{0}} \times 30 = 42$ (Divide by 100 to find 1% and then multiply by 30 to find 30%.)

Find 12% of 75. $\frac{75}{100}^{\,3} \times 12^{\,3} = 9$ (Divide by 100 to find 1% and then multiply by 12 to find 12%.)

Find 30% of these numbers.

620 → $\frac{620}{100} \times 30 = 186$ 240 → $\frac{240}{100} \times 30 = 72$

80 → $\frac{80}{100} \times 30 = 24$ 160 → $\frac{160}{100} \times 30 = 48$

Find 60% of these numbers.

60 → $\frac{60}{100} \times 60 = 36$ 100 → $\frac{100}{100} \times 60 = 60$

160 → $\frac{160}{100} \times 60 = 96$ 580 → $\frac{580}{100} \times 60 = 348$

Find 45% of these numbers.

80 oz → $\frac{80}{100} \times 45 = 36$ oz   40 in. → $\frac{40}{100} \times 45 = 18$ in.

240 fl oz → $\frac{240}{100} \times 45 = 108$ fl oz   600 mi → $\frac{600}{100} \times 45 = 270$ mi

Find 12% of these numbers.

$150 → $\frac{150}{100} \times 12 = 18 $600 → $\frac{600}{100} \times 12 = 72

125 ft → $\frac{125}{100} \times 12 = 15$ ft   775 ft → $\frac{775}{100} \times 12 = 93$ ft

The most common error when finding percentages is to reverse the operation, i.e. to divide by the percentage required and multiply by 100. Explain again that if the whole is 100% we divide the number by 100 to find 1% and then multiply by the percentage we want.

Addition

Work out the answer to each problem.

```
  ¹ ¹              ¹ ³¹
   634            1,472
 4,812               96
+1,428            8,391
──────          + 564
 6,874          ──────
                10,523
```

Remember to regroup if you need to.

Find each sum.

```
 5,831     3,724     9,994       524
 8,375     9,942     7,358     7,034
+ 219     + 623     + 471      + 95
──────    ──────    ──────    ──────
14,425    14,289    17,823     7,653
```

```
 7,341     9,328     7,159       208
   299       347        39     4,943
+5,143    +8,222     + 748      + 55
──────    ──────    ──────    ──────
12,783    17,897     7,946     5,206
```

Find each sum.

```
 8,594     7,362     3,041     7,641
   629       843       571        93
 9,878     4,732     5,210     8,521
+  96     +  53     +  71     + 843
──────    ──────    ──────    ──────
19,197    12,990     8,893    17,098
```

```
 8,795     6,043        27       146
   659         4       153     3,714
 3,212       147     8,612        26
+ 961     +8,948     + 127    +5,003
──────    ──────    ──────    ──────
13,627    15,142     8,919     8,889
```

This page should be fairly straightforward, but errors may creep in as the lists get longer towards the end. Errors will most likely be mistakes in adding the longer lists, adding across place value, or a failure to carry.

More addition ⭐

Work out the answer to each problem.

```
 ¹¹ ¹            ¹²¹
23,714          11,541
 9,024             861
+  348          29,652
──────         +     5
33,086         ──────
                42,059
```

Remember to regroup if you need to.

Find each sum.

```
17,203    29,521    65,214    25,046
   112     6,211       973        15
+5,608    +   58    +1,291    +  263
──────    ──────    ──────    ──────
22,923    35,790    67,478    25,324
```

```
 6,958    73,009    11,536    87,019
    71         3        48       127
+16,911   +  581    +2,435    +5,652
──────    ──────    ──────    ──────
23,940    73,593    14,019    92,798
```

Find each sum.

```
79,622    64,599     6,940    72,148
 8,011       122       936       999
47,391     6,375    58,274     7,481
+    7    +   91    +   36    +21,685
──────    ──────    ──────    ──────
135,031    71,187    66,186   102,313
```

```
58,975    36,403         8        23
   858        73    22,849    99,951
 8,423       712       502       358
+   27    +6,229    +4,034    +6,231
──────    ──────    ──────    ──────
68,283    43,417    27,393   106,563
```

Any problems on this page will be similar to those encountered on the previous page. As the numbers get larger, errors are more likely to occur.

Dividing by ones

477 ÷ 2 can be written in two ways:

$238\frac{1}{2}$ or $238 \text{ r } 1$

$2\overline{)477}$ $2\overline{)477}$

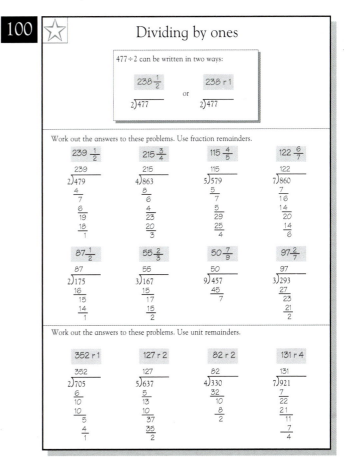

Work out the answers to these problems. Use fraction remainders.

$239\frac{1}{2}$, $215\frac{3}{4}$, $115\frac{4}{5}$, $122\frac{6}{7}$

$87\frac{1}{2}$, $55\frac{2}{3}$, $50\frac{7}{9}$, $97\frac{2}{7}$

Work out the answers to these problems. Use unit remainders.

$352 \text{ r } 1$, $127 \text{ r } 2$, $82 \text{ r } 2$, $131 \text{ r } 4$

Children may think that the two types of division represent different procedures. Point out that the only difference is in how to write the remainder.

Dividing by tens

$361 \div 20$ can be written in two ways:

$$18\frac{1}{20} \qquad \text{or} \qquad 18\,r\,1$$
$$20\overline{)361} \qquad\qquad 20\overline{)361}$$

Work out the answers to these problems. Use fraction remainders.

8
$$\begin{array}{r} 8 \\ 40\overline{)320} \\ \underline{320} \\ 0 \end{array}$$

7
$$\begin{array}{r} 7 \\ 70\overline{)490} \\ \underline{490} \\ 0 \end{array}$$

$4\frac{29}{80}$
$$\begin{array}{r} 4 \\ 80\overline{)349} \\ \underline{320} \\ 29 \end{array}$$

$6\frac{7}{90}$
$$\begin{array}{r} 6 \\ 90\overline{)547} \\ \underline{540} \\ 7 \end{array}$$

$80\frac{7}{10}$
$$\begin{array}{r} 80 \\ 10\overline{)807} \\ \underline{80} \\ 7 \end{array}$$

$21\frac{17}{20}$
$$\begin{array}{r} 21 \\ 20\overline{)437} \\ \underline{40} \\ 37 \\ \underline{20} \\ 17 \end{array}$$

$94\frac{3}{10}$
$$\begin{array}{r} 94 \\ 10\overline{)943} \\ \underline{90} \\ 43 \\ \underline{40} \\ 3 \end{array}$$

$12\frac{1}{30}$
$$\begin{array}{r} 12 \\ 30\overline{)361} \\ \underline{30} \\ 61 \\ \underline{60} \\ 1 \end{array}$$

Work out the answers to these problems. Use unit remainders.

$8\,r\,17$
$$\begin{array}{r} 8 \\ 50\overline{)417} \\ \underline{400} \\ 17 \end{array}$$

9
$$\begin{array}{r} 9 \\ 90\overline{)810} \\ \underline{810} \\ 0 \end{array}$$

$10\,r\,3$
$$\begin{array}{r} 10 \\ 30\overline{)303} \\ \underline{300} \\ 3 \end{array}$$

$9\,r\,6$
$$\begin{array}{r} 9 \\ 40\overline{)366} \\ \underline{360} \\ 6 \end{array}$$

$38\,r\,8$
$$\begin{array}{r} 38 \\ 20\overline{)768} \\ \underline{60} \\ 168 \\ \underline{160} \\ 8 \end{array}$$

14
$$\begin{array}{r} 14 \\ 70\overline{)980} \\ \underline{70} \\ 280 \\ \underline{280} \\ 0 \end{array}$$

$13\,r\,7$
$$\begin{array}{r} 13 \\ 60\overline{)787} \\ \underline{60} \\ 187 \\ \underline{180} \\ 7 \end{array}$$

$29\,r\,7$
$$\begin{array}{r} 29 \\ 10\overline{)297} \\ \underline{20} \\ 97 \\ \underline{90} \\ 7 \end{array}$$

Children may have trouble deciding where to place digits in the quotient. Have them place the digit directly above the number being subtracted in that step.

Dividing by larger numbers

$589 \div 15$ can be written in two ways:

$$39\frac{4}{15} \qquad \text{or} \qquad 39\,r\,4$$
$$15\overline{)589} \qquad\qquad 15\overline{)589}$$

Work out the answers to these problems. Use fractions remainders.

$9\frac{3}{48}$
$$\begin{array}{r} 9 \\ 48\overline{)435} \\ \underline{432} \\ 3 \end{array}$$

$17\frac{2}{21}$
$$\begin{array}{r} 17 \\ 21\overline{)359} \\ \underline{21} \\ 149 \\ \underline{147} \\ 2 \end{array}$$

$7\frac{53}{57}$
$$\begin{array}{r} 7 \\ 57\overline{)452} \\ \underline{399} \\ 53 \end{array}$$

11
$$\begin{array}{r} 11 \\ 72\overline{)792} \\ \underline{72} \\ 72 \\ \underline{72} \\ 0 \end{array}$$

$31\frac{7}{30}$
$$\begin{array}{r} 31 \\ 30\overline{)937} \\ \underline{90} \\ 37 \\ \underline{30} \\ 7 \end{array}$$

$12\frac{19}{65}$
$$\begin{array}{r} 12 \\ 65\overline{)799} \\ \underline{65} \\ 149 \\ \underline{130} \\ 19 \end{array}$$

17
$$\begin{array}{r} 17 \\ 17\overline{)289} \\ \underline{17} \\ 119 \\ \underline{119} \\ 0 \end{array}$$

$16\frac{48}{51}$
$$\begin{array}{r} 16 \\ 51\overline{)854} \\ \underline{50} \\ 354 \\ \underline{306} \\ 48 \end{array}$$

Work out the answers to these problems. Use unit remainders.

$8\,r\,21$
$$\begin{array}{r} 8 \\ 79\overline{)653} \\ \underline{632} \\ 21 \end{array}$$

$22\,r\,17$
$$\begin{array}{r} 22 \\ 24\overline{)545} \\ \underline{48} \\ 65 \\ \underline{48} \\ 17 \end{array}$$

14
$$\begin{array}{r} 14 \\ 68\overline{)952} \\ \underline{68} \\ 272 \\ \underline{272} \\ 0 \end{array}$$

$11\,r\,15$
$$\begin{array}{r} 11 \\ 36\overline{)411} \\ \underline{36} \\ 51 \\ \underline{36} \\ 15 \end{array}$$

73
$$\begin{array}{r} 73 \\ 12\overline{)876} \\ \underline{84} \\ 36 \\ \underline{36} \\ 0 \end{array}$$

$8\,r\,29$
$$\begin{array}{r} 8 \\ 96\overline{)797} \\ \underline{768} \\ 29 \end{array}$$

$43\,r\,11$
$$\begin{array}{r} 43 \\ 17\overline{)742} \\ \underline{68} \\ 62 \\ \underline{51} \\ 11 \end{array}$$

$12\,r\,42$
$$\begin{array}{r} 12 \\ 45\overline{)582} \\ \underline{45} \\ 132 \\ \underline{90} \\ 42 \end{array}$$

See the notes for page 101.

Everyday problems

A plumber has 6 m of copper tubing. If he uses 2.36 m, how much will he have left?

3.64 m

$$\begin{array}{r} {}^{5}6.^{9}0^{10}0 \\ -\ 2.36 \\ \hline 3.64 \end{array}$$

If he buys another 4.5 m of copper tubing, how much will he now have?

8.14 m

$$\begin{array}{r} {}^{1}3.64 \\ +\ 4.50 \\ \hline 8.14 \end{array}$$

A man spends $35.65, $102.43, $68.99 and $36.50 in 4 different stores. How much money did he spend altogether?

$243.57

$$\begin{array}{r} {}^{1\,2\,2\,1}35.65 \\ 102.43 \\ 68.99 \\ +\ 36.50 \\ \hline \$243.57 \end{array}$$

A gas station has 10,400 gallons of gasoline delivered on Monday, 13,350 gal on Tuesday, 14,755 gal on Wednesday, 9,656 gal on Thursday, and 15,975 gal on Friday. How much did they have delivered from Monday through Friday?

64,136 gal

$$\begin{array}{r} {}^{2\,2\,3}10,400 \\ 13,350 \\ 14,755 \\ 9,656 \\ +\ 15,975 \\ \hline 64,136 \end{array}$$

If they sold 59,248 gallons that week, how much gasoline did they have left?

4,888 gal

$$\begin{array}{r} {}^{5\,13\,10\,12\,16}64,136 \\ -\ 59,248 \\ \hline 4,888 \end{array}$$

Daniel runs 22.56 km in a charity fun run. Sandra runs 8,420 m less. How far does Sandra run?

14.14 km

$$\begin{array}{r} 22.56 \\ -\ 8.42 \\ \hline 14.14 \end{array}$$

What is the combined distance run by Daniel and Sandra?

36.7 km

$$\begin{array}{r} {}^{1}22.56 \\ +\ 14.14 \\ \hline 36.70 \end{array}$$

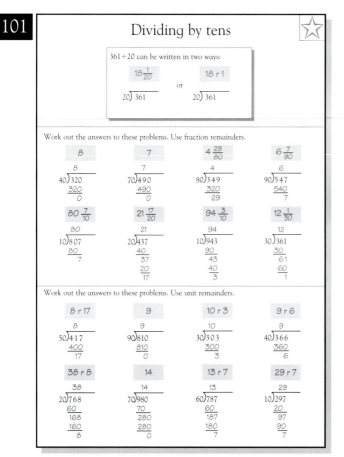

Dianne is 4 ft 10 in. tall. Tania is 5 ft 1 in. tall. How much taller is Tania?

3 in.

5 ft 1 in. = 4 ft 13 in.
$$\begin{array}{r} 4\ \text{ft}\ 13\ \text{in.} \\ -\ 4\ \text{ft}\ 10\ \text{in.} \\ \hline 3\ \text{in.} \end{array}$$

Children will apply subtraction and addition skills to real-life problems. If they are unsure about which operation to use, discuss whether the answer will be larger (addition) or smaller (subtraction). Take care when units of measurement need to be converted.

Real-life problems

A man walks 18.34 km on Saturday and 16.57 km on Sunday. How far did he walk that weekend?

34.91 km

$$\begin{array}{r} {}^{1\ 1}18.34 \\ +\ 16.57 \\ \hline 34.91 \end{array}$$

How much farther did he walk on Saturday?

1.77 km

$$\begin{array}{r} {}^{7\ 12\ 14}18.34 \\ -\ 16.57 \\ \hline 1.77 \end{array}$$

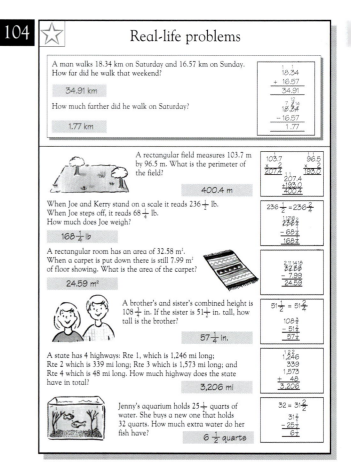

A rectangular field measures 103.7 m by 96.5 m. What is the perimeter of the field?

400.4 m

$$\begin{array}{r} 103.7 \\ \times\ 2 \\ \hline 207.4 \end{array} \qquad \begin{array}{r} 96.5 \\ \times\ 2 \\ \hline 193.0 \end{array}$$
$$\begin{array}{r} 207.4 \\ +193.0 \\ \hline 400.4 \end{array}$$

When Joe and Kerry stand on a scale it reads $236\frac{1}{2}$ lb. When Joe steps off, it reads $68\frac{1}{4}$ lb. How much does Joe weigh?

$168\frac{1}{4}$ lb

$$236\frac{1}{2} = 236\frac{2}{4}$$
$$\begin{array}{r} {}^{1}236\frac{2}{4} \\ -\ 68\frac{1}{4} \\ \hline 168\frac{1}{4} \end{array}$$

A rectangular room has an area of 32.58 m². When a carpet is put down there is still 7.99 m² of floor showing. What is the area of the carpet?

24.59 m²

$$\begin{array}{r} {}^{2\ 11\ 14\ 18}32.58 \\ -\ 7.99 \\ \hline 24.59 \end{array}$$

A brother's and sister's combined height is $108\frac{1}{4}$ in. If the sister is $51\frac{1}{2}$ in. tall, how tall is the brother?

$57\frac{1}{4}$ in.

$$51\frac{1}{2} = 51\frac{2}{4}$$
$$\begin{array}{r} 108\frac{1}{4} \\ -\ 51\frac{2}{4} \\ \hline 57\frac{1}{4} \end{array}$$

A state has 4 highways: Rte 1, which is 1,246 mi long; Rte 2 which is 339 mi long; Rte 3 which is 1,573 mi long; and Rte 4 which is 48 mi long. How much highway does the state have in total?

3,206 mi

$$\begin{array}{r} {}^{1\,2\,2}1,246 \\ 339 \\ 1,573 \\ +\ 48 \\ \hline 3,206 \end{array}$$

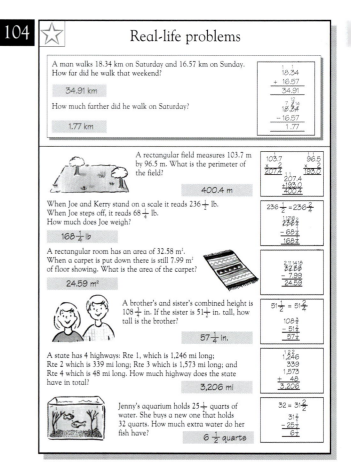

Jenny's aquarium holds $25\frac{1}{2}$ quarts of water. She buys a new one that holds 32 quarts. How much extra water do her fish have?

$6\frac{1}{2}$ quarts

$$32 = 31\frac{2}{2}$$
$$\begin{array}{r} 31\frac{2}{2} \\ -\ 25\frac{1}{2} \\ \hline 6\frac{1}{2} \end{array}$$

This page once again tests the skills of children in real-life problems. In the first question, make sure that they are finding the perimeter and not the area.

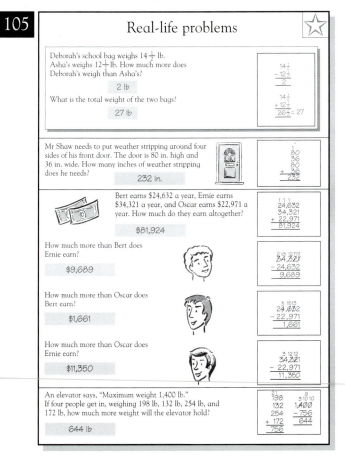

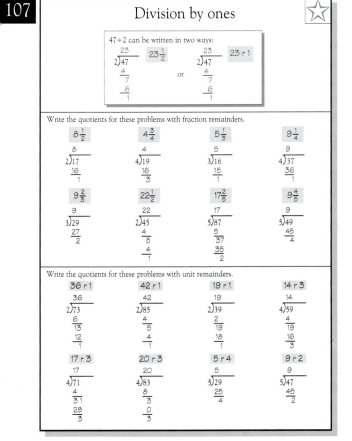

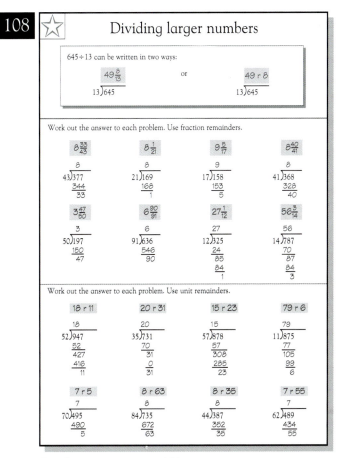

Real-life problems

Deborah's school bag weighs $14\frac{1}{4}$ lb. Asha's weighs $12\frac{1}{4}$ lb. How much more does Deborah's weigh than Asha's?

2 lb

$$14\frac{1}{4}$$
$$-12\frac{1}{4}$$
$$2$$

What is the total weight of the two bags?

27 lb

$$14\frac{1}{4}$$
$$+12\frac{1}{4}$$
$$26\frac{2}{4} = 27$$

Mr Shaw needs to put weather stripping around four sides of his front door. The door is 80 in. high and 36 in. wide. How many inches of weather stripping does he needs?

232 in.

$$\begin{array}{r}1\\80\\36\\80\\+36\\\hline232\end{array}$$

Bert earns $24,632 a year, Ernie earns $34,321 a year, and Oscar earns $22,971 a year. How much do they earn altogether?

$81,924

$$\begin{array}{r}1\,1\,1\\24,632\\34,321\\+22,971\\\hline81,924\end{array}$$

How much more than Bert does Ernie earn?

$9,689

$$\begin{array}{r}2\ 13\ 12\ 11\ 11\\\cancel{34,321}\\-24,632\\\hline9,689\end{array}$$

How much more than Oscar does Bert earn?

$1,661

$$\begin{array}{r}3,\ 15\,13\\24,\cancel{632}\\-22,971\\\hline1,661\end{array}$$

How much more than Oscar does Ernie earn?

$11,350

$$\begin{array}{r}3\ 12\,12\\34,\cancel{321}\\-22,971\\\hline11,350\end{array}$$

An elevator says, "Maximum weight 1,400 lb." If four people get in, weighing 198 lb, 132 lb, 254 lb, and 172 lb, how much more weight will the elevator hold?

644 lb

$$\begin{array}{r}21\\198\\132\\254\\+172\\\hline756\end{array} \qquad \begin{array}{r}3\ 9\\3\,\cancel{10}\,\cancel{10}\\1,\cancel{4}\cancel{0}\cancel{0}\\-756\\\hline644\end{array}$$

See the notes for page 104.

Multiplication by 2-digit numbers

Work out the answer to each problem.

$$\begin{array}{r}527\\\times\ 76\\\hline3,162\\36,890\\\hline40,052\end{array} \qquad \begin{array}{r}834\\\times\ 58\\\hline41,700\\6,672\\\hline48,372\end{array}$$

Work out the answer to each problem.

$$\begin{array}{r}426\\\times\ 84\\\hline1,704\\34,080\\\hline35,784\end{array} \quad \begin{array}{r}895\\\times\ 65\\\hline4,475\\53,700\\\hline58,175\end{array} \quad \begin{array}{r}632\\\times\ 39\\\hline5,688\\18,960\\\hline24,648\end{array} \quad \begin{array}{r}778\\\times\ 49\\\hline7,002\\31,120\\\hline38,122\end{array}$$

$$\begin{array}{r}597\\\times\ 46\\\hline3,582\\23,880\\\hline27,462\end{array} \quad \begin{array}{r}994\\\times\ 37\\\hline6,958\\29,820\\\hline36,778\end{array} \quad \begin{array}{r}632\\\times\ 64\\\hline2,528\\37,920\\\hline40,448\end{array} \quad \begin{array}{r}747\\\times\ 75\\\hline3,735\\52,290\\\hline56,025\end{array}$$

$$\begin{array}{r}428\\\times\ 95\\\hline2,140\\38,520\\\hline40,660\end{array} \quad \begin{array}{r}147\\\times\ 62\\\hline294\\8,820\\\hline9,114\end{array} \quad \begin{array}{r}236\\\times\ 87\\\hline1,652\\18,880\\\hline20,532\end{array} \quad \begin{array}{r}145\\\times\ 33\\\hline435\\4,350\\\hline4,785\end{array}$$

$$\begin{array}{r}346\\\times\ 85\\\hline1,730\\27,680\\\hline29,410\end{array} \quad \begin{array}{r}529\\\times\ 72\\\hline1,058\\37,030\\\hline38,088\end{array} \quad \begin{array}{r}485\\\times\ 29\\\hline4,365\\9,700\\\hline14,065\end{array} \quad \begin{array}{r}763\\\times\ 84\\\hline3,052\\61,040\\\hline64,092\end{array}$$

Explain that multiplying by 84 means multiplying by 80, then by 4, and then adding the answers together. Multiplying by 10 (or 80) means adding a zero and multiplying by 1 (or 8). Multiplying by the tens digit first, saves having to remember to put the zero later.

Division by ones

$47 \div 2$ can be written in two ways:

$$\begin{array}{r}23\\2\overline{)47}\\4\\\hline7\\6\\\hline1\end{array} \quad 23\frac{1}{2} \qquad or \qquad \begin{array}{r}23\\2\overline{)47}\\4\\\hline7\\6\\\hline1\end{array} \quad 23\ r\ 1$$

Write the quotients for these problems with fraction remainders.

$$8\frac{1}{2}\quad\begin{array}{r}8\\2\overline{)17}\\16\\\hline1\end{array} \qquad 4\frac{3}{4}\quad\begin{array}{r}4\\4\overline{)19}\\16\\\hline3\end{array} \qquad 5\frac{1}{3}\quad\begin{array}{r}5\\3\overline{)16}\\15\\\hline1\end{array} \qquad 9\frac{1}{4}\quad\begin{array}{r}9\\4\overline{)37}\\36\\\hline1\end{array}$$

$$9\frac{2}{3}\quad\begin{array}{r}9\\3\overline{)29}\\27\\\hline2\end{array} \qquad 22\frac{1}{2}\quad\begin{array}{r}22\\2\overline{)45}\\4\\\hline5\\4\\\hline1\end{array} \qquad 17\frac{2}{5}\quad\begin{array}{r}17\\5\overline{)87}\\5\\\hline37\\35\\\hline2\end{array} \qquad 9\frac{4}{5}\quad\begin{array}{r}9\\5\overline{)49}\\45\\\hline4\end{array}$$

Write the quotients for these problems with unit remainders.

$$36\ r\ 1\quad\begin{array}{r}36\\2\overline{)73}\\6\\\hline13\\12\\\hline1\end{array} \qquad 42\ r\ 1\quad\begin{array}{r}42\\2\overline{)85}\\4\\\hline5\\4\\\hline1\end{array} \qquad 19\ r\ 1\quad\begin{array}{r}19\\2\overline{)39}\\2\\\hline19\\18\\\hline1\end{array} \qquad 14\ r\ 3\quad\begin{array}{r}14\\4\overline{)59}\\4\\\hline19\\16\\\hline3\end{array}$$

$$17\ r\ 3\quad\begin{array}{r}17\\4\overline{)71}\\4\\\hline31\\28\\\hline3\end{array} \qquad 20\ r\ 3\quad\begin{array}{r}20\\4\overline{)83}\\8\\\hline3\\0\\\hline3\end{array} \qquad 5\ r\ 4\quad\begin{array}{r}5\\5\overline{)29}\\25\\\hline4\end{array} \qquad 9\ r\ 2\quad\begin{array}{r}9\\5\overline{)47}\\45\\\hline2\end{array}$$

By now children will be comfortable with remainders. In the second section, they have to place a decimal point after the number being divided and add one or two zeros. Encourage them to use the last section as practice for the operation they found most difficult.

Dividing larger numbers

$645 \div 13$ can be written in two ways:

$$49\frac{8}{13}\quad\begin{array}{r}\\13\overline{)645}\end{array} \qquad or \qquad 49\ r\ 8\quad\begin{array}{r}\\13\overline{)645}\end{array}$$

Work out the answer to each problem. Use fraction remainders.

$$8\frac{33}{43}\quad\begin{array}{r}8\\43\overline{)377}\\344\\\hline33\end{array} \qquad 8\frac{1}{21}\quad\begin{array}{r}8\\21\overline{)169}\\168\\\hline1\end{array} \qquad 9\frac{5}{17}\quad\begin{array}{r}9\\17\overline{)158}\\153\\\hline5\end{array} \qquad 8\frac{40}{41}\quad\begin{array}{r}8\\41\overline{)368}\\328\\\hline40\end{array}$$

$$3\frac{47}{50}\quad\begin{array}{r}3\\50\overline{)197}\\150\\\hline47\end{array} \qquad 6\frac{90}{91}\quad\begin{array}{r}6\\91\overline{)636}\\546\\\hline90\end{array} \qquad 27\frac{1}{12}\quad\begin{array}{r}27\\12\overline{)325}\\24\\\hline85\\84\\\hline1\end{array} \qquad 56\frac{3}{14}\quad\begin{array}{r}56\\14\overline{)787}\\70\\\hline87\\84\\\hline3\end{array}$$

Work out the answer to each problem. Use unit remainders.

$$18\ r\ 11\quad\begin{array}{r}18\\52\overline{)947}\\52\\\hline427\\416\\\hline11\end{array} \qquad 20\ r\ 31\quad\begin{array}{r}20\\35\overline{)731}\\70\\\hline31\\0\\\hline31\end{array} \qquad 15\ r\ 23\quad\begin{array}{r}15\\57\overline{)878}\\57\\\hline308\\285\\\hline23\end{array} \qquad 79\ r\ 6\quad\begin{array}{r}79\\11\overline{)875}\\77\\\hline105\\99\\\hline6\end{array}$$

$$7\ r\ 5\quad\begin{array}{r}7\\70\overline{)495}\\490\\\hline5\end{array} \qquad 8\ r\ 63\quad\begin{array}{r}8\\84\overline{)735}\\672\\\hline63\end{array} \qquad 8\ r\ 35\quad\begin{array}{r}8\\44\overline{)387}\\352\\\hline35\end{array} \qquad 7\ r\ 55\quad\begin{array}{r}7\\62\overline{)489}\\434\\\hline55\end{array}$$

See the notes on page 101.

Division of 3-digit decimal numbers

Work out these division sums.

```
    0.89              0.74
3)2.67            4)2.96
  24                28
  27                16
  27                16
   0    0.89         0    0.74
```

Work out these division problems.

```
   1.47          1.83          1.53          1.62
2)2.94        4)7.32        4)6.12        2)3.24
  2             4             4             2
  9            33            21            12
  8            32            20            12
 14            12            12            04
 14            12            12             4
  0             0             0             0
```

```
   4.99          3.24          1.56          1.87
2)9.98        3)9.72        4)6.24        4)7.48
  8             9             4             4
 19            07            22            34
 18             6            20            32
 18            12            24            28
 18            12            24            28
  0             0             0             0
```

```
   0.56          0.74          0.75          0.87
4)2.24        3)2.22        3)2.25        3)2.61
 20            21            21            24
 24            12            15            21
 24            12            15            21
  0             0             0             0
```

On this page, the decimal point has been incorporated into the middle of the number being divided. After the previous two pages, carrying across the decimal point should be familiar to children. No additional zeros need to be added on in this section.

Division of 3-digit decimal numbers

Work out these division problems.

```
    1.99             1.61
5)9.95           6)9.66
  5                6
  49               36
  45               36
   45               6
   45               6
    0   1.99         0   1.61
```

Work out these division problems.

```
   1.63          1.85          1.27          1.52
5)8.15        5)9.25        5)6.35        6)9.12
  5             5             5             6
 31            42            13            31
 30            40            10            30
 15            25            35            12
 15            25            35            12
  0             0             0             0
```

```
   0.36          1.26          0.69          0.74
6)2.16        7)8.82        7)4.83        8)5.92
 18             7            42            56
 36            18            63            32
 36            14            63            32
  0            42             0             0
               42
                0
```

```
   1.09          0.91          0.63          1.06
8)8.72        9)8.19        9)5.67        6)6.36
 8             81            54             6
 72             9            27            36
 72             9            27            36
  0             0             0             0
```

The comments on the previous page also apply to this one, but as the dividing numbers are larger any weakness in multiplication facts for 6, 7, 8, and 9 times tables will show up.

Real-life problems

A builder uses 1,600 lb of sand a day. How much will he use in 5 days?

8,000 lb

```
   3
 1,600
 x   5
 8,000
```

If he uses 9,500 lb the next week, how much more has he used than the week before?

1,500 lb

```
 9,500
-8,000
 1,500
```

An electrician uses 184 ft of cable while working on four houses. If he uses the same amount on each house, how much does he use on one house?

46 ft

```
  46
4)184
 16
 24
 24
  0
```

A family looks at vacations in two different resorts. The first one costs $846.95. The second costs $932. How much will the family save if they choose the cheaper resort?

$85.05

```
 8 2 11 9 10
 932.00
-846.95
  85.05
```

Doris has 5 sections of fence, each 36 in. wide. If she puts them together, how much of her yard can she fence off?

180 in.

```
   3
  36
 x  5
 180
```

Shula goes on a sponsored walk and collects $15.95 from her mother, $8.36 from her uncle, $4.65 from her brother, and $2.75 from her aunt. How much does she collect altogether?

$31.71

```
 2 2 2
 15.95
  8.36
  4.65
+ 2.75
 31.71
```

A taxi company has 9 cars. If each car holds 16.4 gallons of gasoline, how many gallons will it take to fill all of the cars?

147.6 gallons

```
  5 3
 16.4
 x  9
 147.6
```

This page provides an opportunity to apply the skills practiced. Children will need to select the operation necessary. If they are unsure about which operation to use, discuss whether the answer will be larger or smaller, which narrows down the options.

Rounding money

Round to the nearest dollar.

$3.95 rounds to $4

$2.25 rounds to $2

Round to the nearest ten dollars.

$15.50 rounds to $20

$14.40 rounds to $10

Round to the nearest dollar.

$2.60 rounds to $3 $8.49 rounds to $8 $3.39 rounds to $3

$9.55 rounds to $10 $1.75 rounds to $2 $4.30 rounds to $4

$7.15 rounds to $7 $6.95 rounds to $7 $2.53 rounds to $3

Round to the nearest ten dollars.

$37.34 rounds to $40 $21.75 rounds to $20 $85.03 rounds to $90

$71.99 rounds to $70 $66.89 rounds to $70 $52.99 rounds to $50

$55.31 rounds to $60 $12.79 rounds to $10 $15.00 rounds to $20

Round to the nearest hundred dollars.

$307.12 rounds to $300 $175.50 rounds to $200 $115.99 rounds to $100

$860.55 rounds to $900 $417.13 rounds to $400 $650.15 rounds to $700

$739.10 rounds to $700 $249.66 rounds to $200 $367.50 rounds to $400

If children have difficulty, have them decide which are the two nearest hundred dollars, and which is closest to the number.

Estimating sums of money

Round to the leading digit. Estimate the sum.

$3.26 → \$3
+ \$4.82 → + \$5
is about   \$8

$68.53 → \$70
+ \$34.60 → + \$30
is about   \$100

Round to the leading digit. Estimate the sum.

$52.61 → \$50
+ \$27.95 → + \$30
is about   \$80

$19.20 → \$20
+ \$22.13 → + \$20
is about   \$40

$70.75 → \$70
+ \$12.49 → + \$10
is about   \$80

$701.34 → \$700
+ \$100.80 → + \$100
is about   \$800

$339.50 → \$300
+ \$422.13 → + \$400
is about   \$700

$160.07 → \$200
+ \$230.89 → + \$200
is about   \$400

$25.61 → \$30
+ \$72.51 → + \$70
is about   \$100

$61.39 → \$60
+ \$19.50 → + \$20
is about   \$80

$18.32 → \$20
+ \$13.90 → + \$10
is about   \$30

$587.35 → \$600
+ 251.89 → + \$300
is about   \$900

$109.98 → \$100
+ \$210.09 → + \$200
is about   \$300

$470.02 → \$500
+ \$203.17 → + \$200
is about   \$700

Round to the leading digit. Estimate the sum.

$75.95 + $17.95 → \$100

$41.67 + $20.35 → \$60

$49.19 + $38.70 → \$90

$784.65 + $101.05 → \$900

$516.50 + $290.69 → \$800

$58.78 + $33.25 → \$90

$82.90 + $11.79 → \$90

$90.09 + $14.50 → \$100

In section 2, children need to estimate by rounding mentally. If they have trouble, have them write the rounded numbers above the originals first, and then add them.

Estimating differences of money

Round the numbers to the leading digit. Estimate the differences.

$8.75 → \$9
− \$5.10 → − \$5
is about   \$4

$61.47 → \$60
+ \$35.64 → − \$40
is about   \$20

Round the numbers to the leading digit. Estimate the differences.

$17.90 → \$20
− \$12.30 → − \$10
is about   \$10

$6.40 → \$6
− \$3.75 → − \$4
is about   \$2

$87.45 → \$90
− \$54.99 →− \$50
is about   \$40

$34.90 → \$30
− \$12.60 → − \$10
is about   \$20

$8.68 → \$9
− \$4.39 → − \$4
is about   \$5

$363.24 → \$400
− \$127.66 → − \$100
is about   \$300

$78.75 → \$80
− \$24.99 → − \$20
is about   \$60

$64.21 → \$60
− \$28.56 → − \$30
is about   \$30

$723.34 → \$700
− \$487.12 → − \$500
is about   \$200

Round the numbers to the leading digit. Estimate the differences.

$8.12 − $1.35
→ $8 − $1   =   \$7

$49.63 − $27.85
→ $50 − $30   \$20

$7.50 − $3.15
→ $8 − $3   =   \$5

$85.15 − $42.99
→ $90 − $40   \$50

$5.85 − $4.75
→ $6 − $5   =   \$1

$634.60 − $267.25
→ $600 − $300   \$300

$37.35 − $16.99
→ $40 − $20   \$20

$842.17 − $169.54
→ $800 − $200   \$600

$56.95 − $20.58
→ $60 − $20 =   \$40

$628.37 − $252.11
→ $600 − $300 =   \$300

See the comments on page 113.

Estimating sums and differences

Round the numbers to the leading digit. Estimate the sum or difference.

3,576 → 4,000
+ 1,307 → +1,000
is about   5,000

198,248 → 200,000
− 116,431 → − 100,000
is about   100,000

Round the numbers to the leading digit. Estimate the sum or difference.

685 → 700
+ 489 → + 500
is about   1,200

21,481 → 20,000
− 12,500 → − 10,000
is about   10,000

7,834 → 8,000
+ 3,106 → + 3,000
is about   11,000

682,778 → 700,000
+ 130,001 → + 100,000
is about   800,000

58,499 → 60,000
− 22,135 → − 20,000
is about   40,000

902,276 → 900,000
− 615,999 → − 600,000
is about   300,000

46,801 → 50,000
+ 34,700 → + 30,000
is about   80,000

9,734 → 10,000
− 8,306 → − 8,000
is about   2,000

65,606 → 70,000
+ 85,943 → + 90,000
is about   160,000

5,218 → 5,000
− 3,673 → − 4,000
is about   1,000

745 → 700
+ 451 → + 500
is about   1,200

337,297 → 300,000
− 168,931 → − 200,000
is about   100,000

Write < or > for each problem.

329 + 495   >   800

11,569 − 6,146   <   6,000

563 − 317   <   300

8,193 − 6,668   >   1,000

41,924 − 12,445   <   50,000

634,577 + 192,556   >   800,000

18,885 + 12,691   >   30,000

713,096 − 321,667   <   400,000

In section 2, children need to think about their estimates more carefully if the estimate is very close to the number on the right side of the equation. Have them look at the numbers in the next place to the right to adjust their estimates up or down.

Estimating products

Round to the leading digit. Estimate the product.

3,456 x 6
3,000 x 6 =   18,000

73 x 46
70 x 50 =   3,500

Round to the leading digit. Estimate the sum.

1,908 x 8
2,000 x 8 = 16,000

5 x 6,099
5 x 6,000 = 30,000

7 x 1,108
7 x 1000 = 7,000

5,239 x 9
5,000 x 9 = 45,000

81 x 32
80 x 30 = 2,400

19 x 62
20 x 60 = 1,200

39 x 44
40 x 40 = 1,600

94 x 12
90 x 10 = 900

Estimate the product.

6 x 7,243 42,000	4,785 x 4 20,000	3 x 8,924 27,000
2,785 x 5 15,000	6,298 x 4 24,000	7 x 7,105 49,000
8 x 2,870 24,000	4,176 x 7 28,000	5 x 4,803 25,000
6,777 x 9 63,000	6 x 8,022 48,000	3,785 x 4 16,000
42 x 51 2,000	54 x 28 1,500	23 x 75 1,600
16 x 32 600	47 x 54 2,500	59 x 52 3,000
17 x 74 1,400	33 x 22 600	81 x 18 1,600
31 x 91 2,700	38 x 87 3,600	46 x 77 4,000

Have children try to estimate the answer mentally. If they have trouble, have them write the rounded numbers first.

Estimating quotients

Round to compatible numbers. Estimate the quotient.

$3,156 \div 6$
$3,000 \div 6 = \boxed{500}$

$2,159 \div 5$
$2,500 \div 5 = \boxed{500}$

Round to compatible numbers. Estimate the quotient.

$1,934 \div 8$
$1,600 \div 8 = 200$

$4,066 \div 5$
$4,000 \div 5 = 800$

$1,108 \div 4$
$1,200 \div 4 = 300$

$5,657 \div 9$
$5,400 \div 9 = 600$

$3,998 \div 6$
$4,200 \div 6 = 700$

$5,525 \div 7$
$5,600 \div 7 = 800$

$1,701 \div 3$
$1,500 \div 3 = 500$

$1,304 \div 2$
$1,200 \div 2 = 600$

Estimate the quotient.

$4,798 \div 7$ 700	$8,205 \div 9$ 900	$5,022 \div 5$ 1,000
$3,785 \div 4$ 900	$5,528 \div 6$ 900	$2,375 \div 8$ 300
$1,632 \div 3$ 500	$4,251 \div 4$ 1,000	$4,754 \div 9$ 500
$7,352 \div 8$ 900	$1,774 \div 2$ 900	$3,322 \div 7$ 500
$3,591 \div 6$ 600	$2,887 \div 5$ 600	$5,746 \div 2$ 3,000
$3,703 \div 3$ 1,200	$2,392 \div 6$ 400	$6,621 \div 8$ 800

Children should round the dividend to a nearby number that can easily be divided by the divisor. Compatible numbers are ones that are just multiples of the divisor. Knowledge of basic division facts should allow these estimations to be done mentally.

Rounding mixed numbers

Round to the closest whole number.

$2\frac{5}{6}$

$\frac{5}{6}$ is more than $\frac{1}{2}$, so, $2\frac{5}{6}$ rounds up to 3.

$3\frac{2}{5}$

$\frac{2}{5}$ is less than $\frac{1}{2}$, so, $3\frac{2}{5}$ rounds down to 3.

Circle the fractions that are more than $\frac{1}{2}$.

$\frac{3}{7}$ $\frac{2}{9}$ (⑥⁄₇) $\frac{6}{7}$ (⑤⁄₉) $\frac{5}{9}$ $\frac{3}{8}$ $\frac{1}{7}$ (②⁄₃) $\frac{2}{3}$ (④⁄₇) $\frac{4}{7}$

(⑦⁄₁₀) $\frac{7}{10}$ $\frac{2}{5}$ $\frac{1}{3}$ (⑤⁄₆) $\frac{5}{6}$ (③⁄₄) $\frac{3}{4}$ $\frac{2}{9}$ (⑤⁄₈) $\frac{5}{8}$ (③⁄₅) $\frac{3}{5}$

Circle the fractions that are less than $\frac{1}{2}$.

(①⁄₈) $\frac{1}{8}$ (③⁄₉) $\frac{3}{9}$ $\frac{4}{5}$ (②⁄₇) $\frac{2}{7}$ $\frac{3}{5}$ (②⁄₅) $\frac{2}{5}$ $\frac{7}{10}$ (②⁄₉) $\frac{2}{9}$

$\frac{3}{4}$ (①⁄₃) $\frac{1}{3}$ (④⁄₉) $\frac{4}{9}$ (③⁄₁₀) $\frac{3}{10}$ $\frac{5}{6}$ (①⁄₄) $\frac{1}{4}$ (③⁄₇) $\frac{3}{7}$ $\frac{5}{9}$

Round to the closest whole number.

$4\frac{3}{8}$ 4	$2\frac{6}{7}$ 3	$5\frac{3}{4}$ 6	$3\frac{2}{9}$ 3
$2\frac{5}{6}$ 3	$1\frac{7}{8}$ 2	$2\frac{2}{5}$ 2	$5\frac{1}{7}$ 5
$3\frac{1}{6}$ 3	$5\frac{3}{8}$ 5	$3\frac{3}{5}$ 4	$7\frac{8}{13}$ 8
$6\frac{3}{5}$ 7	$1\frac{1}{4}$ 1	$4\frac{5}{6}$ 5	$9\frac{3}{4}$ 10
$5\frac{2}{3}$ 6	$3\frac{3}{7}$ 3	$1\frac{6}{7}$ 2	$6\frac{3}{4}$ 7

If children have trouble rounding, explain that if the numerator is less than half as big as the denominator, the fraction is less than one-half.

Calculate the mean

What is the mean of 6 and 10?
$(6+10) \div 2 = 8$

David is 9, Asha is 10, and Daniel is 5. What is their mean age?
$(9 + 10 + 5) \div 3 = 8$ years

Calculate the mean of these amounts.

9 and 5	7	6 and 8	7
5 and 7	6	11 and 7	9
8 and 12	10	13 and 15	14
19 and 21	20	40 and 60	50

Calculate the mean of these amounts.

5, 7, and 3	5	11, 9, and 7	9
14, 10, and 6	10	12, 8, and 4	8
7, 3, 5, and 9	6	\$1, \$1.50, \$2.50, and \$3	\$2
16¢, 9¢, 12¢, and 3¢	10¢	5 g, 7 g, 8 g, and 8 g	7 g

Calculate these answers.

The mean of two numbers is 7. If one of the numbers is 6, what is the other number? **8**

The mean of three numbers is 4. If two of the numbers are 4 and 5, what is the third number? **3**

The mean of four numbers is 12. If three of the numbers are 9, 15, and 8, what is the fourth number? **16**

Two children record their last five spelling-test scores.

Gayle	17	18	16	14	15
Sally	19	20	12	13	11

Which child has the best mean score? **Gayle**

The average of a number list is known as the 'mean'. Children should add the list and divide by the amount of numbers. In part 3, explain that if the mean is 7, the total must have been 14, so if they take away the number given they will find the number required.

Mean, median, and mode

Sian throws a dice 7 times. Here are her results:
4, 2, 1, 2, 4, 2, 6
What is the mean? $(4 + 2 + 1 + 2 + 4 + 2 + 6) \div 7 = 3$

What is the median? Put the numbers in order of size and find the middle number, example, 1, 2, 2, 2, 4, 4, 6.
The median is 2.

What is the mode? The most common result, which is 2.

A school soccer team scores the following number of goals in their first 9 matches:
2, 2, 1, 3, 2, 1, 2, 4, 1

What is the mean score? **2**

What is the median score? **2**

Write down the mode for their results. **2**

The ages of the local hockey players are:
17, 15, 16, 19, 17, 19, 22, 17, 18, 21, 17

What is the mean of their ages? **18**

What is their median age? **17**

Write down the mode for their ages. **17**

The results of Susan's last 11 spelling tests were:
15, 12, 15, 17, 11, 16, 19, 11, 3, 11, 13

What is the mean of her scores? **13**

What is her median score? **13**

Write down the mode for her scores. **11**

The work on this page leads on from previous work on the mean, but also expands it to the median and the mode. The biggest problem children may have is remembering which is which. Encourage them to develop a system that works for them.

Line graphs

Look at this graph.

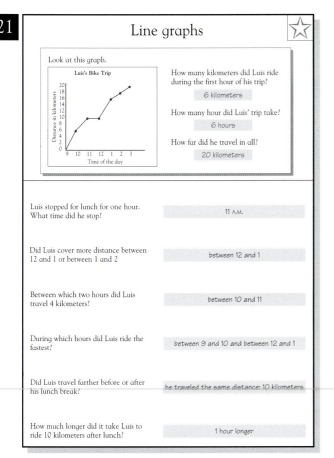

How many kilometers did Luis ride during the first hour of his trip?

6 kilometers

How many hour did Luis' trip take?

6 hours

How far did he travel in all?

20 kilometers

Luis stopped for lunch for one hour. What time did he stop?

11 A.M.

Did Luis cover more distance between 12 and 1 or between 1 and 2

between 12 and 1

Between which two hours did Luis travel 4 kilometers?

between 10 and 11

During which hours did Luis ride the fastest?

between 9 and 10 and between 12 and 1

Did Luis travel farther before or after his lunch break?

he traveled the same distance: 10 kilometers

How much longer did it take Luis to ride 10 kilometers after lunch?

1 hour longer

Children may have trouble deciding how far Luis traveled between two times. Have them find the distance at the starting and ending times, and then subtract to get the answer.

Coordinates

Write the coordinates of:

A **(2, 4)**

B **(3, 1)**

C **(1, 1)**

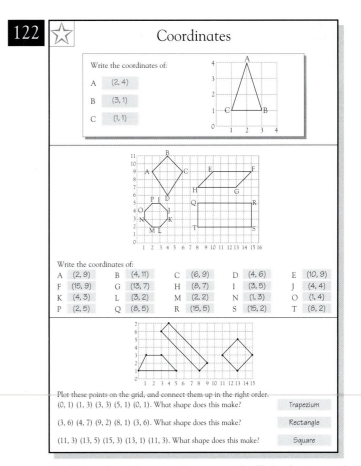

Write the coordinates of:

A	(2, 9)	B	(4, 11)	C	(6, 9)	D	(4, 6)	E	(10, 9)
F	(15, 9)	G	(13, 7)	H	(8, 7)	I	(3, 5)	J	(4, 4)
K	(4, 3)	L	(3, 2)	M	(2, 2)	N	(1, 3)	O	(1, 4)
P	(2, 5)	Q	(8, 5)	R	(15, 5)	S	(15, 2)	T	(8, 2)

Plot these points on the grid, and connect them up in the right order.

(0, 1) (1, 3) (3, 3) (5, 1) (0, 1). What shape does this make? **Trapezium**

(3, 6) (4, 7) (9, 2) (8, 1) (3, 6). What shape does this make? **Rectangle**

(11, 3) (13, 5) (15, 3) (13, 1) (11, 3). What shape does this make? **Square**

Children should remember to read off the horizontal coordinate first. In the second section, it is important that they join the coordinates in the order in which they are written, to produce the shape intended.

Drawing angles

Acute angles are between 0° and 90°.   Obtuse angles are between 90° and 180°.

When you get to 180° you have a straight line.

Use a protractor to draw these angles. Remember to mark the angle you have drawn.

150°

135°

45°

110°

10°

20°

To do the work on this page and the next, children require a 360° protractor. Check that they read the protractor from the right direction. Remind children to mark the angles. This is important to avoid confusion when drawing reflex angles.

Reading and writing numbers

264,346 in words is **Two hundred sixty-four thousand, three hundred forty-six**

One million, three hundred twelve thousand, five hundred two is **1,312,502**

Write each of these numbers in words.

326,208 **Three hundred twenty-six thousand, two hundred eight**

704,543 **Seven hundred four thousand, five hundred forty-three**

240,701 **Two hundred forty thousand, seven hundred one**

278,520 **Two hundred seventy-eight thousand, five hundred twenty**

Write each of these in numbers.

Five hundred seventeen thousand, forty-two **517,042**

Six hundred ninety-four thousand, seven hundred eleven **694,711**

Eight hundred nine thousand, two hundred three **809,203**

Nine hundred thousand, four hundred four **900,404**

Write each of these numbers in words.

9,307,012 **Nine million, three hundred seven thousand, twelve**

5,042,390 **Five million, forty-two thousand, three hundred ninety**

9,908,434 **Nine million, nine hundred eight thousand, four hundred thirty-four**

8,400,642 **Eight million, four hundred thousand, six hundred forty-two**

Write each of these in numbers.

Eight million, two hundred fifty-one **8,000,251**

Two million, forty thousand, four hundred four **2,040,404**

Seven million, three hundred two thousand, one hundred one **7,302,101**

Two million, five hundred forty-one thousand, five **2,541,005**

Children may use zeros incorrectly in numbers. In word form, zeros are omitted, but children should take care to include them when writing numbers in standard form.

Multiplying and dividing by 10

Write the answer in the box.
26 x 10 = 260
40 ÷ 10 = 4

Write the answer in the box.
76 x 10 = 760   43 x 10 = 430   93 x 10 = 930
66 x 10 = 660   13 x 10 = 130   47 x 10 = 470
147 x 10 = 1,470   936 x 10 = 9,360   284 x 10 = 2,840
364 x 10 = 3,640   821 x 10 = 8,210   473 x 10 = 4,730

Write the answer in the box.
30 ÷ 10 = 3   20 ÷ 10 = 2   70 ÷ 10 = 7
60 ÷ 10 = 6   50 ÷ 10 = 5   580 ÷ 10 = 58
310 ÷ 10 = 31   270 ÷ 10 = 27   100 ÷ 10 = 10
540 ÷ 10 = 54   890 ÷ 10 = 89   710 ÷ 10 = 71

Write the number that has been multiplied by 10.
37 x 10 = 370   64 x 10 = 640   74 x 10 = 740
81 x 10 = 810   10 x 10 = 100   83 x 10 = 830
714 x 10 = 7,140   307 x 10 = 3,070   529 x 10 = 5,290
264 x 10 = 2,640   829 x 10 = 8,290   648 x 10 = 6,480

Write the number that has been divided by 10.
30 ÷ 10 = 3   20 ÷ 10 = 2   90 ÷ 10 = 9
420 ÷ 10 = 42   930 ÷ 10 = 93   740 ÷ 10 = 74
570 ÷ 10 = 57   380 ÷ 10 = 38   860 ÷ 10 = 86

Children should realize that multiplying a whole number by 10 means writing a zero at the end. To divide a multiple of ten by 10, simply take the final zero off the number. In the two final sections, the inverse operation is used for solving the problems.

Identifying patterns

Continue each pattern.
Steps of 9:   5   14   23   32   41   50
Steps of 14:   20   34   48   62   76   90

Continue each pattern.

21	38	55	72	89	106	123	140
13	37	61	85	109	133	157	181
7	25	43	61	79	97	115	133
32	48	64	80	96	112	128	144
12	31	50	69	88	107	126	145
32	54	76	98	120	142	164	186
24	64	104	144	184	224	264	304
4	34	64	94	124	154	184	214
36	126	216	306	396	486	576	666
12	72	132	192	252	312	372	432
25	45	65	85	105	125	145	165
22	72	122	172	222	272	322	372
25	100	175	250	325	400	475	550
60	165	270	375	480	585	690	795
8	107	206	305	404	503	602	701
10	61	112	163	214	265	316	367
26	127	228	329	430	531	632	733
48	100	152	204	256	308	360	412

Children should determine what number to add to the first number to make the second number, and check to make sure that adding the same number turns the second number into the third. They can then continue the pattern.

Recognizing multiples of 6, 7, and 8

Circle the multiples of 6.
8   (12)   15   (18)   20   (24)

Circle the multiples of 6.
8   22   14   (18)   (36)   40
16   38   44   25   (30)   (60)
(6)   21   19   (54)   56   (24)
(12)   (48)   10   20   35   26
(42)   39   23   28   (36)   32

Circle the multiples of 7.
(7)   17   24   59   (42)   55
15   20   (21)   46   12   (70)
(14)   27   69   36   47   (49)
65   19   57   (28)   38   (63)
33   34   (35)   37   60   (56)

Circle the multiples of 8.
(40)   26   15   25   38   (56)
26   (8)   73   41   (64)   12
75   58   62   (24)   31   (72)
12   (80)   (32)   46   38   78
(16)   42   66   28   (48)   68

Circle the number that is a multiple of 6 and 7.
18   54   (42)   21   28   63

Circle the numbers that are multiples of 6 and 8.
16   (24)   36   (48)   54   42

Circle the number that is a multiple of 7 and 8.
24   32   40   28   42   (56)

Success on this page will basically depend on a knowledge of multiplication tables. Where children experience difficulties, multiplication table practice should be encouraged.

Factors of numbers from 1 to 30

The factors of 10 are   1   2   5   10
Circle the factors of 4.   (1) (2)   3   (4)

Write all the factors of each number.
The factors of 26 are   1, 2, 13, 26
The factors of 30 are   1, 2, 3, 5, 6, 10, 15, 30
The factors of 9 are   1, 3, 9
The factors of 12 are   1, 2, 3, 4, 6, 12
The factors of 15 are   1, 3, 5, 15
The factors of 22 are   1, 2, 11, 22
The factors of 20 are   1, 2, 4, 5, 10, 20
The factors of 21 are   1, 3, 7, 21
The factors of 24 are   1, 2, 3, 4, 6, 8, 12, 24

Circle all the factors of each number.
Which numbers are factors of 14?   (1)(2) 3 5 (7) 9 12 (14)
Which numbers are factors of 13?   (1) 2 3 4 5 6 7 8 9 10 11 (13)
Which numbers are factors of 7?   (1) 2 3 4 5 6 (7)
Which numbers are factors of 11?   (1) 2 3 4 5 6 7 8 9 10 (11)
Which numbers are factors of 6?   (1)(2)(3) 4 5 (6)
Which numbers are factors of 8?   (1)(2) 3 (4) 5 6 7 (8)
Which numbers are factors of 17?   (1) 2 5 7 12 14 16 (17)
Which numbers are factors of 18?   (1)(2)(3) 4 5 (6) 8 (9)10 12 (18)

Some numbers only have factors of 1 and themselves. They are called prime numbers. Write down all the prime numbers that are less than 30 in the box.

2, 3, 5, 7, 11, 13, 17, 19, 23, 29

Encourage a systematic approach such as starting at and working forward to the number that is half of the number in question. Children often forget that 1 and the number itself are factors of a given number. You may need to point out that 1 is not a prime number.

Recognizing equivalent fractions ☆

Make each pair of fractions equal by writing a number in the box.

$\frac{1}{2} = \frac{2}{4}$ $\frac{1}{3} = \frac{2}{6}$

Make each pair of fractions equal by writing a number in the box.

$\frac{1}{2} = \frac{5}{10}$ $\frac{3}{4} = \frac{6}{8}$ $\frac{1}{3} = \frac{3}{9}$

$\frac{2}{3} = \frac{8}{12}$ $\frac{6}{12} = \frac{3}{6}$ $\frac{4}{8} = \frac{1}{2}$

$\frac{1}{5} = \frac{2}{10}$ $\frac{4}{12} = \frac{2}{6}$ $\frac{3}{5} = \frac{6}{10}$

$\frac{1}{4} = \frac{2}{8}$ $\frac{6}{18} = \frac{1}{3}$ $\frac{3}{12} = \frac{1}{4}$

$\frac{3}{9} = \frac{1}{3}$ $\frac{4}{10} = \frac{2}{5}$ $\frac{3}{4} = \frac{9}{12}$

$\frac{4}{16} = \frac{1}{4}$ $\frac{15}{20} = \frac{3}{4}$ $\frac{6}{12} = \frac{1}{2}$

$\frac{3}{5} = \frac{6}{10}$ $\frac{3}{6} = \frac{1}{2}$ $\frac{9}{12} = \frac{3}{4}$

Make each row of fractions equal by writing a number in each box.

$\frac{1}{2} = \frac{2}{4} = \frac{3}{6} = \frac{4}{8} = \frac{5}{10} = \frac{6}{12}$

$\frac{1}{4} = \frac{2}{8} = \frac{3}{12} = \frac{4}{16} = \frac{5}{20} = \frac{6}{24}$

$\frac{3}{4} = \frac{6}{8} = \frac{9}{12} = \frac{12}{16} = \frac{15}{20} = \frac{18}{24}$

$\frac{1}{3} = \frac{2}{6} = \frac{3}{9} = \frac{4}{12} = \frac{5}{15} = \frac{12}{36}$

$\frac{1}{5} = \frac{2}{10} = \frac{3}{15} = \frac{4}{20} = \frac{5}{25} = \frac{6}{30}$

$\frac{2}{3} = \frac{4}{6} = \frac{6}{9} = \frac{8}{12} = \frac{10}{15} = \frac{14}{21}$

If children have problems with this page, point out that fractions remain the same as long as you multiply both the numerator and denominator by the same number, or divide the numerator and denominator by the same number.

☆ Rounding decimals

Round each decimal to the nearest whole number.

3.4 → 3

5.7 → 6

4.5 → 5

If the whole number has 5 after it, round it to the whole number above.

Round each decimal to the nearest whole number.

6.2	6	2.5	3	1.5	2	3.8	4
5.5	6	2.8	3	3.2	3	8.5	9
5.4	5	7.9	8	3.7	4	2.3	2
1.1	1	8.6	9	8.3	8	9.2	9
4.7	5	6.3	6	7.3	7	8.7	9

Round each decimal to the nearest whole number.

14.4	14	42.3	42	74.1	74	59.7	60
29.9	30	32.6	33	63.5	64	96.4	96
18.2	18	37.5	38	39.6	40	76.3	76
40.1	40	28.7	29	26.9	27	12.5	13
29.5	30	38.5	39	87.2	87	41.6	42

Round each decimal to the nearest whole number.

137.6	138	423.5	424	426.2	426	111.8	112
641.6	642	333.5	334	805.2	805	246.8	247
119.5	120	799.6	800	562.3	562	410.2	410
682.4	682	759.6	760	531.5	532	829.9	830
743.4	743	831.1	831	276.7	277	649.3	649

If children experience difficulties, you might want to use a number line showing tenths. Errors often occur when a number with 9 in the ones column is rounded up. Children also often neglect to alter the tens digit in a number such as 19.7.

Real-life problems ☆

Write the answer in the box.

Yasmin has $4.60 and she is given another $1.20. How much money does she have?

$5.80

$\begin{array}{r} \$4.60 \\ + \$1.20 \\ \hline \$5.80 \end{array}$

David has 120 marbles. He divides them equally among his 5 friends. How many marbles does each get?

24

$\begin{array}{r} 24 \\ 5\overline{)120} \\ \underline{10} \\ 20 \\ \underline{20} \\ 0 \end{array}$

TOYS

Write the answer in the box.

Michael buys a ball for $5.50 and a flashlight for $3.65. How much does he spend?

$9.15

How much does he have left from $10?

$0.85

The 32 children of a class bring in $5 each for a school trip. What is the total of the amount brought in?

$160

A set of 5 shelves can be made from a piece of wood 4 yards long. What fraction of a yard will each shelf be?

$\frac{4}{5}$ yard

Each of 5 children has $16. How much do they have altogether?

$80

If the above total were shared among 8 children, how much would each child have?

$10

This page tests children's ability to choose the operation required to solve real-life problems, mostly involving money. Discussing whether the answer will be larger or smaller than the question will help children decide on their choice of operation.

☆ Real-life problems

Find the answer to each problem.

A box is 16 in. wide. How wide will 6 boxes side by side be?

96 in.

$\begin{array}{r} \overset{3}{16} \text{ in.} \\ \times 6 \\ \hline 96 \text{ in.} \end{array}$

Josh is 1.20 m tall. His sister is 1.55 m tall. How much taller than Josh is his sister?

0.35 m

$\begin{array}{r} 1.55 \text{ m} \\ - 1.20 \text{ m} \\ \hline 0.35 \text{ m} \end{array}$

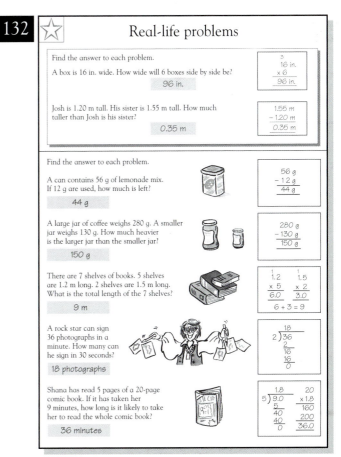

Find the answer to each problem.

A can contains 56 g of lemonade mix. If 12 g are used, how much is left?

44 g

$\begin{array}{r} 56 \text{ g} \\ - 12 \text{ g} \\ \hline 44 \text{ g} \end{array}$

A large jar of coffee weighs 280 g. A smaller jar weighs 130 g. How much heavier is the larger jar than the smaller jar?

150 g

$\begin{array}{r} 280 \text{ g} \\ - 130 \text{ g} \\ \hline 150 \text{ g} \end{array}$

There are 7 shelves of books. 5 shelves are 1.2 m long. 2 shelves are 1.5 m. What is the total length of the 7 shelves?

9 m

$\begin{array}{r} \overset{1}{1.2} \\ \times 5 \\ \hline 6.0 \end{array}$ $\begin{array}{r} \overset{1}{1.5} \\ \times 2 \\ \hline 3.0 \end{array}$

$6 + 3 = 9$

A rock star can sign 36 photographs in a minute. How many can he sign in 30 seconds?

18 photographs

$\begin{array}{r} 18 \\ 2\overline{)36} \\ \underline{2} \\ 16 \\ \underline{16} \\ 0 \end{array}$

Shana has read 5 pages of a 20-page comic book. If it has taken her 9 minutes, how long is it likely to take her to read the whole comic book?

36 minutes

$\begin{array}{r} 1.8 \\ 5\overline{)9.0} \\ \underline{5} \\ 40 \\ \underline{40} \\ 0 \end{array}$ $\begin{array}{r} 20 \\ \times 1.8 \\ \hline 160 \\ 200 \\ \hline 36.0 \end{array}$

This page continues with real-life problems but with units other than money. Note that children must perform three operations to solve the third problem.

Problems involving time ⭐

Find the answer to this problem.

A train leaves the station at 7:30 A.M. and arrives at the end of the line at 10:45 A.M. How long did the journey take?

3 hours 15 minutes

7:30 → 10:30 = 3 h
10:30 → 10:45 = 15 min
Total = 3 h 15 min

Find the answer to each problem.

A film starts at 7:00 P.M. and finishes at 8:45 P.M. How long is the film?

1 hour 45 minutes

7:00 → 8:00 = 1 h
8:00 → 8:45 = 45 min
Total = 1 h 45 min

A cake takes 2 hours 25 minutes to bake. If it begins baking at 1:35 P.M., at what time will the cake be done?

4:00 P.M.

1:35 + 2 h = 3:35
3:35 + 25 min = 4:00

Sanjay needs to clean his bedroom and wash the car. It takes him 1 hour 10 minutes to clean his room and 45 minutes to clean the car. If he starts at 10:00 A.M., at what time will he finish?

11.55 A.M.

10:00 + 1 h = 11:00
11:00 + 10 min = 11:10
11:10 + 45 min = 11:55

A car is taken in for repair at 7:00 A.M. It is finished at 1:50 P.M. How long did the repairs take?

6 hours 50 minutes

7:00 → 1:00 = 6 h
1:00 → 1:50 = 50 min
Total = 6 h 50 min

Claire has to be at school by 8:50 A.M. If she takes 1 hour 30 minutes to get ready, and the trip takes 35 minutes, at what time does she need to get up?

6.45 A.M.

8:50 − 1 h = 7:50
7:50 − 30 min = 7:20
7:20 − 35 min = 6:45

A bus leaves the bus station at 8:45 A.M. and arrives back at 10:15 A.M. How long has its trip taken?

1 hour 30 minutes

8:45 → 9:45 = 1 h
9:45 → 10:15 = 30 min
Total = 1 h 30 min

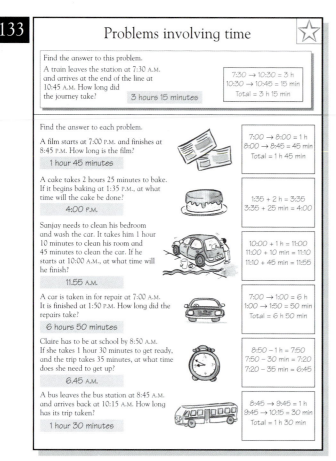

Children must remember that hours are based on units of 60 rather than of 10, so when they regroup, they will add 60 to the minutes instead of the 10 they would add when regrouping numbers.

⭐ Elapsed time

Write the answer in the box.

10:40   11:40   12:40   1:20

1 hour   1 hour   40 minutes

Carmen's gymnastics class starts at 10:40 A.M. and ends at 1:20 P.M. How long does it last? **2 hours and 40 minutes**

Write the answer in the box.

The ferry leaves the mainland at 11:00 A.M. and docks on the island at 3 P.M. How long is the ride?

4 hours

The movie starts at 6:05 P.M. and ends at 9:17 P.M. How long is it?

3 hours 12 minutes

Pat works an 8-hour shift at the fairgrounds. If he starts work at 9 A.M., at what time is he finished?

5 P.M.

Keesha wants to videotape a program that starts at 11:30 P.M. It lasts 1 hour and 45 minutes. What time will it end?

1:15 A.M.

Mai finished painting her porch at 4:25 P.M. The instructions said she should wait at least 15 hours to paint the trim. What is the earliest time when she could start painting the trim?

7:25 A.M.

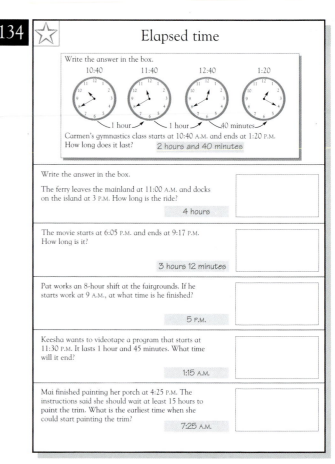

If children have trouble keeping track of the changes in hours or minutes, have them write down each step as in the diagram.

Recognizing multiples ⭐

Circle the multiples of 10.

14   ⃝20   25   ⃝30   47   ⃝60

Circle the multiples of 6.
20   ⃝48   56   ⃝72   25   35
1   3   ⃝6   16   26   ⃝36

Circle the multiples of 7.
⃝14   24   ⃝35   27   47   ⃝49
⃝63   ⃝42   52   37   64   71

Circle the multiples of 8.
25   31   ⃝48   84   ⃝32   ⃝8
18   54   ⃝64   35   ⃝72   28

Circle the multiples of 9.
17   ⃝81   ⃝27   35   92   106
⃝45   53   ⃝108   ⃝90   33   95
64   ⃝9   28   ⃝18   ⃝36   98

Circle the multiples of 10.
15   35   ⃝20   46   ⃝90   ⃝100
44   37   ⃝30   29   ⃝50   45

Circle the multiples of 11.
24   ⃝110   123   54   ⃝66   90
45   ⃝33   87   98   ⃝99   ⃝121
43   ⃝44   65   ⃝55   21   ⃝22

Circle the multiples of 12.
136   134   ⃝144   109   ⃝108   ⃝132
⃝24   34   58   68   ⃝48   ⃝60
35   29   ⃝72   74   ⃝84   94

Success on this page basically depends on knowledge of multiplication tables. Where children experience difficulties, it may be necessary to reinforce multiplication tables.

⭐ Bar graphs

Use this bar graph to answer each question.

What color cap was sold the most?   **red**

How many more green caps were sold than blue caps?   **10**

Use this bar graph to answer each question.

How many tickets were sold on May 1?   **80 tickets**

How many more tickets were sold on May 2 than on May 4?   **20 more tickets**

On which date were 90 tickets sold?   **May 3**

Use this bar graph to answer each question.

Which runner ran 14 miles?   **Max**

Which runner ran the same distance as Annie?   **Jill**

How much farther did Ivan run than Max?   **4 miles**

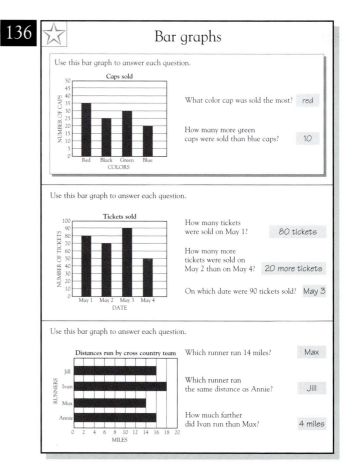

Children will be required to read information, to look for specific information, and to manipulate the information they read on a bar graph, to answer the questions. They may need to be reassured that a horizontal bar graph can be read in much the same way as a vertical bar graph.

Triangles

Look at these different triangles.

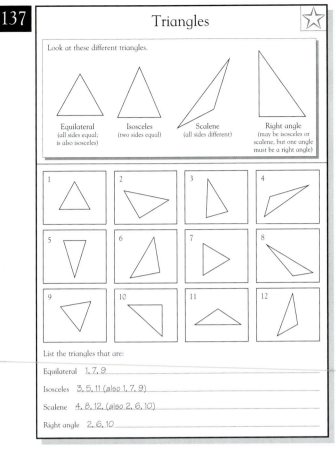

Equilateral
(all sides equal;
is also isosceles)

Isosceles
(two sides equal)

Scalene
(all sides different)

Right angle
(may be isosceles or
scalene, but one angle
must be a right angle)

1	2	3	4
5	6	7	8
9	10	11	12

List the triangles that are:

Equilateral   1, 7, 9

Isosceles   3, 5, 11 (also 1, 7, 9)

Scalene   4, 8, 12, (also 2, 6, 10)

Right angle   2, 6, 10

This page will highlight any gaps in children's ability to recognize and name triangles. Make sure that children can identify the triangles that have been rotated.

Place value to 10,000,000

How many hundreds are there in 7,000?   70   hundreds
(70 x 100 = 7,000)

What is the value of the 9 in 694?   90   (because the 9 is in the tens column)

Write how many tens there are in:

400	40	tens	600	60	tens	900	90	tens
200	20	tens	1,300	130	tens	4,700	470	tens
4,800	480	tens	1,240	124	tens	1,320	132	tens
2,630	263	tens	5,920	592	tens	4,350	435	tens

What is the value of the 7 in these numbers?

| 76 | 70 | 720 | 700 | 137 | 7 |
| 7,122 | 7,000 | 74,301 | 70,000 | 724 | 700 |

What is the value of the 3 in these numbers?

| 324,126 | 300,000 | 3,927,141 | 3,000,000 | 214,623 | 3 |
| 8,254,320 | 300 | 3,711,999 | 3,000,000 | 124,372 | 300 |

Write how many hundreds there are in:

6,400	64	hundreds	8,500	85	hundreds
19,900	199	hundreds	36,200	362	hundreds
524,600	5,246	hundreds	712,400	7,124	hundreds

What is the value of the 8 in these numbers?

| 8,214,631 | 8,000,000 | 2,398,147 | 8,000 | 463,846 | 800 |
| 287,034 | 80,000 | 8,110,927 | 8,000,000 | 105,428 | 8 |

Explain to children that finding how many tens there are in a number is the same as dividing by 10. In the number 400, for example, there are 40 tens, because 400 divided by 10 is 40.

Multiplying and dividing by 10

Write the answer in the box.

37 x 10 =   370   58 ÷ 10 =   5.8

Write the product in the box.

94 x 10 =	940	13 x 10 =	130	37 x 10 =	370
36 x 10 =	360	47 x 10 =	470	54 x 10 =	540
236 x 10 =	2,360	419 x 10 =	4,190	262 x 10 =	2,620
531 x 10 =	5,310	674 x 10 =	6,740	801 x 10 =	8,010

Write the quotient in the box.

92 ÷ 10 =	9.2	48 ÷ 10 =	4.8	37 ÷ 10 =	3.7
18 ÷ 10 =	1.8	29 ÷ 10 =	2.9	54 ÷ 10 =	5.4
345 ÷ 10 =	34.5	354 ÷ 10 =	35.4	723 ÷ 10 =	72.3
531 ÷ 10 =	53.1	262 ÷ 10 =	26.2	419 ÷ 10 =	41.9

Find the missing factor.

23	x 10 = 230	75	x 10 = 750	99	x 10 = 990
48	x 10 = 480	13	x 10 = 130	25	x 10 = 250
52	x 10 = 520	39	x 10 = 390	27	x 10 = 270
62	x 10 = 620	86	x 10 = 860	17	x 10 = 170

Find the dividend.

47	÷ 10 = 4.7	68	÷ 10 = 6.8	124	÷ 10 = 12.4
257	÷ 10 = 25.7	362	÷ 10 = 36.2	314	÷ 10 = 31.4
408	÷ 10 = 40.8	672	÷ 10 = 67.2	809	÷ 10 = 80.9
924	÷ 10 = 92.4	327	÷ 10 = 32.7	563	÷ 10 = 56.3

Remind children that multiplying by 10 adds a 0 to the original figure. Dividing by 10 moves the decimal one place to the left. Whole numbers can be written with a decimal point (e.g. 16 as 16.0). Inverse operations in the later sections give the number that begins the equation.

Appropriate units of measure

Choose the best units to measure the length of each item.

| inches | feet | yards |

| notebook | car | swimming pool |
| inches | feet | yards |

Choose the best units to measure the length of each item.

| inches | feet | yards |

| bed | bicycle | toothbrush | football field |
| feet | feet | inches | yards |

| shoe | driveway | canoe | fence |
| inches | feet or yards | feet | yards |

The height of a door is about 7   feet   .

The length of a pencil is about 7   inches   .

The height of a flagpole is about 7   yards   .

Choose the best units to measure the weight of each item.

| ounces | pounds | tons |

| train | kitten | watermelon | tennis ball |
| tons | ounces | pounds | ounces |

| shoe | bag of potatoes | elephant | washing machine |
| ounces | pounds | tons | pounds |

The weight of a hamburger is about 6   ounces   .

The weight of a bag of apples is about 5   pounds   .

The weight of a truck is about 4   tons   .

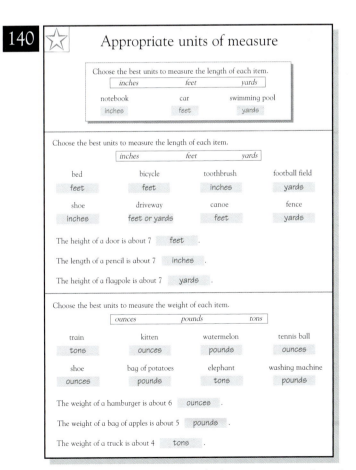

Children might come up with their own examples of items that measure about 1 inch, 1 foot, and 1 yard, as well as items that weigh about 1 ounce, 1 pound, and 1 ton. They can use these as benchmarks to find the appropriate unit.

141 Identifying patterns

Continue each pattern.

Intervals of 6:	1	7	13	19	25	31	37
Intervals of 3:	27	24	21	18	15	12	9

Continue each pattern.

0	10	20	30	40	50	60
15	20	25	30	35	40	45
5	7	9	11	13	15	17
2	9	16	23	30	37	44
4	7	10	13	16	19	22
2	10	18	26	34	42	50

Continue each pattern.

44	38	32	26	20	14	8
33	29	25	21	17	13	9
27	23	19	15	11	7	3
56	48	40	32	24	16	8
49	42	35	28	21	14	7
28	25	22	19	16	13	10

Continue each pattern.

36	30	24	18	12	6	0
5	14	23	32	41	50	59
3	8	13	18	23	28	33
47	40	33	26	19	12	5
1	4	7	10	13	16	19

Point out that some of the patterns show an increase and some a decrease. Children should see what operation turns the first number into the second, and that the same operation turns the second number into the third. They can then continue the pattern.

142 Factors of numbers from 31 to 65

The factors of 40 are 1 2 4 5 8 10 20 40

Circle the factors of 56.

① ② 3 ④ 5 6 ⑦ ⑧ ⑭ ㉘ 32 (56)

Find all the factors of each number.

The factors of 31 are 1, 31

The factors of 47 are 1, 47

The factors of 60 are 1, 2, 3, 4, 5, 6, 10, 12, 15, 20, 30, 60

The factors of 50 are 1, 2, 5, 10, 25, 50

The factors of 42 are 1, 2, 3, 6, 7, 14, 21, 42

The factors of 32 are 1, 2, 4, 8, 16, 32

The factors of 48 are 1, 2, 3, 4, 6, 8, 12, 16, 24, 48

The factors of 35 are 1, 5, 7, 35

The factors of 52 are 1, 2, 4, 13, 26, 52

Circle all the factors of each number.

Which numbers are factors of 39?

① 2 ③ 4 5 8 9 10 ⑬ 14 15 20 25 ㊴

Which numbers are factors of 45?

① ③ 4 ⑤ 8 ⑨ 12 ⑮ 16 21 24 36 40 44 ㊺

Which numbers are factors of 61?

① 3 4 5 6 10 15 16 18 20 26 31 40 (61)

Which numbers are factors of 65?

① 2 4 ⑤ 6 8 9 10 12 ⑬ 14 15 30 60 (65)

Some numbers have only factors of 1 and themselves. They are called prime numbers. Write all the prime numbers between 31 and 65 in the box.

31, 37, 41, 43, 47, 53, 59, 61

Children often miss some of the factors of a number, especially when the number is large. Encourage a systematic method of finding factors. Children may forget that 1 and the number itself are factors of the number. If needed, discuss prime numbers with them.

143 Greatest common factor

Circle the common factors.
Write the greatest common factor (GCF).

24: ①, ②, ③, 4, ⑥, 8, 12, 24
60: ①, ②, ③, 4, 5, ⑥, 8, 10, 12, 60 The GCF is 6
42: ①, ②, ③, ⑥, 7, 14

Find the factors. Circle the common factors.

45: ①, ③ 5, ⑨ 15, 45
36: ①, 2, ③, 4, 6, 8, ⑨, 12, 18, 36

28: ①, ② 4, 7, 14, 28
54: ①, ② 3, 6, 9, 18, 54

Find the factors. Write the GCF.

35: ①, ⑤ 7, 35
The GCF is 5
80: ①, 2, 4, ⑤ 8, 10, 20, 40, 80

32: ①, ②, ④, ⑧, ⑯, ㉜
The GCF is 32
64: ①, ②, ④, ⑧, ⑯, ㉜, 64

12: ①, 2, ③, 4, 6, 12
44: ①, 2, ③, 4, 6, 8, 12, 24
15: 1, 3, ⑤, ⑮
The GCF is 3

54: 1, 2, 3, 6, 9, 18, 27, 54
72: 1, 2, 3, 4, 6, 8, 9, 12, 18, 24, 36
18: 1, 2, 3, 6, 9, 18
The GCF is 18

It is common for children to skip some of the factors of a number. Have them test factors systematically, beginning with 2, and then 3, and so on.

144 Writing equivalent fractions

Make these fractions equal by writing the missing number.

$\frac{20}{100} = \frac{2}{10} = \frac{1}{5}$

$\frac{5}{15} = \frac{1}{3}$

Make these fractions equal by writing a number in the box.

$\frac{10}{100} = \frac{1}{10}$ $\frac{8}{100} = \frac{2}{25}$ $\frac{4}{100} = \frac{1}{25}$

$\frac{2}{20} = \frac{1}{10}$ $\frac{5}{100} = \frac{1}{20}$ $\frac{6}{20} = \frac{3}{10}$

$\frac{3}{5} = \frac{12}{20}$ $\frac{5}{6} = \frac{10}{12}$ $\frac{2}{8} = \frac{6}{24}$

$\frac{2}{3} = \frac{16}{24}$ $\frac{2}{18} = \frac{1}{9}$ $\frac{4}{50} = \frac{2}{25}$

$\frac{11}{12} = \frac{33}{36}$ $\frac{12}{15} = \frac{4}{5}$ $\frac{8}{20} = \frac{2}{5}$

$\frac{2}{12} = \frac{1}{6}$ $\frac{5}{20} = \frac{1}{4}$ $\frac{5}{8} = \frac{10}{16}$

$\frac{7}{8} = \frac{21}{24}$ $\frac{15}{100} = \frac{3}{20}$ $\frac{6}{24} = \frac{1}{4}$

$\frac{5}{25} = \frac{1}{5}$ $\frac{8}{20} = \frac{2}{5}$ $\frac{15}{20} = \frac{3}{4}$

$\frac{5}{30} = \frac{1}{6}$ $\frac{12}{14} = \frac{6}{7}$ $\frac{1}{5} = \frac{4}{20}$

$\frac{9}{18} = \frac{1}{2}$ $\frac{24}{30} = \frac{4}{5}$ $\frac{25}{30} = \frac{5}{6}$

$\frac{1}{8} = \frac{2}{16} = \frac{3}{24} = \frac{4}{32} = \frac{5}{40} = \frac{6}{48}$

$\frac{20}{100} = \frac{5}{25} = \frac{2}{10} = \frac{1}{5} = \frac{10}{50} = \frac{40}{200}$

$\frac{2}{5} = \frac{6}{15} = \frac{8}{20} = \frac{10}{25} = \frac{20}{50} = \frac{40}{100}$

$\frac{1}{6} = \frac{2}{12} = \frac{3}{18} = \frac{4}{24} = \frac{5}{30} = \frac{6}{36}$

$\frac{2}{3} = \frac{16}{24} = \frac{24}{36} = \frac{14}{21} = \frac{6}{9} = \frac{200}{300}$

Remind children that fractions retain the same value if you multiply both the numerator and denominator by the same number or divide the numerator and denominator by the same number.

Fraction models

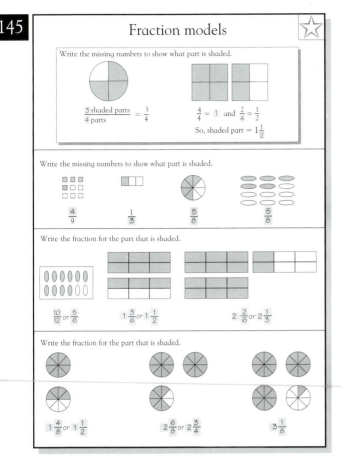

Write the missing numbers to show what part is shaded.

$\frac{3 \text{ shaded parts}}{4 \text{ parts}} = \frac{3}{4}$

$\frac{4}{4} = 1$ and $\frac{2}{4} = \frac{1}{2}$
So, shaded part = $1\frac{1}{2}$

Write the missing numbers to show what part is shaded.

$\frac{4}{9}$ $\frac{1}{3}$ $\frac{5}{8}$ $\frac{5}{8}$

Write the fraction for the part that is shaded.

$\frac{10}{12}$ or $\frac{5}{6}$ $1\frac{3}{6}$ or $1\frac{1}{2}$ $2\frac{2}{6}$ or $2\frac{1}{3}$

Write the fraction for the part that is shaded.

$1\frac{4}{8}$ or $1\frac{1}{2}$ $2\frac{6}{8}$ or $2\frac{3}{4}$ $3\frac{1}{8}$

Some children may need further explanation of the models of mixed numbers. Point out that when all the parts of a model are shaded, the model shows the number 1.

Multiplying by one-digit numbers

Find each product. Remember to regroup.

$465 \times 3 = 1,395$ $391 \times 4 = 1,564$ $278 \times 5 = 1,390$

Find each product.

563 × 3 = 1,689	910 × 2 = 1,820	437 × 3 = 1,311	812 × 2 = 1,624
572 × 4 = 2,288	831 × 3 = 2,493	406 × 5 = 2,030	394 × 6 = 2,364

Find each product.

318 × 3 = 954	223 × 4 = 892	542 × 4 = 2,168	217 × 3 = 651
127 × 4 = 508	275 × 5 = 1,375	798 × 6 = 4,788	365 × 6 = 2,190
100 × 5 = 500	372 × 4 = 1,488	881 × 4 = 3,524	953 × 3 = 2,859

Solve each problem.

A middle school has 255 students. A high school has 6 times as many students. How many children are there at the high school?

1,530 students $255 \times 6 = 1,530$

A train can carry 365 passengers. How many could it carry on
four trips?   1,460 passengers
six trips?   2,190 passengers

$365 \times 4 = 1,460$ $365 \times 6 = 2,190$

Make sure children understand the convention of multiplication, i.e. multiply the ones first and work left. Problems on this page may result from gaps in knowledge of the 2, 3, 4, 5, and 6 times tables. Errors will also occur if children neglect to regroup.

Multiplying by one-digit numbers

Find each product. Remember to regroup.

$456 \times 6 = 2,736$ $823 \times 8 = 6,584$ $755 \times 9 = 6,795$

Find each product.

394 × 7 = 2,758	736 × 7 = 5,152	827 × 8 = 6,616	943 × 9 = 8,487
643 × 6 = 3,858	199 × 6 = 1,194	821 × 7 = 5,747	547 × 8 = 4,376
501 × 7 = 3,507	377 × 8 = 3,016	843 × 8 = 6,744	222 × 9 = 1,998
471 × 9 = 4,239	223 × 8 = 1,784	606 × 6 = 3,636	513 × 7 = 3,591
500 × 9 = 4,500	800 × 9 = 7,200	900 × 8 = 7,200	200 × 9 = 1,800

Solve each problem.

A crate holds 550 apples. How many apples are there in 8 crates?

4,400 apples $550 \times 8 = 4,400$

Keyshawn swims 760 laps each week. How many laps does he swim in 5 weeks?

3,800 people $760 \times 5 = 3,800$

Problems encountered will be similar to the previous page. Gaps in knowledge of the 6, 7, 8, and 9 times table will result in children's errors.

Real-life problems

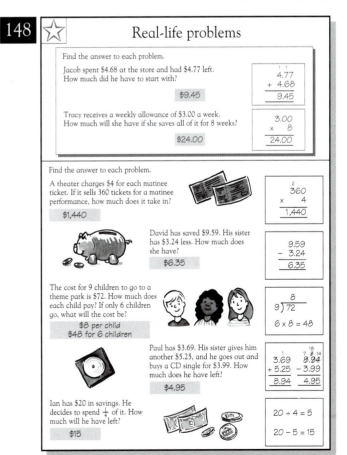

Find the answer to each problem.

Jacob spent $4.68 at the store and had $4.77 left. How much did he have to start with?

$9.45 $4.77 + 4.68 = 9.45$

Tracy receives a weekly allowance of $3.00 a week. How much will she have if she saves all of it for 8 weeks?

$24.00 $3.00 \times 8 = 24.00$

Find the answer to each problem.

A theater charges $4 for each matinee ticket. If it sells 360 tickets for a matinee performance, how much does it take in?

$1,440 $360 \times 4 = 1,440$

David has saved $9.59. His sister has $3.24 less. How much does she have?

$6.35 $9.59 - 3.24 = 6.35$

The cost for 9 children to go to a theme park is $72. How much does each child pay? If only 6 children go, what will the cost be?

$8 per child
$48 for 6 children

$9)\overline{72} = 8$ $6 \times 8 = 48$

Paul has $3.69. His sister gives him another $5.25, and he goes out and buys a CD single for $3.99. How much does he have left?

$4.95 $3.69 + 5.25 = 8.94$ $8.94 - 3.99 = 4.95$

Ian has $20 in savings. He decides to spend $\frac{1}{4}$ of it. How much will he have left?

$15 $20 \div 4 = 5$ $20 - 5 = 15$

This page and the next provide children an opportunity to apply the skills they have practiced. They will need to select the appropriate operation. If they are unsure, discuss whether the answer should be larger or smaller. This can help them decide on the operation.

Real-life problems

Find the answer to each problem.

Nina has an hour to do her homework. She plans to spend ⅓ of her time on math. How many minutes will she spend doing math?

20 minutes

1 hour is 60 minutes

$$\begin{array}{r} 20 \\ 3\overline{)60} \end{array}$$

In gym class, David makes 2 long jumps of 1.78 m and 2.19 m. How far does he jump altogether?

3.97 m

$$\begin{array}{r} 1.78\,m \\ +\,2.19\,m \\ \hline 3.97\,m \end{array}$$

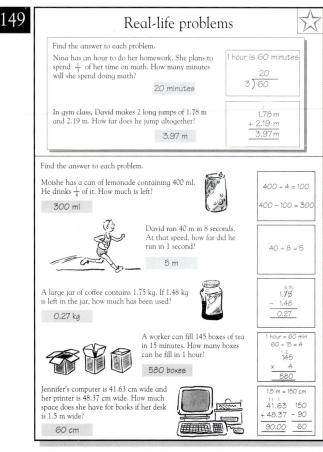

Find the answer to each problem.

Moishe has a can of lemonade containing 400 ml. He drinks ¼ of it. How much is left?

300 ml

400 ÷ 4 = 100

400 − 100 = 300

David ran 40 m in 8 seconds. At that speed, how far did he run in 1 second?

5 m

40 ÷ 8 = 5

A large jar of coffee contains 1.75 kg. If 1.48 kg is left in the jar, how much has been used?

0.27 kg

$$\begin{array}{r} {}^{6}\,1.\cancel{7}^{15} \\ -\,1.48 \\ \hline 0.27 \end{array}$$

A worker can fill 145 boxes of tea in 15 minutes. How many boxes can he fill in 1 hour?

580 boxes

1 hour = 60 min
60 ÷ 15 = 4
$$\begin{array}{r} {}^{1\,2}145 \\ \times\quad 4 \\ \hline 580 \end{array}$$

Jennifer's computer is 41.63 cm wide and her printer is 48.37 cm wide. How much space does she have for books if her desk is 1.5 m wide?

60 cm

1.5 m = 150 cm
$$\begin{array}{r} {}^{1\,1}41.63 \quad 150 \\ +\,48.37 \quad -\,90 \\ \hline 90.00 \quad 60 \end{array}$$

This page deals with units other than money. Note that solving the final problem requires two operations.

Problems involving time

Find the answer to each problem.

Caitlin spends 35 minutes on her homework each day. How many minutes does she spend on her homework in one week from Monday through Friday?

175 minutes

$$\begin{array}{r} {}^{2}35 \\ \times\quad 5 \\ \hline 175 \end{array}$$

Jenny spends 175 minutes on her homework from Monday through Friday. How much time does she spend on homework each day?

35 minutes

$$\begin{array}{r} 35 \\ 5\overline{)175} \end{array}$$

Find the answer to each problem.

Amy works from 9 A.M. until 5 P.M. She has a lunch break from noon until 1 P.M. How many hours does she work in a 5-day week?

35 hours

8 − 1 = 7

7 × 5 = 35

School children have a 15-minute break in the morning and a 10-minute break in the afternoon. How many minutes of break do they have in a week?

125 minutes

$$\begin{array}{r} 15 \\ +\,10 \\ \hline 25 \end{array} \qquad \begin{array}{r} {}^{2}25 \\ \times\quad 5 \\ \hline 125 \end{array}$$

It takes 2 hours for one person to do a job. If John shares the work with 3 of his friends, how long will it take?

30 minutes

2 × 60 = 120

$$\begin{array}{r} 30 \\ 4\overline{)120} \\ 12 \\ \hline 00 \end{array}$$

Mr. Tambo spent 7 days building a patio. If he worked a total of 56 hours and he divided the work evenly among the seven days, how long did he work each day?

8 hours

56 ÷ 7 = 8

It took Ben 45 hours to build a remote-controlled airplane. If he spent 5 hours a day working on it:

How many days did it take? **9 days**

How many hours per day would he have needed to finish it in 5 days?

9 hours

45 ÷ 5 = 9

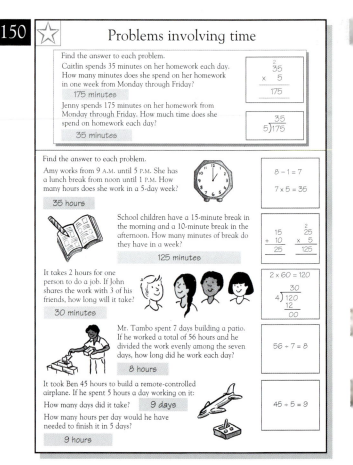

For the second problem, children should realize that a school week is 5 days. For the third problem, check that children divide by 4 rather than 3.

Multiplying and dividing

Write the answer in the box.

26 × 10 = **260**   26 × 100 = **2,600**

400 ÷ 10 = **40**   400 ÷ 100 = **4**

Write the product in the box.

33 × 10 = **330**   21 × 10 = **210**   42 × 10 = **420**

94 × 100 = **9,400**   36 × 100 = **3,600**   81 × 100 = **8,100**

416 × 10 = **4,160**   204 × 10 = **2,040**   513 × 10 = **5,130**

767 × 100 = **76,700** 821 × 100 = **82,100** 245 × 100 = **24,500**

Write the quotient in the box.

120 ÷ 10 = **12**   260 ÷ 10 = **26**   470 ÷ 10 = **47**

300 ÷ 100 = **3**   800 ÷ 100 = **8**   400 ÷ 100 = **4**

20 ÷ 10 = **2**   30 ÷ 10 = **3**   70 ÷ 10 = **7**

500 ÷ 100 = **5**   100 ÷ 100 = **1**   900 ÷ 100 = **9**

Write the number that has been multiplied by 100.

59 × 100 = 5,900   **714** × 100 = 71,400

721 × 100 = 72,100   **234** × 100 = 23,400

11 × 100 = 1,100   **470** × 100 = 47,000

84 × 100 = 8,400   **441** × 100 = 44,100

Write the number that has been divided by 100.

200 ÷ 100 = 2   **800** ÷ 100 = 8

2,100 ÷ 100 = 21   **1,800** ÷ 100 = 18

8,600 ÷ 100 = 86   **2,100** ÷ 100 = 21

1,000 ÷ 100 = 10   **5,900** ÷ 100 = 59

Children should realize that multiplying a whole number by 10 or 100 means writing one or two zeros at the end of the number. To divide a multiple of ten by 10, simply take the final zero off. In the two final sections, solve by using the inverse operation.

Identifying patterns

Continue each pattern.

Steps of 2: ½   2½   4½   **6½**   **8½**   **10½**

Steps of 5: 3.5   8.5   13.5   **18.5**   **23.5**   **28.5**

Continue each pattern.

5½	10½	15½	**20½**	**25½**	**30½**
1¼	3¼	5¼	**7¼**	**9¼**	**11¼**
8⅓	9⅓	10⅓	**11⅓**	**12⅓**	**13⅓**
55¾	45¾	35¾	**25¾**	**15¾**	**5¾**
42½	38½	34½	**30½**	**26½**	**22½**
7.5	6.5	5.5	**4.5**	**3.5**	**2.5**
28.4	25.4	22.4	**19.4**	16.4	**13.4**
81.6	73.6	65.6	**57.6**	**49.6**	**41.6**
6.3	10.3	14.3	**18.3**	**22.3**	**26.3**
12.1	13.1	14.1	**15.1**	**16.1**	17.1
14.6	21.6	28.6	**35.6**	**42.6**	**49.6**
11½	10½	9½	**8½**	**7½**	**6½**
8.4	11.4	14.4	**17.4**	20.4	**23.4**
7¾	13¾	19¾	**25¾**	**31¾**	**37¾**
57.5	48.5	39.5	**30.5**	**21.5**	**12.5**

The patterns on this page are formed by adding or subtracting whole numbers but the items in each row are mixed numbers or decimals. Children should see what operation turns the first number into the second, and the second into the third, and then continue the pattern.

Products with odd and even numbers ☆

Find the products of these numbers.

3 and 4 | The product of 3 and 4 is 12. | 6 and 8 | The product of 6 and 8 is 48.

Find the products of these odd and even numbers.

5 and 6	The product of 5 and 6 is 30.	3 and 2	The product of 3 and 2 is 6.
7 and 4	The product of 7 and 4 is 28.	8 and 3	The product of 8 and 3 is 24.
6 and 3	The product of 6 and 3 is 18.	2 and 9	The product of 2 and 9 is 18.
10 and 3	The product of 10 and 3 is 30.	12 and 5	The product of 12 and 5 is 60.

What do you notice about your answers? The product of odd and even numbers is always an even number.

Find the products of these odd numbers.

5 and 7	The product of 5 and 7 is 35.	3 and 9	The product of 3 and 9 is 27.
5 and 11	The product of 5 and 11 is 55.	7 and 3	The product of 7 and 3 is 21.
9 and 5	The product of 9 and 5 is 45.	11 and 7	The product of 11 and 7 is 77.
13 and 3	The product of 13 and 3 is 39.	1 and 5	The product of 1 and 5 is 5.

What do you notice about your answers? The product of two odd numbers is always an odd number.

Find the products of these even numbers.

2 and 4	The product of 2 and 4 is 8.	4 and 6	The product of 4 and 6 is 24.
6 and 2	The product of 6 and 2 is 12.	4 and 8	The product of 4 and 8 is 32.
10 and 2	The product of 10 and 2 is 20.	4 and 10	The product of 4 and 10 is 40.
6 and 10	The product of 6 and 10 is 60.	6 and 8	The product of 6 and 8 is 48.

What do you notice about your answers? The product of two even numbers is always an even number.

Can you write a rule for the products with odd and even numbers?
The product of two numbers will always be even unless both numbers are odd.

Children may need help answering the questions on what they notice about the products. Accept any rule about products that children write, as long as it indicates that they have grasped the concept.

☆ Factors of numbers from 66 to 100

The factors of 66 are   1   2   3   6   11   22   33   66
Circle the factors of 94.   (1) (2) 28   32   43   (47) 71   86   (94)

Write the factors of each number in the box.

The factors of 70 are	1, 2, 5, 7, 10, 14, 35, 70
The factors of 85 are	1, 5, 17, 85
The factors of 69 are	1, 3, 23, 69
The factors of 83 are	1, 83
The factors of 75 are	1, 3, 5, 15, 25, 75
The factors of 96 are	1, 2, 3, 4, 6, 8, 12, 16, 24, 32, 48, 96
The factors of 63 are	1, 3, 7, 9, 21, 63
The factors of 99 are	1, 3, 9, 11, 33, 99
The factors of 72 are	1, 2, 3, 4, 6, 8, 9, 12, 18, 24, 36, 72

Circle the factors of 68.
(1) (2) 3 (4) 5 6 7 8 9 11 12 (17) (34) 35 62 (68)

Circle the factors of 95.
(1) 2 3 4 (5) 15 16 17 (19) 24 37 85 90 (95) 96

Circle the factors of 88.
(1) (2) 3 (4) 5 6 (8) 10 (11) 15 (22) 25 27 (44) 87 (88)

Circle the factors of 73.
(1) 2 4 5 6 8 9 10 12 13 14 15 30 60 (73)

A prime number only has two factors, 1 and itself.
Write all the prime numbers between 66 and 100 in the box.

67, 71, 73, 79, 83, 89, 97

Children often miss some of the factors of a number, especially for large numbers. Encourage a systematic method of finding factors. Children may forget that 1 and the number itself are factors of a number. If necessary, discuss prime numbers with children.

Multiplying by two-digit numbers ☆

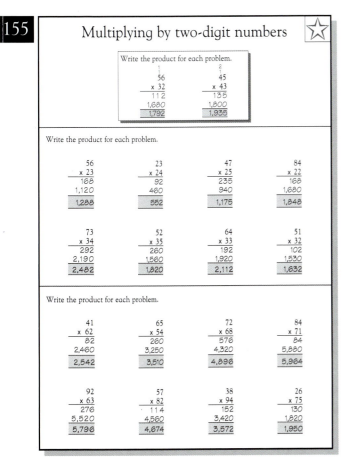

Write the product for each problem.

```
  1              2
  1              1
  56             45
x 32          x 43
 112           135
1,680         1,800
1,792         1,935
```

Write the product for each problem.

```
   56         23          47          84
 x 23       x 24        x 25        x 22
  168         92         235         168
1,120        460         940       1,680
1,288        552       1,175       1,848
```

```
   73         52          64          51
 x 34       x 35        x 33        x 32
  292        260         192         102
2,190      1,560       1,920       1,530
2,482      1,820       2,112       1,632
```

Write the product for each problem.

```
   41         65          72          84
 x 62       x 54        x 68        x 71
   82        260         576          84
2,460      3,250       4,320       5,880
2,542      3,510       4,896       5,964
```

```
   92         57          38          26
 x 63       x 82        x 94        x 75
  276        114         152         130
5,520      4,560       3,420       1,820
5,796      4,674       3,572       1,950
```

Children should understand that multiplying a number by 32 is the same as multiplying the number by 2 and then by 30, and adding the two products.

☆ Multiplying by two-digit numbers

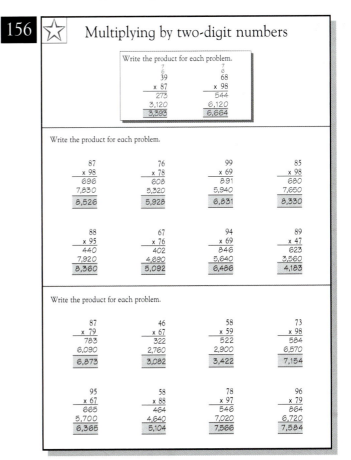

Write the product for each problem.

```
  7              7
  6              6
  39             68
x 87          x 98
 273           544
3,120         6,120
3,393         6,664
```

Write the product for each problem.

```
   87         76          99          85
 x 98       x 78        x 69        x 98
  696        608         891         680
7,830      5,320       5,940       7,650
8,526      5,928       6,831       8,330
```

```
   88         67          94          89
 x 95       x 76        x 69        x 47
  440        402         846         623
7,920      4,690       5,640       3,560
8,360      5,092       6,486       4,183
```

Write the product for each problem.

```
   87         46          58          73
 x 79       x 67        x 59        x 98
  783        322         522         584
6,090      2,760       2,900       6,570
6,873      3,082       3,422       7,154
```

```
   95         58          78          96
 x 67       x 88        x 97        x 79
  665        464         546         864
5,700      4,640       7,020       6,720
6,365      5,104       7,566       7,584
```

This page gives further practice of multiplication as on the previous page. Make sure that children do not neglect to regroup when necessary.